Pathways to Economic Development

To Sandy, Andy, Adam, and Nikki

Pathways to Economic Development

Richard Grabowski
Professor of Economics, Southern Illinois University, USA

Edward Elgar
Cheltenham, UK • Northampton, MA, USA

Published by
Edward Elgar Publishing Limited
Glensanda House
Montpellier Parade
Cheltenham
Glos GL50 1UA
UK

Edward Elgar Publishing, Inc.
136 West Street
Suite 202
Northampton
Massachusetts 01060
USA

A catalogue record for this book
is available from the British Library

Library of Congress Cataloguing in Publication Data
Grabowski, Richard, 1949-
    Pathways to economic development / Richard Grabowski.
    Includes index.
    1. Economic development. 2. Economic development–Social aspects.
    3. Economic development–Political aspects. I. Title.
    HD75.G714 1999
    338.9—dc21   99–12124
                                                             CIP

ISBN 1 84064 112 6

Printed and bound in Great Britain by MPG Books Ltd, Bodmin, Cornwall

Contents

List of Figures   *vi*
List of Tables   *vii*
Preface   *viii*

1. Role of Agriculture   1

2. Traders' Dilemma   30

3. Market Integration and Industrial Revolutions   68

4. Market Integration and Catching up: the State   103

5. Developmental Entrepreneurial Groups   150

6. Conclusions   182

Index   189

List of Figures

1.1 The Lewis Model   3

1.2 Circular Flow   18

1.3 Transaction Costs   20

1.4 Traders' Dilemma   21

2.1 Traders' Dilemma   31

2.2 Technologies for Generating Information   39

3.1 Neoclassical Growth Theory   70

3.2 Classical Growth Theory   71

3.3 Smithian Growth Theory   72

3.4 Risk and Growth   85

4.1 Catching Up   103

4.2 Low-Tech Equilibrium   126

4.3 Specialization and Relative Prices   126

4.4 Multiple Equilibria   128

4.5 State and Entrepreneurs: A Prisoners' Dilemma   130

List of Tables

5.1 Average Annual Growth Rates (%)   151

5.2 Gross Domestic Investment (Share in GDP)   152

5.3 Agricultural Growth Rates   155

5.4 Taxation on Agriculture (%, annual average)   156

5.5 Incremental Capital to Output Ratios (ICOR)   173

5.6 Investment Rates (% of GDP)   174

5.7 Thailand: Manufacturing, Wage and Productivity Indices   175

Preface

Economic analysis of the process of development has traditionally focused on a limited number of explanatory factors: capital accumulation, population growth, technical change and technical innovation, international trade and investment, and the distribution of income both within and between nations. Recently significant attention has been focused on the effects of limited market development or missing markets. All of this generally aimed at drawing policy conclusions.

There has been, however, very little analysis of where markets come from or how they evolve. Specifically, this book seeks to analyze how integrated national market systems can arise and how they have arisen in the past. It emphasizes the crucial role that the agricultural sector plays in this process. This represents one path by which economic development can occur. Two other paths involve bypassing the domestic market and instead using networks of social relationships within the context of large firms or groups of firms linked by these networks. Although all three paths have been utilized by various countries, it will be argued that there are advantages to the rural development path.

This book is the outcome of my research over the last few years. It was originally presented in seminar to graduate students taking the field courses in economic development. The core of the book is Chapter 2 and it is based on two papers which were originally published in *New Political Economy* and the *Canadian Journal of Development Studies*. The first paper was entitled "Traders' Dilemma and Development: A Variety of Solutions" and the second "Agriculture, Markets, and Economic Development." I would like to thank the editors of both journals for allowing me to use this material.

In closing, I would like to thank Nancy Mallett for typing the original manuscript and for preparing it for publication. Without her tireless efforts, this book would never have come about. Finally, thanks to Sandy McRoy for keeping us laughing.

1. Role of Agriculture

1. INTRODUCTION

The role of agriculture in the process of economic development has been a much debated topic. Historically, there is significant evidence for agricultural revolutions preceding or occurring simultaneously with significant expansions in industrial production. For example, the industrial revolution in the late 18th and early 19th centuries in England was preceded by a long-run increase in agricultural productivity in the 17th and early 18th centuries. In Japan the historical evidence seems to indicate that in the 17th and 18th centuries agriculture experienced a slow but steady increase in agricultural production. This was followed by rapid industrial growth accompanied by continued expansion in agricultural productivity.

More recent experiences with economic development also indicate that agricultural growth is associated with overall economic development. For example, both South Korea and Taiwan experienced rapid agricultural growth in the 19th and 20th centuries. This growth again preceded and then occurred concurrently with rapid growth in manufacturing.

Alternatively, slow overall economic development is usually associated with slow agricultural growth. For example, large areas of South Asia, Central and South America, and Africa have been characterized by sluggish growth of the agricultural sector and agonizingly slow growth in overall per capita income and manufacturing production. Even more pointedly, the policies followed by the governments of these nations have often been biased against the agricultural sector and in favor of industry. Lipton (1976) has characterized this as urban bias. These policies have involved the allocation of resources for public infrastructure, schools, medical care and so on and Lipton argues that these resources have been more readily allocated to the provision of goods and services for urban inhabitants, at the expense of rural dwellers. In addition, exchange rate and macroeconomic policies have often resulted in an indirect diversion of resources from agriculture to industry. Complementing the indirect diversion of resources policies have often directly turned the relative terms of trade between agriculture and manufacturing in favor of the latter at the expense of the former. Thus these sorts of policy have created stagnant agricultural sectors posing significant barriers to long-run economic development.

2.   THEORETICAL PERSPECTIVES

Historical as well as recent experience seems to indicate a relationship between agricultural growth and overall growth and development. This has not escaped the notice of scholars seeking to develop theories of the process of overall economic development. The dualistic model of economic development first put forward by Lewis (1954) is an example of such theorizing. In his model the economy of a developing nation is divided into a traditional and modern sector. The former produces commodities where decision making is governed by tradition instead of profit maximization, thus output is shared (labor receives its average rather than marginal product) and surplus labor exists. By the latter it is meant that there are workers in the traditional sector where the marginal product is below the wage rate and possibly even zero or negative. Alternatively, in the modern sector, labor is paid its marginal product and profits are maximized. Savings result only from the profit of the industrial sector which serves as the engine of capital accumulation.

In this model, at a wage rate slightly above that paid in the traditional sector, there will be, in the short to medium term, an unlimited supply of labor available to the modern sector without raising the wage rate. Thus as capital is accumulated in the modern sector labor is pulled out of the traditional sector. Given the constancy of the wage rate, the share of modern sector profit in the economy increases, resulting in further increases in savings and capital accumulation. As labor continues to be drawn out of the traditional sector, its marginal productivity rises until eventually it equals the wage rate. At this point commercialization of the traditional sector occurs and the Lewis model ceases to be relevant. The model briefly outlined above seeks to answer the basic question posed by Lewis concerning how a rise in the savings rate, which is necessary for rapid economic growth, could occur. In his model, it arises from a change in the functional distribution of income.

The operation of this model is illustrated in Figure 1.1. This represents the labor market in the modern sector with AB representing the marginal product of labor (demand for labor). It slopes downwards in the short run because the supply of capital is fixed and the supply of labor is variable. WS represents the unlimited supply of labor available to the modern sector from the traditional sector at a wage rate slightly above what is available in the traditional sector (OW). Labor will be hired up to the point where the wage, OW, is equal to the marginal product, which occurs at OL^*. This is the quantity of labor which maximizes total profit with the latter being represented by the triangle *WAC*.

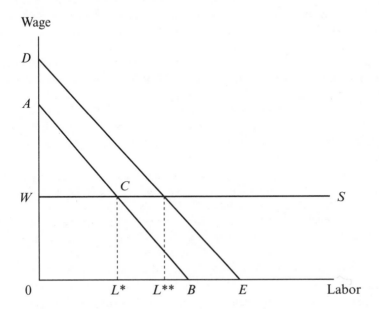

Figure 1.1   The Lewis Model

As mentioned previously, the profit is presumed to be invested in capital for the modern sector. This shifts the marginal product of labor curve to *DE*, the employment level rises to OL^{**} and the total profit triangle increases in size.

In terms of the role of agriculture in the model it must first be remembered that Lewis hypothesized that the traditional sector included both agricultural and manufacturing activities and that the same holds for the modern sector. The main distinction between these two sectors concerns not what is produced, but how it is produced. The technologies are different in that the modern sector utilizes capital and labor whereas the traditional sector uses only land and labor. More importantly, the process of decision making differs with profit maximizing dominating the modern sector and other mechanisms dominating the traditional sector.

However, Lewis did introduce agriculture more directly by allowing for the possibility that the two sectors might produce different types of goods: food in the traditional sector and manufacturing in the modern sector. Thus, as the modern sector expands, increases in the relative price of food may cause such a deterioration in the profits of the modern sector that the transition to rapid growth via increased savings might be inhibited or prevented altogether. The relative price of food would rise as long as the marginal product of labor in the food-producing traditional sector is positive, therefore as labor is drawn from this sector the supply of food would decline relative to the supply of manufactured goods.

Ranis and Fei (1961) developed a dualistic model similar in structure to that of Lewis. The traditional sector is identified with the production of agricultural goods while the modern sector is explicitly identified with industry. Now the terms of trade play a central role in the development process. As long as the marginal product in the agricultural sector is zero, expansion of the modern sector can draw labor out of agriculture without causing any fall in output in the latter sector. This represents an example in which economic growth is essentially free from a society's point of view. Industrial output can expand without giving up any agricultural output and this is the first stage of the development process.

A few comments need to be made concerning this first stage. As labor leaves agriculture, output there does not fall. Thus agricultural output per person rises in the agricultural sector since output remains unchanged but there are fewer workers in agriculture. It follows then that the expansion of the industrial sector, driven by profits there (Ranis and Fei assume, like Lewis, that savings comes from profit income), may cause rising opportunity cost for labor from the traditional sector. The labor supply curve facing the industrial sector would not be horizontal meaning that rising wages would immediately cut into industrial profits and expansion. If the agricultural sector is producing food then this can be interpreted as a problem of transferring the food surplus to the industrial sector without reducing profits there. One obvious way to do this would be to tax the agricultural sector and use the proceeds of the tax to finance the expansion of the industrial sector in stage one of the development process.

In stage two the marginal product of labor in agriculture is positive, but less than the wage rate. Here, once again, the profit of the expanding industrial sector may be threatened. Since the marginal product of labor in agriculture is now positive, industrial expansion now comes at the expense of agricultural output and if this represents food, the relative price of food will rise pushing up wages in the industrial sector. It is at this point that Ranis and Fei introduce the notion of balanced growth. As the terms of trade turn against the industrial sector, it will become profitable for investment to flow into the agricultural sector increasing production there. This may involve both the introduction of capital into agriculture and the application of new techniques of production. This will cause the price of agricultural goods to fall relative to industrial goods, increasing the profitability of industrial expansion, thus industry and agriculture must expand in a balanced manner if overall economic development is to be successful.

The flows of investment between the two sectors, necessary for balanced growth, may occur via the operation of markets and private decision making. Specifically, as the rate of return to investment in industry falls relative to investment in agriculture, private investors redirect investment flows into the agricultural sector. However, if markets are not well developed then the state must play an important role in redirecting investment flows so as to assure a long-run balanced growth path between agriculture and industry.

One objection raised by many to these dualistic models concerned the assumptions generally made concerning decision making in the traditional, agricultural (food-producing) sector. Here profits are not maximized and the output is distributed in a traditional manner. For simplicity, most of these models assumed that output was equally distributed among family members so that wages equaled the average product of labor. Jorgenson (1961) drops this view and assumes that farmers are also maximizers. He combines this with a Malthusian assumption concerning population growth. If wages are above some stipulated subsistence level, population will grow at some maximum rate. Within the context of this model, the creation of a modern industrial sector becomes dependent upon the ability of the agricultural sector to produce an agricultural surplus necessary to feed an industrial working class. Ultimately, industrial success is dependent upon the ability of agriculture to produce a surplus to feed the expansion of the modern sector.

Drawing together the ideas put forward in the above theoretical work, Johnston and Mellor (1961) argued that agriculture has five roles to perform in the development process. First, since the bulk of the population in developing nations resides in and earns its income in agriculture, it is no surprise that the bulk of the urban labor force comes from this sector via migration. Second, agriculture provides the food necessary to feed the urban industrial labor force. Third, rising incomes in agriculture can serve as the market for the manufactured goods produced in the industrial sector. Fourth, in all of the dualistic models discussed above the driving force in the industrialization process was savings. Agriculture can provide savings to the industrial sector via private savings or investment decisions or as a result of government efforts to extract such savings via various forms of taxation. Finally, since most developing countries export agricultural commodities, agriculture can generate the foreign exchange necessary to import the foreign produced capital necessary for rapid growth.

Johnston and Mellor (1961) emphasized that all five roles discussed above are of equal importance and they also recognized that successful long-run development was the result of balanced growth between agriculture and industry. The authors recognized that a dynamic agricultural sector can provide resources for the expansion of industry. The expansion of the latter is likely to require significant investment in agriculture. However, the development process in agriculture must be of a unimodal rather than bimodal type. In a bimodal strategy a two-tier farm structure is promoted with large farms being provided with access to new technologies and resources while the bulk of smaller farmers are left behind. This strategy is often justified by arguing that it is less costly to concentrate on the large farmers compared to the efforts necessary to reach a myriad of small farmers. A unimodal strategy requires that resources are concentrated on the bulk of the farmers whose average size is relatively small.

The importance of a unimodal strategy is in terms of its effects on equity as well as the structure of demand emanating from the agricultural sector. Obviously a unimodal strategy will have a more equitable effect on the distribution of income in the rural sector. More importantly, as incomes rise among the bulk of the farmers a large proportion of the increased income is likely to be spent on manufactured goods. It is hypothesized that the type of goods demanded are likely to be technologically simple and produced by labor-intensive techniques. As a result, rural based manufacturing is likely to grow rapidly providing additional employment opportunities for the rural poor.

Evidence for the above assertions is provided by empirical work aimed at analyzing the linkages between agriculture and the nonagricultural sector. These are often classified as being backward, forward or consumption linkages. Backward linkages exist when the expansion of one production sector requires inputs produced in another production sector. Thus as agriculture expands, it often requires machinery, machinery repair, fertilizers, seeds and so on. Forward linkage exists when the expansion of production in one sector provides the materials that can be further processed through activities in another production sector, therefore as food production expands, it enhances the opportunities for rural-based firms to process such materials into finished products. The third category concerns consumption linkages. As income is generated through production in one sector, that income, or parts of it, is spent on output produced in other sectors.

Empirical estimates of these linkages running from agricultural to nonagricultural production have been made. Hazell and Haggblade (1991) have derived rural agricultural multipliers for India. The results suggest that a 100-rupee increase in agricultural income will result in an increase of 64 rupees in rural nonfarm income. Haggblade et al. (1987) have reviewed evidence concerning linkages in Africa compared to those in Asia. In terms of magnitude, Africa's rural agricultural growth multipliers are in the area of 1.5, a US $1 increase in agricultural income leading to about a 50-cent increase in nonagricultural income. Thus linkage effects from agriculture to the rest of the economy appear to be strong.

Myint (1975) has criticized the five roles outlined in the work of Johnston and Mellor. The first criticism is that such approaches fail to clearly distinguish between the notions of voluntary and compulsory contributions by agriculture. Myint interprets the idea of agriculture's roles or functions in terms of what agriculture can be made to do by means of a deliberate policy. Then the emphasis on all five roles implies the advocacy of policies designed to increase agriculture's ability to make all five contributions or all five roles simultaneously. From this perspective, an immediate contradiction arises in an open economy setting. If a country does not possess a comparative advantage in food production (agriculture), the policy of promoting increased food production would take resources away from production for exports, thus foreign exchange earnings would decline rather than increase.

Even if a less-developed nation has a potential comparative advantage in food production and can, therefore, be made to increase the supply of food and foreign exchange via investment in agriculture, this will not necessarily lead to increased spending on domestically produced manufactured goods. In an open economy setting much of the increased income may be spent on imported goods. Agriculture could be made to spend the increased income on domestic manufactured goods by putting a tariff on imports. This would raise the relative price of manufactured goods thus turning the terms of trade against the agricultural sector. This in turn extracts resources from agriculture which would tend to make it more difficult to expand food production and generate additional foreign exchange. Thus there seems to exist another fundamental contradiction among the roles for agriculture outlined in the literature.

A final potential contradiction occurs between agriculture's proposed role of providing a market for manufactured goods as well as providing savings for the expansion of the industrial sector. Obviously, if rising agricultural income is to provide a market for industrial goods it must be spent, rather than saved. Alternatively, if agriculture is to provide savings to the modern sector consumption must be suppressed, thus these two functions or roles for agriculture are contradictory in nature.

In summary, it would seem that in an open economy setting, the various roles for agriculture outlined by Johnston and Mellor are contradictory in nature. Subsequent authors have generally dropped the notion that agriculture can play all of these roles simultaneously. Instead, they emphasize that the role of agriculture changes as the development process unfolds. For example, Adelman (1984) has stressed that an inflow of resources into agriculture is necessary in the initial stages of economic development. This would require investments in physical infrastructure and the development of new agricultural technologies. In addition, the incentives to develop and utilize new technologies will have to be maintained and this will require a terms of trade policy which allows farmers to reap increased income from increased output. She justifies these policies based upon the notion that many developing nations possess potential comparative advantages in agricultural production.

The rising incomes of the agricultural sector would, in the second stage of development, provide internal demand for intermediate and consumer goods. Adelman believes that there are strong linkages between agriculture and manufacturing production. However, the crucial question concerns the nature of these linkages. Adelman presumes that large farms are most likely to have demand linkages with foreign firms, that is, large farmers generally use capital-intensive methods, often involving importation of inputs. Alternatively, small farmers generally use labor-intensive techniques and are more likely to spend their increased income on domestically produced manufactured goods, thus small farmers are more likely to have demand linkages with domestic producers. A development strategy, therefore, which emphasized raising the productivity and income levels of small farmers in the first stage would lead to the development of domestic manufacturing in the second stage. Adelman's strategy has been labeled as an agricultural-demand-led-industrialization programme (ALDI).

The emphasis on agriculture as a market for the manufacturing industry, especially rural manufacturing, also plays an important role in Mundle's (1985) analysis. He is especially concerned with trying to understand the comparative performances of Japan and India in terms of economic development. In terms of the transfer of savings from agriculture to industry, he finds that the experience of Japan and India are similar. From 1885 to World War II a savings surplus was transferred out of agriculture in Japan and also from the mid-1950s to the 1970s in India. As a proportion of value added in agriculture the magnitude of these transfers was similar in both countries. The transfer of this surplus was part of a larger strategy of industrialization pursued by both the Japanese and Indian governments. However, development succeeded in Japan and failed in India. Mundle concludes that the relative success of development in Japan could not be attributed to transferring surplus or savings to the industrial sector.

Mundle offers an alternative explanation. When the transfer of surplus began in the 1880s in Japan, nonagricultural production already accounted for 60 per cent of aggregate output, while in the 1950s in India agriculture still accounted for well over half of total production. Thus Japan was, even in the 1880s, much more advanced, in a structural sense, than India was in the 1950s. This advanced industrial structure evolved prior to the Meiji industrialization which began in the 1880s. What is the explanation for this phenomenon? Mundle argues that the answer lies in a long agrarian revolution in Japan starting in the middle of the 17th century which led to the development of significant amounts of small-scale, labor-intensive, industrial activity, sometimes referred to as protoindustry.

The overall conclusion that Mundle draws is that in countries where the size of the market is the binding constraint on manufacturing output growth, this rate of growth is crucially dependent on agriculture. This dependence operates via two routes. One is the large share of manufacturing output which is sold to agriculture and the other is the large share of manufacturing sector expenditure which is put on food and raw materials from the agricultural sector. Thus raising agricultural growth is the key to the development of manufacturing. Mundle further argues that the growth of agriculture is strongly dependent upon its structural or institutional organization.

Mundle's analysis does not ignore the possibility that a nation could break the agricultural constraint on the size of market via international trade. However, he argues that 'industrialization, however initiated, must sooner or later base itself on the home market; which implies that an agrarian revolution is a necessary condition for sustained industrialization' (Mundle, 1985, p.77). Further, 'industrialization dependent on external markets is precocious and fragile development which will collapse sooner or later with shifts in the commodity/region composition of world trade' (Mundle, 1985, p.77).

Murphy et al. (1989) have developed a model incorporating increasing returns which also has agriculture performing a critical role in the overall process of development. In their model food is a necessity implying that below a certain income level all income is spent on food. As individual's income rises above this minimum, expenditure is diversified into manufactured goods, thus richer people consume all the things that poorer people do, plus some. On the production side food is produced subject to diminishing returns. Manufactured goods can be produced in two types of setting, utilizing a constant return to scale technology or an increasing return to scale technology. At small levels of production (small market size), the constant returns to scale technology is superior. At large levels of production (large market size), the increasing returns to scale technology is superior. Industrialization is then defined to be the substitution of increasing returns for constant returns technologies in the production of manufactured goods.

Within the context of this model, productivity growth in agriculture can precipitate industrialization. This results from the growth in market size which allows firms in the manufacturing sector to shift from constant to increasing returns to scale technology. The model also indicates when industrialization may fail to occur. This happens in the case of too much equality or too much inequality. With extreme equity, all consumers will be buying (under certain conditions) only food. There will be no market for manufacturing. Alternatively, too much inequality implies that the market for manufacturing output will be too small to make the switch to increasing returns profitable.

Murphy et al. do not ignore open economy issues in their analysis. If international trade is costly, then agriculture will play a significant role in industrialization. These costs of trade stem from such factors as transportation, marketing, establishing a reputation in product markets and overcoming trade barriers. However, if these costs are low enough, exports may also play a role in the industrialization process. Specifically, 'exports of cash crops, minerals, or light manufacturing (small scale, constant returns) enable a country to substitute efficient export production and food imports for inefficient domestic food production, so that food can be obtained in a roundabout and cheaper way' (Murphy et al. 1989, p.557). The net result is that the wages of individuals will allow them to buy more food and will likely push poorer individuals above the food minimum implying increased expenditures on manufactured goods. In addition, those in the middle classes who have income from profits will find that as the profits earned by exports rise they will be able to buy additional amounts of manufactured goods. Both of these factors will likely promote industrialization.

However, there is one warning to draw from the analysis above. Export production allows the importation of cheaper food, thus incomes in food production will decline relative to those in the export sector, but the net effect on income would be positive, implying a larger market for manufactured goods and a greater probability of industrialization. However, if the returns from exports are more unequally distributed than those from food production, the increased inequality may reduce the size of the domestic market for manufactured goods, reducing the likelihood of industrialization (switching to increasing returns technology). Thus whether or not export production will bring about industrialization will be dependent on how broadly based such production is. In the same manner, growth in agricultural production will lead to industrialization only if it is broadly based with the income gains widespread among the rural population.

3.   MARKET LIMITATIONS: AGRICULTURE AND DEVELOPMENT

The focus of the previous section has been on the role agriculture can play in the overall development process. However, much of the analysis is constructed upon the implicit assumption that markets mostly operate well in rural areas. Governments have caused agricultural stagnation by discriminating against the agricultural sector in favor of the urban sector. This has often been labeled urban bias (discussed at the beginning of the chapter) and has resulted in the general conclusion that governments should follow a border price paradigm approach. That is, the best price policy for governments to follow is to allow the relative prices of agricultural goods to be determined by international prices and thus correctly reflect social opportunity cost. Any attempt to interfere with or cause a deviation from the international price of an agricultural commodity reduces total economic welfare in a country. Following a border price policy would, for most developing countries, result in a rise in the relative prices of agricultural goods. As this occurred, agriculture could then effectively play one or more of the roles outlined in the previous section.

There has, of course, generally been a recognition that one kind of market failure, in particular, tends to plague agriculture in developing countries. Specifically, technologies often used in the agricultural sector have the characteristics of a public good. Public goods are thought to be both nonrival and nonexclusionary in nature. They are nonrival in the sense that the use of a public good by one individual does not affect its availability for use to others. A public good is nonexclusionary in the sense that if one individual has access to the good, others cannot be prevented from using it even though they have not paid for it.

Biochemical technologies in agriculture are thought to possess both of these characteristics. This type of technology generally involves the substitution of labor and industrial inputs for land. This substitution may occur through increased recycling of soil fertility by more labor-intensive cultivation systems utilizing increased use of chemical fertilizers, better husbandry practices and the utilization of higher yielding seeds. The utilization of such a package of inputs also generally requires irrigation. This type of technology is generally nonrival and is easily copied (implying the inability to exclude others who have not paid), thus incentives for private firms to develop such technologies would likely be limited. Thus Hayami and Ruttan (1985) believe that there is a role for the state to play in fostering agricultural research. However, this conclusion does not detract from the conclusion of the previous paragraph that once relative prices reflect border (international) prices, then agriculture and its contribution to development will be adequately valued.

Timmer (1993) has vigorously disagreed with this position. He argues that there are four reasons agricultural commodity markets and border prices fail to provide developing countries appropriate signals for valuing their agricultural sectors. First, agricultural markets fail to reflect the importance to countries of maintaining food security. Second, the markets do not reflect the value of the learning by doing that is occurring in this sector. This learning by doing results in both better government policy and better entrepreneurial skills. Third, agricultural markets undervalue the indirect positive effects which agricultural growth has on total factor productivity for the entire economy. Fourth, markets ignore the special role of the agricultural sector in alleviating poverty.

With regard to price stabilization in agriculture, especially for staple crops, the economics profession has generally concluded, on theoretical grounds, that while the welfare gains from price stabilization are generally positive, empirically they are not very important (Newbery and Stiglitz, 1981). However, this conclusion is very much at odds with the importance which governments place on stabilization of food prices. Timmer argues that wherever one finds a goal considered to be universally important by governments and society in general in developing nations, there is usually an economic rationale.

Some insight into this issue can be gained by viewing farmers as investors rather than just managers or allocators of an existing supply of resources. From this perspective, risk would greatly influence the patterns of investment in physical and human capital. Specifically, Timmer (1989) believes that food price instability would likely cause reduced investment at various levels of the economy. At the farm level, price instability leads to lower investments than are optimal in production for the market relative to production of subsistence crops. In addition, investment in processing and marketing equipment (small mills, motorcycles, tractors and so on) will also likely be reduced.

At the industrial level, food price instability also has an important impact. Instability in food prices is likely to lead to instability in wage rates for industrial production. Firms are likely, in response, to substitute machinery for labor thus causing the production process to be more capital-intensive than is optimal. This not only reduces the employment impact of industrial growth, but it also reduces the long-run growth rate, derived from Solow's (1956) theory of neoclassical growth, by raising the capital to output ratio.

Price instability also has some negative impacts on consumers. Perhaps, most importantly, there is a universal fear of food shortages in urban areas. 'Governments are held accountable for provisioning cities at reasonable costs, and citizens have repeatedly demonstrated their capacity to bring down governments that fail in this obligation' (Timmer, 1989, p.23). An environment in which price stability occurs contributes to the overall stability of the society with its spillover effects on investor expectations. Thus the interplay between domestic production, food imports and price movements would seem to be crucial to the overall development process.

It was pointed out above that agriculture's role in food price stabilization and the spillover benefits of such stabilization on overall growth are undervalued by the marketplace. Agriculture's true social value is undervalued, in a second way. Timmer (1992) argues that governments are not automatically born knowing how to carry out effective policies for increasing productivity and growth. Instead, governments must learn by doing and Timmer believes that this can be most effectively carried out in the agricultural sector. 'The hypothesis here is that governments learn these tasks first and most efficiently by learning how to design and implement agricultural development strategies that reach small farmers with rural infrastructure, new technology, modern inputs, and stable, profitable prices' (Timmer, 1992, p.46). He argues that the ability of East and Southeast Asian countries to promote rapid economic growth is linked to their strong need to provide a supply of food (rice) at a reasonably stable price level. To achieve this goal a unimodal strategy of agricultural development was pursued which required the governments of these nations to design institutions and mechanisms for the provision of investment, credit, new technology, roads, and so on to a myriad of small farmers. These lessons can then be applied to the rest of the economy creating positive externalities.

Dawe[1] argues that there are similar opportunities for managerial learning by doing to be achieved by rural households as well as by governmental units. One of the difficulties faced by managers of large firms involves agency problems, that is, principals who make the managerial decisions must delegate decision making authority to agents. This leads to an interaction problem, often called the problem of moral hazard. In this kind of situation the benefit of a transaction to one party depends on actions taken by another. The latter may be contractually required to undertake certain actions, but once the contract is signed there may be an incentive to shirk, as with managers hiring workers on fixed wage contracts. Because firms (farms) are generally much smaller in agriculture, the moral hazard problems are likely to be much reduced. In addition, since family members make up much of the work force in agriculture, the problems involved are likely to be less severe. This allows managers in rural areas to gradually learn how to handle moral hazard problems on a small scale. This would then allow these manager-entrepreneurs to eventually branch out into nonagricultural activities, rural-based manufacturing. In fact, this is one of the characteristics of development in parts of East and Southeast Asia, that is, many of these regions are characterized by a vibrant sector of small-scale firms producing a wide variety of goods in both rural areas and urban areas. This activity has often occurred while the population maintains strong connections to agricultural production.

In this context the undervaluation of agriculture causes the economy to suffer in two distinct ways. First, governments will fail to learn how to create institutional structures which will allow effective mobilization of large numbers of economic actions. In addition, the bulk of the population in the rural areas will not learn to become effective managers and entrepreneurs. Both of these have spillover effects which influence the overall process of economic development.

Markets undervalue agriculture in a third sense. Agriculture has a number of indirect effects on total factor productivity that are not appropriately valued by the market. This can, perhaps, best be explained by reference to the following equation (Timmer, 1993):

$$G = TFP + X(1)L + X(2)K, \qquad (1.1)$$

where G is the growth rate of domestic product, $X(1)$ and $X(2)$ are the elasticities of output with respect to labor and capital, L and K are the growth rates of labor and capital respectively, and TFP is the change in total factor productivity. Agricultural growth has a roundabout effect on growth via its effect on total factor productivity and this is done through several mechanisms.

One of the important lessons from the recent success of the Chinese economy is the idea that economic reforms should begin with agriculture, which is due to the fact that rural households are highly efficient mainly because they almost always face hard budget constraints. Any failure to pay attention to prices, input availability and technology threatens not only low income, but possible starvation. Rural households also have the greatest amount of knowledge concerning land quality, whether irrigation is needed, what problems are likely to arise and so on. As a result, an economic strategy which places additional resources in the hands of these households will result in overall increases in productivity (TFP will rise). Related to this is the fact that in most developing nations the opportunity cost of labor is quite low. Labor has been applied to existing land and stocks of capital such that the marginal product of that labor is quite low and, therefore, the return to new resources (irrigation, new seeds, fertilizers) is quite high. Thus additional income allocated into the hands of small farmers will likely lead to spending and investment in areas having very high returns.

In order to fully understand this last point more must be said concerning the problems of missing markets, in particular the capital market, in the rural areas of less-developed nations. Markets cannot function unless there is a clear vision of what the underlying social contract is as well as a mechanism for punishment when the rules are broken. In terms of a capital market in which money is to be borrowed now and paid back in the future, there must be assets which the lender can take from the borrower if the borrower defaults on payment of the loan. In societies where wealth is very unequally distributed, poor rural families may find it impossible to access credit markets because they lack collateral. If credit is necessary to start a small business, educate family members, buy inputs and other necessary items for entrepreneurial activity, then poorer families will face insurmountable obstacles to becoming entrepreneurs. As Ray emphasizes credit markets may shut down for individuals with relatively little collateral because 'these individuals cannot credibly convince their creditors that they will not default on their debt obligations' (Ray, 1998, p.229).

A rural development strategy which puts access to resources in the hands of the bulk of the agricultural population can allow this difficulty to be partially overcome. Resources can now be directly saved and invested by households behaving as entrepreneurs. Fertilizers, new seeds and so on can be purchased and pumps used for irrigation so as to raise overall productivity. Without some sort of broadly based strategy for rural development, the pre-existing inequality will, according to Ray, tend to perpetuate itself. This is due to the fact that if a majority of individuals are shut out of access to credit, these individuals will likely increase the supply of labor to the labor market causing wages to fall. The latter falls not only from the increased supply of labor, but also from the reduction in demand. The reduction in demand stems from the lack of investment by large numbers of potential producers who are unable to produce for lack of credit. Thus people earning subsistence wages will likely be unable to acquire wealth while those that already have it will find their profits enhanced via higher profits stemming from lower wages.

The conclusion to be drawn from the above is *not* that increasing inequality is bad. Instead, the idea to be seen is that inequality and increases in inequality are inefficient in an environment in which the bulk of the population is unable to access credit markets. It is inefficient in that it limits the extent of entrepreneurship and, therefore, productivity growth that can occur in the society at large, thus lowering TFP.

To summarize, the third set of reasons markets undervalue agriculture's contribution to economic development all revolve around its effects on productivity (TFP). Small, household farmers are very efficient, both technically and allocatively, thus allocating more resources to them will likely raise overall productivity. In addition, increased resources to this sector acts as a second best solution to the lack of functioning credit markets. Entrepreneurial activity will be enhanced and productivity will grow.

The fourth reason that markets undervalue the agricultural sector is that they fail to adequately recognize the important role that agriculture plays in reducing poverty. Most of the poverty in poor countries is located in rural areas and much of the rural poor earn their livelihood in agricultural production or related occupations. Thus improvements in agricultural productivity, if broadly based, are likely to have significant negative effects on levels of poverty.

The previous section of this chapter examined various theories concerning the role of agriculture in overall economic development. Although these theorists certainly recognized that market imperfections and limitations exist in rural areas of developing countries, they did not explicitly address them. In the same manner most of these theorists implicitly saw a role for the state to play in the development process. Specifically, the state must cease to discriminate against the agricultural sector so as to allow resources to flow back into the agricultural sector and this would certainly involve acceptance of the border price paradigm. Beyond this, the state would certainly need to invest in any agricultural technology which has the characteristics of a public good, but there is little further to be derived from these theories.

Timmer, however, argues that there is a widespread failure of markets to adequately value agriculture's contribution to agricultural growth. It fails to adequately value agricultural price stability, the learning by doing that occurs in the agricultural sector, the indirect effects of agricultural growth on overall factor productivity and the significant role this sector plays in reducing poverty. The existence of this widespread market failure implies that allowing relative agriculture prices to equal international prices (the border price paradigm) will not be enough. Timmer argues that there are 'very few examples where a strategy of merely providing agriculture with the same incentives seen in world markets has led to rapid and sustained growth. By contrast, no poor country that has "overvalued" agriculture has failed to perform extremely well in terms of economic growth and poverty alleviation' (Timmer, 1993, p.28).

The discussion above of market failure and limitations leads to the heart of this study. Market failures imply that development will be blocked until such failures are dealt with. However, even this approach fails to get at the root of the problem. What are the foundations of market exchange? How do they get established? It is argued in this study that it is in rural areas that integrated national markets generally first evolve. The evolution of such markets is fundamentally intertwined with the transition from agriculture to manufacturing. The next section introduces this topic.

4.   AGRICULTURE AND MARKETS

Many of the models discussed earlier in this chapter emphasize the dualistic nature of the economies of developing nations. Myint (1985) suggests that there are a variety of different versions of dualism. The best known version is that developed by Lewis (1954) and Ranis and Fei (1961) and is based on dualism in the labor market. A second version is financial dualism which concentrates on the interest rate differential between the organized and unorganized capital markets. It seeks to analyze the limitations on flows of funds between these two sectors. A third version is technological dualism which concentrates on the scale of production and factor proportions adopted in the modern and traditional sectors. Finally, there is the notion of sociological dualism which seeks to explain the incomplete specialization of traditional sector participants through appeal to substitutes for the behavioral assumption of profit maximization (perhaps sociological explanations).

Myint (1985) seeks to explain what is common in these various versions of dualism and tries to integrate them into a general conceptual framework. The characteristic of dualism which he concentrates on is the existence of wide price differentials for the same factor of production or commodity in the traditional and modern sectors. One could extend this notion by concentrating on that part of any price differential between different factors of production or different commodities that is not explained by differences in marginal productivity or differences in marginal utility (or marginal rates of substitution among commodities). Myint recognizes that some of these price differentials could be explained by price distortions, stemming from obstacles to the operation of perfect competition, for example the existence of monopoly and monopsony. These involve mainly imperfectly competitive market structures, unions and government regulations. However, he argues that there are considerable price differentials to be explained even after accounting for such noncompetitive distortions.

The analytical device which Myint uses to analyze the price differentials which characterize dualism is the concept of organizational dualism. He characterizes a fully organized economy in the form of a circular flow diagram similar to that in Figure 1.2. He sees the various sectors of the economy as being connected by pipelines which allow goods, factors of production and financial resources to freely flow throughout the economy. There are business firms which hire labor from households and pay wages. The households use this and other income to buy goods and services from the businesses. There are also financial institutions which collect savings from households and businesses and in turn provide both sectors with loans. A government sector, not pictured in Figure 1.2, collects taxes and spends revenues to provide services. Finally, firms can sell their production in the international sector.

In this simple view of a completely organized economy, the pipelines, represented by the arrows, exist and are clear. It is presumed that goods and services can flow frictionlessly from sector to sector in the economy. Thus price differentials between factors of production should reflect only differ-

Figure 1.2   Circular Flow

ences in relative marginal productivities and differences in commodity prices should reflect only differences in marginal rates of substitution.

Note that the crucial assumption above is that the connecting pipes exist and that factors and commodities flow frictionlessly among sectors of the economy. In an economy characterized by organizational dualism, these assumptions only characterize a part of the economy, often called the modern sector. This sector is only loosely connected to the traditional economy where the latter is made up of small-scale units of production, generally household or extended family firms. They produce both agricultural and manufactured commodities and these households are presumed to maximize household or extended family utility. Thus the people in the traditional sector are presumed to be every bit as economically rational as individuals in the modern sector.

The significant difference is that the pipelines connecting households within the traditional sector to other households in the traditional and/or modern sector often do not exist. Or if they do exist factors of production and commodities moving through them are subject to considerable friction, reducing the speed of flow or preventing the flows from occurring. Thus wide price differentials for goods and factors of production will exist, price differentials that cannot be explained by differences in marginal rates of substitution and marginal products. In addition, households in the traditional sector are only partly engaged in the market and much production is subsistence-oriented. However, this is not the result of some irrationality on their part, but 'merely the result of applying the ordinary maximizing behavior to their local economic circumstances' (Myint, 1985). These circumstances concern the structure of the local economy which they find themselves in. Using Myint's analogy, the decisions that households make reflect the constraints stemming from the lack of pipelines connecting various sectors or the degree of friction which acts to slow down or clog flows of resources and outputs.

In order to give further meaning to Myint's analogy the concept of transactions cost[2] must be introduced. In much of economic analysis markets and transacting in them is taken for granted, thus emphasis is placed on distortions which can arise within an existing market system. However, there are costs to transacting in markets and if these costs get too high, the market can actually cease to function.

Transaction costs can be classified based on the different phases of the exchange process. The first step requires that the parties seeking to exchange must search each other out and this is a costly process. Once the parties have found each other, information concerning exchange possibilities must be shared. This information includes characteristics of the product's quality, uses and so on. If large numbers of individuals are involved, additional costs must be incurred in coordinating the plans of individuals and costly bargaining will be required to determine the terms of trade. After a bargain has been struck, it must be monitored and enforced to ensure that the stipulated obligations are carried out. In summary, there are search costs, bargaining and decision costs, and policing and enforcement costs. There must, therefore, be a set of rules limiting the type of behavior that will be allowed to occur in the search, bargaining and enforcement phases. This set of rules represents the institutional structure which underlays the operation of markets.

A simpler way of looking at this may be to realize that the underlying problem of human relations is the uncertainty concerning what can be expected about the behavior of others around us. This uncertainty makes exchange costly and in Myint's analysis creates friction in the movement of output and resources. Thus rules must be created to limit and direct human behavior to create an environment in which people can engage in exchange with some confidence as to what the response of the exchange partners is likely to be.

The effects of transaction costs can be visualized by referring to Figure 1.3. As can be seen, the diagram utilizes supply and demand curves for a particular commodity and determines the equilibrium price and quantity which will result. Much of economic analysis presumes no friction or zero transaction costs, thus attention is concentrated on equilibrium. However, to allow for transaction costs, a wedge will have to be driven between what the buyer is willing to pay and what the seller is willing to accept. In the diagram, this wedge is represented first by the distance *AB*. This represents the cost per unit of carrying out exchange involving *OY* units of output. Additional exchange in the market will be foregone because the costs of exchange are too great. As transaction costs per unit increase to *CD*, the amount of exchange conducted on the marketplace will decline to *OX*. As can be seen, if transaction costs rise high enough, market exchange can disappear altogether.

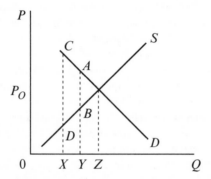

Figure 1.3   Transaction Costs

Thus what distinguishes the traditional from the modern sector is the extent of transaction costs. Then markets can be viewed on a spectrum in which one extreme represents markets with zero (or close to zero) transaction costs and the other with transaction costs so high that no market transactions take place. In between these two extremes, there is a varying degree of market exchange and transaction costs. The traditional sector represents those markets towards the end with high transaction cost per unit, while the modern sector represents those markets towards the end with low transaction costs per unit. In much of the discussion in the following chapters it will, for simplicity purposes, be assumed that in the modern sector transaction costs are zero while in the traditional sector they are positive.

The problem of economic development would then seem to revolve around, at least in the early stages, transforming sectors from being traditional to being modern. This will result in a type of economic growth in the short to medium run which in this study is called Smithian growth. This growth stems from productivity increases resulting from increased specialization. The increased specialization follows from the reduction in transaction costs that occur with modernization.

Long-run growth is of a different nature and involves technical change. This is the rate of growth around which neoclassical growth theory (Solow varieties) has been focused. In this perspective increased savings can only temporarily influence growth rates, since the law of diminishing returns always lowers the return to capital back to long-run equilibrium levels and the long-run growth rate of per capita income is limited to the rate of technical change. The latter in the traditional neoclassical growth models is exogenously determined. In this study, it is argued that Smithian growth is the prelude to and provides the foundation for long-run growth based on technical innovation. · This is the long-run phase of economic growth.

The essential questions then will initially be how does Smithian growth begin, how does an economy, where most economic sectors are traditional in nature, transform into one in which most sectors are modern? How is the institutional structure, necessary to reduce transaction costs, to be laid? A simple framework for the analysis of this problem is provided by the prisoners' dilemma game which, from this point on, will be labeled the traders' dilemma. The outlines of the game are illustrated in Figure 1.4. It is presumed that there are two players of this game, a buyer (*B*) and a seller (*S*). There are two strategies available to each player. The buyer can choose strategy one, the honest or cooperative strategy, which involves negotiating and abiding by the terms of any agreement in an honest, trustworthy manner. Or the buyer can choose strategy two and try to cheat the seller in some way. The same sorts of choice are available to the seller in that he can choose to behave in an honest manner (strategy one) or seek to cheat the buyer (strategy two).

		S	
		I	II
B	I	6,6	0,10
	II	10,0	2,2

Figure 1.4   Traders' Dilemma

The numbers in each of the cells of Figure 1.4 show the rewards to *B* and *S* respectively resulting from the strategy choices actually made. This is a traders' dilemma in that the strategy combination which results in the best outcome for the entire group, choosing to behave honestly (strategy one), is not the strategy choice which maximizes the returns to individual players. Specifically, both the buyer and seller have the incentive to cheat (choose strategy two) since this yields the highest individual return to each player. However, if both choose to behave in a noncooperative manner (choose strategy two) the end result is the worst possibility for the group, the payoffs given in the southeastern cell of the diagram. In fact, for this game this latter possibility represents the only equilibrium.

In terms of markets, one can interpret the above in the following manner. For markets to succeed, buyers and sellers must be cooperative and behave honestly in dealing with others in the exchange process. However, each individual participant has an incentive to cheat and the equilibrium solution is the situation in which both buyers and sellers cheat. In this case market exchange cannot survive because the costs of transacting in the market become so high that such exchange is not beneficial and market exchange disappears. Thus households will retreat from market production to subsistence production and specialization will decline and, as a result, Smithian growth will not occur. This is the traders' dilemma.

The solution to this dilemma would be the creation of certain rules which would outline what could and could not be done by buyers and sellers in the exchange process. This represents the institutional infrastructure of a society, without which market exchange cannot flourish. However, where are these rules to come from and how are they to be established?

One immediate answer is that the rules must be created and imposed by an external entity, for example the state. The latter would decide and enforce the rules which will be imposed on buyers and sellers. There is, however, a fundamental problem with this solution. The state in this situation becomes a third player in the game and who will keep the state honest? Specifically, including the state only widens the existing traders' dilemma. If the state imposes rules how can buyers and sellers presume that these rules will be created so as to be unbiased to either party and honestly enforced? It would seem that the state, too, would be tempted to behave in a myriad of dishonest ways. For example, the state could promise to administer the market for a modest fee (tax). However, once the goods are brought to the marketplace, the state will find a strong incentive to behave dishonestly and ask for additional payments (or confiscate goods). Another possibility is that the state could choose to enforce the rules in a manner which favors one group of individuals or another. Buyers and sellers, realizing that the state is subject to these incentives, will refuse to participate in market exchange. Thus who will keep the state or some external power honest?

The implication of the above is that rules governing market exchange cannot be created and imposed from the outside. They must evolve among the players of the traders' dilemma game, they must come from within. It will be argued throughout much of this study that agriculture provides the crucial environment within which this institutional structure can evolve. Thus agriculture's role is not to provide things to other sectors, such as food, savings, labor and foreign exchange. Instead, it is through agricultural development that the institutional structure for market exchange is constructed. It is in turn this institutional infrastructure which serves as the mechanism for medium-term Smithian growth and long-term growth and industrialization.

5. EMPIRICAL EVIDENCE

Up to this point much of the discussion of agriculture's importance in overall development has been theoretical in nature. Although there has been some empirical evidence presented in this discussion, it has been limited. As a result, in this section additional empirical evidence concerning agriculture's role in economic development will be presented.

Hwa (1988) sought to statistically analyze the contribution of agriculture to overall economic development. He used two cross-country samples with the first consisting of 63 countries for the decade of the 1960s and the second consisting of 87 countries for the decade of the 1970s. Assuming a Cobb-Douglas production function and rewriting it in terms of rates of change through time yielded

$$\dot{Y} - \alpha\dot{K} + \beta\dot{L} + \dot{R}, \qquad (1.2)$$

where $\dot{Y}$, $\dot{K}$, and $\dot{L}$ are the rates of growth of GDP, capital and labor. In addition, α and β represent output elasticities and R is the rate of growth of productivity.

The argument that Hwa makes is that the rate of productivity change is positively influenced by agricultural growth and the growth of exports, while negatively influenced by the rate of inflation. Thus equation (1.2) can be rewritten as

$$\dot{Y} - a + \alpha\dot{K} + \beta\dot{L} + \gamma\dot{A} + \theta\dot{X} + \eta\dot{P} + \epsilon, \qquad (1.3)$$

where a is an intercept term, $\dot{A}$ is the growth of agricultural production, $\dot{X}$ is the growth of exports, and $\dot{P}$ is the average annual rate of inflation. The equation is estimated for the two cross-country samples using regression analysis.

The results for the period 1960-1970 indicate that the signs for $\dot{X}$ and $\dot{A}$, and $\dot{P}$ are all as hypothesized. However, only the coefficients for $\dot{X}$ and $\dot{A}$ are statistically significant, with the coefficient for the latter being substantially larger than for the former. For the period 1970-1979 the signs of the coefficients for $\dot{X}$, $\dot{A}$ and $\dot{P}$ are again as hypothesized and all are statistically significant.   Once again the size of the coefficient from $\dot{A}$ exceeds that for $\dot{X}$, thus agricultural growth was more important than export growth in terms of overall growth.

Using a similar approach Block[3] examines African data for 1965-1973, 1973-1980 and 1980-87.   In the early post-colonial period when African economies were growing, agriculture was making a significant contribution to overall growth.   However, the significance of agricultural growth declines in the 1973-1980 period and disappears in the latest period.   This result probably reflects the overall growth disaster that has afflicted Africa.

Timmer (1993) has also undertaken to empirically analyze the impact of agricultural growth.   Using a relatively extensive sample, he estimated the following regression equation:

Nonagricultural Growth Rate = a + b (Agricultural Growth Rate) (1.4)

The time period covered was 1965-1980. The results indicate a statistically significant positive coefficient for the agricultural growth rate which implies that there is a positive statistical relationship between agricultural and industrial growth.

Bautista (1990) examined a sample of food deficit developing nations where agriculture makes up a large share in gross domestic product (GDP) (more than 20 per cent in the early 1970s).   The relevant variables were expressed in average annual rates of change (trend values) over each of two observation periods, 1961-1984 and 1973-1984.   The equation estimated for these two time periods is similar to that used by Timmer and can be written as

$$\dot{V}_n = a + b\dot{V}_a + c\dot{X}, \tag{1.5}$$

where $\dot{V}_n$ is the rate of growth of nonagriculture value added, $\dot{V}_a$ is the rate of growth of agricultural value added, and $\dot{X}$ is the rate of growth of exports. The results indicated that the coefficients for $\dot{V}_a$ and $\dot{X}$ were positive and statistically significant for both sample periods. In addition, the size of the coefficient for $\dot{V}_a$ was greater than that for $\dot{X}$. The implication then is that agricultural growth is a much more important determinant of nonagricultural growth than is exports.

Bautista also sought to estimate the same equation separately for a number of Asian countries for the period 1961-1984. These countries were India, Indonesia, Malaysia, Pakistan, Philippines, South Korea and Sri Lanka. In all these countries the coefficient for $\dot{V}_a$ was positive and significant. With respect to the coefficient for $\dot{X}$, for all the countries it was positive, but it was only statistically significant for India, Indonesia and South Korea. Of these, the size of the coefficient for $\dot{X}$ was smaller than that for $\dot{V}_a$ in the first two. Only in South Korea was the size of the coefficient for $\dot{X}$ larger. Thus for all the Asian countries except South Korea, agricultural growth was a more important influence on nonagricultural growth than was export growth.

Vogel (1994) sought to answer the following empirical question. Does agriculture possess the strong linkages necessary to drive industrialization in developing countries? He estimated open economy social accounting matrices for six groups of countries: low income developing countries (per capita income below $500), middle-income developing countries ($501-$1000), high-income developing countries ($1001-$1500), the newly industrialized countries ($1500-$3000), low-income developed countries ($6000-$8000), and the USA ($11760). He then uses those matrices to calculate agricultural multipliers representing forward and backward linkages (discussed earlier in the chapter). The forward linkage is found to be very small. However, the backward linkage is quite strong even at the lowest levels of economic development. A $1 increase in expenditure in agriculture generates $2.75 in induced demand for nonagricultural inputs and services. Also the value of the backward linkage increases with the level of development.

The second interesting conclusion to emerge from Vogel's work concerns the source of the backward linkage. At low levels of development the strong backward linkage stems from the demand by rural households for nonfarm commodities. However, at higher levels of income the strong backward linkage stems from agriculture's increased purchases of inputs from the nonagricultural sector. Thus this study and the previous ones cited indicate that agriculture is important in the overall development process.

6. SUMMARY

This chapter has reviewed the various roles that scholars have attributed to agriculture in the overall development process. Generally, these theories viewed agriculture as a source of things for the industrialization process. In particular, agriculture can provide the labor, savings, foreign exchange and market for the growth and expansion of the modern industrial sector. More recent contributions to the literature have recognized that the simultaneous pursuit of these roles is contradictory. Thus they have concentrated on one or a subset of these roles. Most often, the recent work has emphasized how agriculture, through growing income, can provide the growing demand which will stimulate industrial production.

The above approach, however, ignores the institutional structure necessary for the creation of an integrated market system. Timmer's work emphasizes these issues both directly and indirectly. He argued that it is agriculture which provides the learning by doing necessary for the development of entrepreneurs as well as for the development of policy-making skills by the state. It is in agriculture that an institutional structure must be created to provide the stability necessary to provide an environment conducive to long-run investments. It is agriculture where a broad-based strategy of development can create an environment in which rapid productivity growth can occur.

This theme is more specifically addressed in this study. Economic growth is seen as proceeding in two stages. Initially growth is Smithian in nature, being driven by the increasing returns stemming from specialization, and ultimately it is neoclassical in nature, being driven by technological innovation. The former is a necessary condition for the latter. For this two-stage process to unfold, integrated development of the market must occur. The problems involved were illustrated in the form of a traders' dilemma problem or game.

In the traders' dilemma game the equilibrium strategy for both buyer and seller is to cheat by behaving dishonestly in exchange relationships. This dramatically increases the transaction cost per unit of output bought and sold, thus market exchange will shrink in its extent and some markets may actually disappear. What is necessary to overcome this dilemma is a set of rules concerning what is acceptable and not acceptable behavior in the market. However, the problem here is who will construct and enforce these rules. It cannot be simply supposed that the state can serve as the external provider of rules and enforcement. For the state would then become a player in the traders' dilemma. It, too, can choose to be cooperative and honest in its dealings with buyers and sellers or it can choose to be noncooperative and cheat buyer and/or seller.

How then do the institutional rules, which form the foundation for markets, arise? This topic is discussed in Chapter 2 within the context of the traders' dilemma, and argues that there are two types of solution, one for small societies and another for large. For the latter market integration via agricultural development is crucial for what is called Smithian Growth. This is the agrarian path for development. It will be contrasted with an alternative path available to large societies which involves bypassing the creation of an integrated domestic market by substituting the already existing international market. Chapter 3 examines the relationship between market integration and industrial revolutions. Industrial revolutions represent economic growth based on technical change and/or technical innovation. A logical connection between market integration, via the rural path, and technological change and innovation will be developed.

Chapter 4 introduces the state into the theoretical analysis. The discussion will occur within the context of catching up with leaders. It argues that the rural path of development provides a foundation for the development of an autonomous, but embedded state capable of making the transition to high-tech production. Taiwan is used as an example to illustrate this process. The alternative path involving substituting the foreign for the domestic market, and the whole process being driven by government-directed learning, is discussed in the context of Korean experience. The weaknesses of this path relative to the agriculturally driven, rural path is analyzed. Chapter 5 discusses a third path of economic development based on Southeast Asian experience. It is a variant on the second path as represented by South Korea. It, too, represents the substitution of the international for the domestic market, but it is not driven by government-directed learning. Instead, this growth process is led by developmental groups, rather than a developmental state. This path is also frought with difficulties. In particular, it is a fragile sort of development in both an economic and social sense. Finally, Chapter 6 summarizes the study. It argues that of the three paths for development outlined (rural, government-directed learning, developmental groups), the most viable choice for developing countries today would seem to be the rural path. However, it is not free of problems and these are briefly discussed in this final chapter.

NOTES

1. The citation to Dawe is provided in Timmer (1995).
2. See North (1990).
3. The citation to Block is provided in Timmer (1992).

REFERENCES

Adelman, I. (1984), 'Beyond Export-Led Growth,' *World Development* 12 (September), 937-949.

Bautista, R.M. (1990), 'Agricultural Growth and Food Imports in Developing Countries: A Reexamination,' in Seiji Naya (ed.), 266-280.

Haggblade, Steven, Peter Hazell, and James Brown (1987), 'Farm/Nonfarm Linkages and Rural Sub-Saharan Africa: Empirical Evidence and Policy Implications,' Discussion Paper (Agricultural and Rural Development Department, World Bank, Washington, D.C.).

Hayami, Yujiro and Vernon Ruttan (1985), *Agricultural Development: An*

International Perspective (Baltimore: Johns Hopkins University Press).

Hazell, Peter and Steven Haggblade (1991), 'Rural-Urban Growth Linkages in India,' Discussion Paper (Agricultural and Rural Development Department, World Bank, Washington, D.C.).

Hwa, Erh-Cheng (1988), 'The Contribution of Agriculture to Economic Growth: Some Empirical Evidence,' *World Development* 16 (November), 1329-1339.

Johnston, B.F. and J.W. Mellor (1961), 'The Role of Agriculture in Economic Development,' *American Economic Review* 51 (September), 566-593.

Jorgenson, D.W. (1961), 'The Development of a Dual Economy,' *Economic Journal* 71 (June), 309-334.

Lewis, W.A. (1954), 'Economic Development with Unlimited Supplies of Labour,' *Manchester School of Economic and Social Studies* 22 (May), 139-191.

Lipton, M. (1976), *Why Poor People Stay Poor: Urban Bias in World Development* (London: Temple Smith).

Mundle, Sudipto (1985), 'The Agrarian Barrier to Industrial Growth,' *Journal of Development Studies* 22 (October), 49-80.

Murphy, K., A. Shleifer, and R. Vishny (1989), 'Income Distribution, Market Size, and Industrialization,' *Quarterly Journal of Economics* 104 (August), 537-564.

Myint, Hla (1975), 'Agriculture and Economic Development in the Open Economy,' in Lloyd G. Reynolds (ed.), *Agriculture in Development Theory*, 327-354 (New Haven, Connecticut: Yale University Press).

Myint, H. (1985), 'Organizational Dualism and Economic Development,' *Asian Development Review* 3, 24-42.

Newbery, D. and J. Stiglitz (1981), *The Theory of Commodity Price Stabilization: A Study in the Economics of Risk* (Oxford: Clarendon Press).

North, D. (1996), 'Institutions,' *Institutional Change and Economic Performance* (Cambridge: Cambridge University Press).

Ranis, G. and J. Fei (1961), 'A Theory of Economic Development,' *American Economic Review* 51 (September), 533-565.

Ray, Debraj (1998), *Development Economics* (Princeton, New Jersey: Princeton University Press).

Solow, Robert (1956), 'A Contribution to the Theory of Economic Growth,' *Quarterly Journal of Economics* 70 (February), 65-94.

Timmer, C.P. (1995), 'Getting Agriculture Moving: Do Markets Provide the Right Signals,' *Food Policy* 20 (October), 455-472.

Timmer, C.P. (1992), 'Agriculture and Economic Development Revisited,' *Agricultural Systems* 40, 21-58.

Timmer, C.P. (1993), *Why Markets and Politics Undervalue the Role of Agriculture in Economic Development* (Madison, Wisconsin: Benjamin Hibbard Memorial Lecture Series, Department of Agricultural Economics).

Vogel, Stephen J. (1994), 'Structural Changes in Agriculture: Production Linkages and Agricultural Demand-Led Industrialization,' *Oxford Economic Papers* 46 (January), 136-156.

2. Traders' Dilemma

1. INTRODUCTION

The previous chapter ended with a discussion of the traders' dilemma problem, the purpose of which was to show that without a set of rules governing behavior in the market, transaction costs are likely to become so high that market exchange is likely to collapse. As a result, households are likely to remain traditional in nature, which means that the bulk of production will be subsistence-oriented rather than market-oriented. The implication is that the increasing returns stemming from increased specialization will not be realized and Smithian growth will not occur.

In this chapter several solutions to the traders' dilemma are explored. The first involves solutions which evolve within the context of small-scale societies. It is argued that rules can evolve through interaction and that informal enforcement mechanisms can arise. However, the small-scale nature of these societies prevents Smithian growth from occurring. In larger societies, the evolution of such rules and enforcement mechanisms face significant coordination problems. Since the bulk of the population in poor nations resides in and earns its living in agriculture, this coordination problem is an agricultural or rural-based problem. Mechanisms for solving this coordination problem are discussed and from this discussion the crucial role for agriculture emerges.

2. SMALL-SCALE SOCIETIES

The traders' dilemma problem of the previous chapter is reproduced in Figure 2.1. The equilibrium solution to this game is for each individual player, buyer and seller, to choose the noncooperative strategy (two) and cheat, this is always the equilibrium result. This is true if you let the buyer and seller communicate with each other and it is true if the game is played sequentially instead of choices being made simultaneously.

S

		I	II
B	I	6,6	0,10
	II	10,0	2,2

Figure 2.1   Traders' Dilemma

The above analysis and result is, however, too simplistic. It presumes that the traders' dilemma game is played only once and in that situation the only solution is the noncooperative equilibrium. However, what happens when the game is played more than once? If both buyer and seller know the number of times the game will be played, then the result is the same. Every player will have an incentive to choose the noncooperative, dishonest strategy in the second to last play of the game. However, if all players are aware of this, then each player will try to choose a noncooperative strategy on the play prior to the next to last play and so on. The result will be that with the first play of the game both players will choose the noncooperative strategy and this will remain the equilibrium throughout all plays of the game.

This situation changes if multiple plays of the game occur and no one knows when the game will end. The same result will occur if the game is played an infinite number of times. The game unfolds in the following manner. On the first play of the game the buyer (seller) must decide whether to play the cooperative strategy, honesty, or the noncooperative strategy, cheat. If he cheats and the seller (buyer) behaves honestly, then he will reap a large gain (10) in the short run, the first play of the game. The gain is significantly larger than he would have got by behaving in a trustworthy manner (6). However, now the buyer (seller) must consider the potential consequences of behaving dishonestly.

The potential consequences involve the possibility of retaliation. In the example above, if the buyer chooses to cheat the seller and the seller on the initial play behaves honestly, then the latter loses. In retaliation, the seller may choose on the next play of the game to behave dishonestly. Now the winnings of the buyer fall from 10 to 2. The buyer in this circumstance certainly wins a large reward in the short run, but this comes at the expense of dramatically lowered gains in the long run. The possibility that the buyer will choose to behave honestly on the first play of the game becomes real and the cooperative solution has become a potential equilibrium.

The above possibility is dependent on how highly gains in the future are valued; how high or how low the discount rate applied to future earnings is.

If the discount rate is very high it implies that the future is very unimportant to the buyer and he will always choose to cheat. Alternatively, if the discount rate is low enough, the buyer will value returns in the future relatively highly, implying that the possibility of losses due to retaliation in the future for cheating take on an importance. In other words, with a low enough discount rate the buyer will likely choose to behave honestly on the first play of the game as well as all future plays of the game. The same sort of logic applies to the seller as well with the result being that if the discount rate is low enough the honesty (cooperative) solution becomes an equilibrium in the traders' dilemma game.

It must be remembered that although the honesty or cooperative solution becomes an equilibrium, the cheating solution also remains an equilibrium.[1] Which equilibrium will prevail will depend on how the actual game unfolds and cannot be predicted. What is essential to see is that allowing for repeated plays of the game, retaliation, and a low discount rate creates the possibility that interaction among buyers and sellers will evolve into a situation in which certain informal rules of behavior are followed. These informal rules of behavior represent the institutional infrastructure of market exchange and evolve within the context of the exchange process itself.

It should be noted that in the above example it is presumed that the same two people are interacting over and over again in the traders' dilemma game. If each time a buyer plays the game they interact with a different seller, then the threat of retaliation would disappear and the possibility that the honesty solution would be an equilibrium solution disappears. However, as Kreps (1990) argues, there is an alternative possibility by which informal rules could evolve which would limit cheating behavior. If one assumes that somehow information concerning the past choices of all players is freely available to any particular player, then cooperative solutions will be one possible equilibrium in the game even when the same players do not interact continuously over long periods of time. In this situation, dishonest behavior (noncooperation) by a player results in the player being designated as being untrustworthy. Thus individuals must once again weigh the short-run gains of cheating against the long-run losses that come from developing a reputation for dishonesty. The long-run losses would stem from the fact that others will refuse to engage in honest exchange with anyone designated as a cheater.

The above is what Platteau (1994) has labeled as the multilateral reputation mechanism. Notice that once again informal rules, institutions, evolve out of the interaction of buyers and sellers with reputation and its threatened loss serving as the enforcement mechanism. This is how traditional, small-scale societies have usually evaded the breakdown of exchange relationships. At the village and regional level dense interactions by members of villages and regional groups create a process through which information about the behavior of others in the trading community is generated and disseminated informally, throughout the community. As Hayami and Kawagoe (1993) describe it, the village is a community in which everyone is watching everyone else. Gossip concerning a person's behavior is circulated rapidly by word of mouth throughout the community. Any individual who violated a contract with a fellow villager would face grave consequences. Not only would he lose benefits from any present contracts but the resulting bad reputation would prevent him from taking advantage of future opportunities to enter into contracts with other members of the village.

These ideas are similar in nature to those that have been developed by economic sociologists such as Granovetter (1985). He argues that trust among or between individuals can actually be produced. He stresses that this can happen through personal interaction among individuals in structures or networks of relationships which generate trust and discourage noncooperative behavior. This occurs through the creation of personal reputations which act as mechanisms to produce trust. Within this context, Granovetter sees activities such as exchange between buyers and sellers as being embedded in dense networks of social relationships. It is the latter which provides the institutional structure supporting market activities.

This is what is meant by the traditional sector in this study. Note how it is different from the notions presented in Chapter 1. Specifically, Myint argued that the traditional sector activities were subsistence-oriented with little relationship to markets and exchange activity. However, it will be argued in this study that the distinction between traditional and modern does not rest on the distinction between subsistence and market-oriented activity. Traditional economic activities also involve market exchange as well as modern economic activities. The very distinction here concerns the scale of such activities.

An analogy may be helpful at this point. The traditional sector can be viewed as being made up of a series of local islands of economic activity. Within each local island informal rules governing exchange are embedded in the social networks making up these islands and reputation serves as an enforcement mechanism. Thus market exchange within these islands is vigorous, competition fierce and, given the relative supplies of factors of production and the local technology, production is generally efficient. However, the rules and institutions are applicable and legitimate only within that small island of economic activity (village, region, kinship group), and, between these islands of economic activity, there are no or few social networks linking them together. Therefore, the institutional structure necessary to support market exchange has not developed and reputational enforcement mechanisms do not function. As a result, exchange between islands of economic activity is forever plagued by the problems of the single play traders' dilemma game with the result being that the noncooperative, cheating solution prevails. Thus members of one island of activity view individuals from other such islands as strangers to be cheated at will.

It follows then that traditional sector activities are not carried out in the absence of markets. Markets exist, vigorous exchange takes place and some specialization in production activities does occur. However, the extent to which this occurs is limited by the size of the local island of economic activity.

Now a perspective exists that clearly describes the essential characteristics of what is meant by traditional sector activities. The policies often used to try to generate economic growth often wreak great destruction within the traditional sector. Specifically, many states have fostered rapid growth by imposing import substitution strategies emphasizing investment in capital-intensive, urban industries at the expense of rural societies. As a result, migration from rural to urban areas grows rapidly, population growth rates increase and resources are extracted from the rural areas to the benefit of urban areas. The impact of this sort of development process is to destroy the informal rules maintaining market exchange in small-scale societies (the islands of economic activity).

Rapid population growth increases the number of transactors who must interact in market exchange. This makes it increasingly difficult for informal rules to evolve through time. In addition, as families are drawn out of a social environment (rural sector) in which the rules guiding behavior are well known and regarded as legitimate, they are thrust into new and strange surroundings (urban areas). In this new environment the rules are new and unfamiliar and may lack legitimacy in the eyes of the newly settled population. As a result a whole new process of evolution through interaction will have to occur. The problem will be that individuals living in densely settled urban areas will be characterized by greater personal anonymity and less subject to fear of lost reputation. In consequence, in traders' dilemma situations, cheating is likely to be the choice of both buyers and sellers with a breakdown in the underlying rules of market exchange. Individuals and their families will seek to pursue their self-interest even if it comes at the expense of the welfare of the group.

This type of growth is, therefore, likely to be characterized by problems of social and economic organization. Workers within firms are likely to shirk and managers are likely to pursue self-interest at the expense of the firm's interests. Within governments, public employees are likely to feel less and less constrained by informal rules defining what is and is not acceptable. Instead, they are likely to manipulate the rules to enrich themselves and their followers. This growth process is destructive of the institutional structure which is the foundation of market exchange. It destroys the old order provided in small-scale societies without replacing it with an institutional structure appropriate to large-scale, modern societies. Thus this type of growth will retard specialization and Smithian growth. How then is the transition from small- to large-scale exchange to be made?

3. LARGE-SCALE SOCIETIES

Some insight into the solution to the problem of exchange on a large scale is provided in the work of Frank (1988). He assumes that there is a large population of individuals and that everyone in the population is of two types, either a cooperator or noncooperator. The cooperators refrain from cheating in traders' dilemma situations while the noncooperators will always cheat when given the opportunity. Within this context Frank is interested in determining what will happen in a struggle for survival between these two groups. It is assumed that the proportion of cooperators will increase as long as their rewards from playing the game exceed those of the noncooperators and vice versa. Finally, assume that the reward structure of the game played resembles Figure 2.1.

If it is assumed that there is no way to distinguish between cooperators and noncooperators, and that individuals are paired up randomly, then no matter what proportion of the population is made up of cooperators (as long as it is less than 100 per cent), noncooperators will always reap relatively higher rewards compared to cooperators and this will cause the latter to disappear.

If it is assumed that there is a mechanism for distinguishing cooperators from noncooperators and that this information is made available to all players of the game, then the situation is altered dramatically. Cooperators will seek out cooperators and refuse to interact with noncooperators. The latter will only be able to interact with fellow noncooperators. Using the payoffs as illustrated in Figure 2.1, it follows that cooperators would gain relative to noncooperators with the latter disappearing from the population.

Frank considers a third possibility. Suppose it is possible to distinguish between the two groups, but this can only be accomplished by paying a cost. In this situation, an equilibrium arises in which a proportion of the population remains cooperative while the rest are noncooperative. The proportion depends on a number of factors, one of which is the cost of gaining information concerning who the cooperators and noncooperators are. The lower this cost, *ceteris paribus*, the larger the proportion of the population made up of cooperators and vice versa.

The contribution of Frank's analysis is that he pinpoints the crux of the problem concerning how to make markets work. A lack of information about who is trustworthy and who is not prevents the evolution of rules necessary for market exchange. In the traditional sector such information was generated via networks of social relationships which transmit information for the formation of reputations. These are pre-existing social relationships and they have generally evolved within the context of kinship groups, extended families and religious associations. Thus these networks evolved in social contexts to address a variety of social problems. However, over time they also came to serve a function in terms of providing the basis of economic exchange, at least in small-scale societies.

In order to extend this analysis it is time to recognize that the traders' dilemma is really a game played among three players: buyers, seller and intermediaries. That is, buyers and sellers generally do not interact directly in the marketplace. Instead, the arranging of exchange is left to intermediaries who in this chapter are called traders. Each trader faces a dilemma with each buyer and seller. It is the traders' function to gather information about the behavior of potential buyers and sellers and use this information to arrange successful exchanges. Traders can then be viewed as producers of information concerning how trustworthy particular buyers and sellers are in the exchange process.

One technology for generating this information has already been discussed in the context of small-scale societies. In these societies traders are able to tap into already existing systems of information that are generated via dense networks of social relationships based on kinship, extended family connections and religious associations. Thus to emphasize, traders link into already existing social systems for generating information.

The method for generating information discussed above is in this study labeled as the traditional technology. Although it is very effective in smaller areas or regions where pre-existing social networks and relationships are strong and pervasive, it ceases to function well between different regional groups, villages, kinship groups and so on. Scholars in economic sociology have analyzed this situation by concentrating on the notion of social networks. 'A network tie is defined as a relation or social bond between two interacting actors' (Davern, 1997). Burt (1993) argues that most social science research indicates that strong, mutual relations tend to develop between people with similar social characteristics such as education, occupation, family background, religious affiliation, income and age. Thus he believes that the natural result of network development is for individuals to accumulate redundant or repetitive contacts. 'Friends introduce you to friends and expect you to like them. As the network grows then the network of relationships certainly tends to become more dense, but certainly more homogeneous and less diverse' (Burt, 1993). Separate groups of these dense networks can be envisioned, representing the islands of economic activity as discussed earlier, being separated from and not connected to each other. The empty space between such groups of networks can be thought of as structural holes which isolate one group of individuals from another.[2]

It would seem then that it is these structural holes which isolate social networks and limit the overall degree of specialization in production. Spanning such structural holes would seem to be the key process involved in creating an alternative technology (alternative to the traditional technology). In this chapter the spanning of such holes is seen to be the result of entrepreneurial activity which establishes *new* social relationships (or bridges) between members of separated social networks. These entrepreneurial activities can be seen as being carried out by merchants, traders and middlemen seeking to enhance their returns by connecting previously isolated groups through *newly* established linkages.

The bridging of structural holes by middlemen entrepreneurs represents a new structure or technology for generating information. The identifying characteristics of this new technology are outlined in the work of Levy (1989) concerning the advantages which intermediaries (traders) have in arranging exchange between buyers and sellers. The advantage stems from the fact that this alternative technology for generating information is subject to increasing returns. This increasing returns stems from a variety of sources. Buyers and sellers are located in different islands of economic activity, separated by structural holes, and have different rules governing exchange. These rules or regulations may be formal in nature, but they may be, and often are, informal. Thus establishing links between these islands would involve learning about the local culture as well as language. Such information involves indivisible set-up costs that would have to be borne by each buyer and seller. Traders would be able to spread these overhead costs among a large number of buyers and sellers, dramatically reducing per unit information costs.

A second source of increasing returns to scale has to do with specific information in connection with particular industries and particular groups of buyers and sellers. Information with regard to buyers about their needs for specific products will be required if sellers are to be able to effectively meet that demand. Buyers seeking to purchase a particular product require information about the attributes of the products produced by particular suppliers. The gathering of this sort of information would, of course, involve significant expenses upon the part of individual buyers and sellers. However, an intermediary can spread these costs over a large number of individual buyers and sellers, once again significantly lowering transaction costs.

A third source of increasing returns and one of more importance to the analysis here concerns the gathering of information on the reputations of particular buyers and sellers. Obviously, as discussed previously, one could use kinship, extended family, or religious associations and relationships to generate that kind of information. However, this is not the mechanism that is relevant. Instead the mechanism for the gathering of information concerning reputation would go beyond kinship, extended family or religious ties. This would involve significant efforts on the part of individual buyers and sellers to gather information since it would require the creation of a myriad of new social relationships between previously isolated groups. In fact, these costs for individual buyers and sellers are likely to be so high as to make it impossible for individuals buyers and sellers to gather the information necessary for extensive market development. However, this information once gathered would be used to select proper (honest) buyers for particular sellers and proper sellers (honest) for particular buyers for a wide variety of transactions involving the same good or service or even different goods and services. Thus an intermediary who bears the cost of establishing new social networks to gather such information would be able to spread this fixed information cost over a large number of transactions, dramatically reducing the cost per transaction. Again, intermediaries acting as traders would be able to reap increasing returns to the accumulation.

A fourth and related source of increasing returns has to do with the financing, warehousing and transportation costs involved in carrying out exchange between buyer and seller. The financial, storage and transportation facilities used to carry out exchange for one type of good can be used for other types of goods as well. Traders could thus also reap economies of scope in terms of dealing in a wide variety of different products. While these are economies of scope when thinking of the output in terms of goods and services, they are economies of scale when the output being considered is the number of transactions. Being able to use financial facilities and transportation services for a wide variety of goods and services allows the trader to dramatically lower the cost per transaction carried out. Thus from the traders' point of view these are economies of scale (given that transactions are the output).

It is now possible to compare the two technologies for generating information. The traditional technology relies upon already existing networks of social relationships based on kinship, extended family and religious associations and other links. These relationships evolved over time as the structure of the nation state evolved. Middlemen and traders merely tapped into this already existing system. It has been argued that this technology or mechanism for generating information is limited in terms of the extent of market exchange that it can support. This characteristic will be represented by assuming that the traditional technology is characterized by decreasing returns to scale. Alternatively, the modern technology or mechanism for generating information arises from the entrepreneurial activities of merchants and middlemen. The latter create new social relationships which allow them to bridge structural holes separating isolated islands of economic activity. This technology or mechanism is subject to increasing returns.

A simple diagram can be used to visualize the difference in technology. In Figure 2.2 the horizontal axis measures the number of transactions carried out by a particular trader and the vertical axis measures the cost per transaction. Curve AC_T represents average cost of the traditional technology while curve AC_M represents the average cost of the modern technology. As can be seen, when transactions take place on a small scale, the per unit cost is lowest for the traditional technology. However, when exchange takes place on a large scale, the per unit cost is lowest for the modern technology. Thus which technology will be best, in terms of transaction costs, will be dependent upon the scale at which transactions take place.

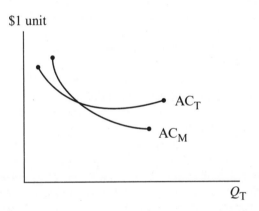

Figure 2.2   Technologies for Generating Information

The above analysis alters the implications of the traders' dilemma significantly. The extent to which buyers or sellers will engage in dishonest behavior was dependent upon the extent to which they could get away with it. Previously, the traditional technology limited this and tended to enforce rules for honest behavior in the market. However, as was just shown, decreasing returns to this technology limits the extent to which it can support market exchange.

With the modern technology the situation changes. If a large number of buyers and sellers agree to simultaneously commit themselves to market exchange, then traders and middlemen will find it profitable to create a new network of social relationships to support this extensive market exchange. They will be able to do this by recouping the benefits of increasing returns to scale (for the modern technology).   However, if the middlemen and traders commit to building the new technology for information-gathering, but few buyers and sellers commit to market exchange, then the traders will fail. Alternatively, if a large number of buyers and sellers commit to market exchange and the middlemen do not, it is the buyers and sellers who will fail. This is a classic example of a coordination problem. This is the topic of the next section of this chapter.

Before closing this section, however, one additional issue needs to be addressed. The distinction between the traditional and modern technologies is that the former involves the use of pre-existing networks of social relationship, whereas the latter views merchants as behaving as entrepreneurs constructing new social relationships linking previously isolated groups. There are decreasing returns to the former and increasing returns to the latter, thus the two technologies are distinct. However, both are dependent on embedding economic exchange in social relationships. This is very similar to the position of Granovetter (1985) who argues that market transactions occurring in developing as well as developed nations, small-scale as well as large-scale societies, are all embedded in networks of social relationships. This view has been strongly attacked in Platteau's (1994) work. He believes that as the scale of exchange grows in terms of the number of individuals involved, the information requirements to make embedded exchange function become overwhelming. Instead, exchange in large-scale societies must be based on some other foundation, other than embeddedness. Exchange in large-scale societies is different in a qualitative sense.

This position is similar to that based on the work of Polanyi (1944). He argued that the development of capitalism involved eliminating the social aspects of exchange, resulting in impersonal exchange. In terms used in this chapter he argued that precapitalist exchange was embedded in social relationships whereas capitalist exchange was disembedded exchange. The approach in this chapter somewhat contradicts this perspective since it argues that merchants establishing new social relationships between previously isolated (socially) groups of buyers and sellers provides the social foundation for integrated market exchange. However, the perspective of this chapter does explain how impersonal exchange can arise as a result of the creation of networks linking previously isolated groups. Thus it can explain how disembedded exchange can arise from embedded exchange.

This explanation follows from viewing societies as being ranked on a scale from less integrated to more integrated. In societies where structural holes are scarce and dense social networks link various groups, market integration will be high. If two strangers meet in the marketplace, because they are unknown to each other the incentive to cheat may be very high. However, in a highly integrated market system (few structural holes), neither player can presume that his opponent is not linked to a large number of others. In fact, the presumption must be that on average each individual *is* linked to a large number of others. Thus each player will be reluctant to cheat and behave dishonestly. Strangers must be respected.

In societies where structural holes predominate and markets are less integrated, it is *less* likely that any individual player in the traders' dilemma game will be linked to many others. As a result, when strangers meet in the marketplace each will assume that the other is linked to few others and thus there is nothing to fear from cheating them. Thus cheating will prevail and exchange between strangers will likely collapse.

The conclusion that results from the above analysis is that if one compares small- and large-scale exchange societies they will appear to be based upon fundamentally different principles: one in which exchange is dependent upon prior existing social relationships and one in which it is not; and one in which exchange occurs only among closely socially related people and one in which exchange occurs among strangers. However, underlying exchange in both types of society are networks of social relationships.

4. SOLVING COORDINATION PROBLEMS

The Agrarian Path

Coordination problems, as outlined in the previous section, are nothing new in development economics. They played an important role in early theorizing on the problems of economic development. Rosenstein-Rodan (1943) argued that the expansion of a single manufacturing industry or firm by itself is likely to fail in a less-developed country. For example, a shoe factory established in isolation will certainly generate enough income to buy all the shoes produced. However, this income is not likely to be spent completely on shoes. Instead, much of the demand would spill over into other commodities and thus the shoe factory would likely fail. However, if a number of investments in different manufacturing fields are carried out simultaneously, then each will provide markets for the production of other sectors. More to the point, investors in potential shoe production hesitate to invest for fear of a lack of market, investors in radio production hesitate for fear of a lack of market and so on. If the investment plans of all of these different industries could be coordinated in the form of a big push, they will all likely succeed.

Murphy et al. (1989) have formalized the big push analysis within the context of imperfect competition with demand spillovers (pecuniary externalities). Within this structure there are two possible equilibria, one with no industrialization (cottage manufacturing) and one with modern industry (utilizing increasing returns to scale technology). The ability to move from one equilibrium to the other depends on the coordination of investment plans.

Within the context of an economy dominated by agricultural production a similar sort of coordination problem exists. Agricultural producers (suppliers) interact with intermediaries (traders). These producers are willing to undertake significant investment in the resources and techniques necessary to rapidly expand production for sale if they can be assured that there will be a market for such output that allows them to profit from investment. In turn, the traders are willing to invest in the modern technology for the gathering of information concerning the reputation of sellers, but only if the number of transactions undertaken by sellers is sufficiently large enough to allow the trader to take advantage of the economics of increasing returns connected with the modern technology. On the other side, buyers will also have to significantly restructure their behavior to extensively participate in market purchases. They will have to switch from a subsistence mode to specialization in production and the reallocation of resources that comes with this. They would then purchase the bulk of their food and other necessary commodities in the market. However, their ability to benefit from this restructuring is dependent upon the extent to which a reliable market for food and other agricultural and nonagricultural commodities exists. This in turn depends upon the ability of traders to assure buyers of an adequate supply of goods and this in turn requires the modern technology for gathering information concerning buyers' reputations. Again, this is only possible if enough buyers and sellers participate so as to allow traders to take advantage of the increasing returns from the modern technology for generating information.

The implication of the above analysis is that some coordination mechanism or stimulus is necessary for an extensive system of integrated market exchange to emerge. It also implies that the development of markets through time is not a linear process in which a society passes from low levels of market development to increasingly larger scales of market exchange until complete commercialization of economic activities occurs. Instead, it may very well be cyclical in nature. Certain stimuli leading to a coordinated entry of buyers and sellers and middlemen into market exchange on a large scale (the use of modern technology for information-gathering), offset by periods of time in which other stimuli prevent coordination and confuse buyers and sellers and middlemen causing them to withdraw from widespread market activity (reverting to the use of traditional technology).

The above sort of analysis has played an important role in Grantham's reevaluation of pre-industrial economic fluctuations. Europe both prior to and during the medieval period experienced a number of expansions and contractions culminating in the industrial revolution. The conventional explanation of the fluctuations is Ricardian in nature. Specifically, capital accumulation drives the expansion process with each phase of the expansion brought to a halt via the operation of the law of diminishing returns. Positive technology shocks driven by human beings' capacity for solving technological problems allow the system to expand until population growth and the law of diminishing returns brings expansion to a halt. This is a supply-side explanation.

Grantham (1996) explains the pre-industrial fluctuations as the result of changing degrees of economic integration. He argues that such integration was dependent on solving the coordination problem and when these solutions failed market disintegration occurred. 'In deciding to undertake specialized production, an individual has to have advance assurance that he will be able to find purchasers; but his potential customers are in exactly the same situation with respect to the market for their own specialties' (Grantham, 1995, p.6). Thus some external coordination mechanism or stimulus was needed so as to push buyers, sellers and middlemen simultaneously into market exchange leading to rapid integration of exchange over significant geographical areas. Alternatively, negative shocks can undo such integration. This is a demand-side explanation of market integration.

As positive shocks occurred economic integration led to increasing returns in production due to productivity gains stemming from growing specialization (Smithian growth). Negative shocks which reduced market integration led to the disintegration of markets and declines in productivity resulting from reduced specialization. Thus growth was cyclical and progress did not unfold in a linear fashion. The fundamental cause of growth (Smithian growth) was a pre-existing economic structure that was highly susceptible to the coordination process.

Grantham intriguingly speculates concerning the European economic breakthrough. 'What is important about the medieval take-off is that in the course of two to three centuries, the basis of specialization widened. Specifically, throughout succeeding centuries the list of goods brought into the integrated systems grew and as it did the high income equilibrium of the European economy became more stable and more robust to shock' (Grantham, 1993, p.30).

The discussion above has tended to imply that coordination stimuli came from outside the economy. Specifically, international trade could provide such a stimulus to an agrarian economy, one in which agricultural activities predominate. If a particular nation has a comparative advantage in the production of particular agricultural commodities for foreign markets this could provide the coordination mechanism to bring about the simultaneous entry by buyers, sellers and middlemen into the market. Traders could then preferably shift to the modern technology for information production and integrate large numbers of individuals into market exchange. However, the key to determining whether or not foreign demand will stimulate widespread market integration is the extent to which rural households are involved in the production process. If the product being exported is grown by a large proportion of the rural population, then the number of potential transactions will be quite high. Thus the export demand would trigger the development of traders utilizing entrepreneurial means to establish new social networks for gathering information concerning trading partners. Cooperators will be linked on both sides of the market (buying and selling) and the proportion of production going through the market system will grow dramatically. Productivity will then grow as a result of the ensuing specialization, what has been called Smithian growth.

Alternatively, if the export crop is grown only by a small proportion of the rural population, the number of transactions involved is likely to be limited. This would in turn pose an obstacle to the use of the modern information-gathering technology by traders. The development of an extensive system of traders is likely to be limited and markets are likely to remain fragmented or undeveloped. The implication would seem to be that coordination, whatever its source, must be directed at the rural production activities that are carried out by the bulk of the rural population. This is most likely to involve the production of foodgrain products that are grown by almost all households. Coordination would involve allocating additional resources to this sector and this would signal buyers, sellers and traders to simultaneously enter the market. Given the large number of transactions that will occur, traders will switch to the modern technology for information-gathering, cooperators will be matched with cooperators, market integration occurs and Smithian growth results.

It was argued above that international trade might play an important role in coordinating the activities of buyers, sellers and middlemen. The coordinating mechanism is the rise in the relative price of the agricultural commodity in which the country has an existing comparative advantage. However the success of such a policy aimed at stimulating the development of an integrated market system will depend on the proportion of the rural population growing the export crop. The lower this proportion, the less likely international trade can serve as a coordinating mechanism. However, the strength of comparative advantage and trade to serve as a coordination mechanism will likely be increased if the state has acted to discriminate against the agricultural sector in the past.

States have discriminated against agriculture, as discussed earlier, in a number of ways. Direct discrimination has often involved establishing marketing boards which push down the prices of important agricultural goods. Indirect discrimination has often involved the use of import substitution policies, which involve levying tariffs on imported manufactured goods, which in turn raise the prices of industrial inputs to farmers. All of these policies tend to turn the internal terms of trade against the agricultural sector. The more discrimination practiced against this sector and the more distorted relative prices are (relative to international prices), the stronger and more effective international trade may serve as a coordinating mechanism stimulating buyers, sellers and middlemen to simultaneously enter into a market exchange on a large scale. However, as previously mentioned, the effectiveness of this coordinating mechanism will be dependent upon the proportion of the population producing the good or goods involved.

The above strategy requires a return to border prices in terms of the pricing of agricultural products. However, as Timmer pointed out, this is in many cases not likely to be enough. He argued that when government discrimination against agriculture is eliminated market prices (border prices) will still tend to undervalue the contribution of agriculture to the overall development process. The same argument is made here, but for reasons that are different from those proposed by Timmer. The analysis in this chapter has argued that countries may very well find themselves in situations in which multiple equilibria (at least two) exist in the agricultural sector. At undistorted relative prices for agricultural goods (no discrimination against the agricultural sector) a country could be caught in a low-level equilibrium at which too few buyers, sellers and middlemen enter into market exchange relationships and thus the traditional mechanisms for generating information are used.

There is another equilibrium at which such a large number of these individuals enter into exchange that it makes it profitable to use the modern technology for information gathering. These equilibriums exist because of the increasing returns to the construction of the social relationships necessary to establish this modern technology. Thus a return to border prices may not be a strong enough signal to solve the coordination problem, especially if the export products are produced in an environment in which the bulk of the population is not involved. The return to border prices may also not be a strong enough coordinating signal in situations where discrimination has been mild or where discrimination has been circumvented due to illegal activities. In the latter case a return to border prices may only legalize markets that already exist rather than stimulate extensive market integration.

In the above context the state may have to play a stronger role in coordination. The coordination process involves increasing the inflow of resources into the agricultural sector. This could be achieved by allowing the relative price of important agricultural goods to rise via protection (raising the relative price above international levels). Important agricultural goods would be those grown by the bulk of the population. This would promote the process of market creation by forcing domestic buyers to purchase domestically produced goods and providing increased incentives for producers to enter the market. Traders, recognizing the increased tendencies for buyers and sellers to enter the market, are more likely to commit the resources necessary to establish the modern technology for generating information.

The point is that the actual mechanisms of coordination will vary significantly given the historical circumstances involved and the precise policy stance of the state to the market. Whatever these historical circumstances may be, it should be emphasized that the initial development of a market system is likely to involve the production and sale of a staple crop, but that this will likely change rapidly as comparative advantages evolve in the countryside. Generally, comparative advantage is analyzed from the supply-side only. That is, the availability of certain resources, skills and so on dictate which agricultural products a region is likely to have a comparative advantage in. However, comparative advantage must be demand-activated, that is, specialization according to relative supply-side advantages cannot occur unless demand grows rapidly enough to make such specialization profitable. Thus rapid growth in markets for staple goods will likely stimulate, via rising income, demands for other agricultural goods (fruit and vegetables) some of which can be produced by local farmers possessing a comparative advantage activated via growing demand.

The above is not to deny that government investment in new agricultural technology and physical infrastructure (roads and communication) are necessary for rapid agricultural development. With regard to the former, technologies developed elsewhere must be adapted to the soil, climate and geographical characteristics of the various regions in developing rural areas. The main point is that government policies aimed at research, road development and other social infrastructure investment need to shift focus as farmers specialize in a variety of new crops.

The above process will be further augmented by a learning by doing process which is just as applicable to agricultural as it is to industrial production. Scholars have generally argued that new technologies for manufactured goods are tacit in nature and cannot be costlessly transferred from developed to less-developed nations. Instead they must be learned via exposure in the actual process of production (Amsden, 1989). However, similar arguments are just as applicable to the use of new technology in agriculture. Such technologies cannot be effectively used unless they are learned and such learning occurs via actual doing. Moreover, there is also an externality involved in the process. Farmers learn from observing the behaviors and activities of their neighbors, thus one learns by doing and using, but also by observing. Knowledge spills over from neighbor to neighbor raising productivity (Foster and Rosenzweig, 1995).

The implication of the above analysis is to further strengthen the notion that comparative advantage or potential comparative advantage must be demand-activated. That is, new technology cannot be effectively learned except through use and use implies that there is a growing demand for a particular product. The faster the growth in demand, the more rapidly the learning occurs.

In addition to the above, as the market for, say, foodgrains develops, the network of traders involved can, as argued previously, use their knowledge (about buyers and sellers) and facilities to coordinate the development of markets not just for other agricultural goods, but also simple manufactured goods. The information gathered and facilities constructed in carrying out trade in important products such as foodgrains dramatically lower the costs of transacting in foodgrains, but the same facilities can dramatically reduce the costs of transacting in other agricultural goods as well as simple manufactured goods.

All of the analysis is quite consistent with the new theoretical work in endogenous growth theory (Locay, 1990). Traditional neoclassical theory implies that increased savings can have no long-run impact on the equilibrium growth rate. This is basically due to the fact that the law of diminishing returns eventually reduces the marginal product of capital. However, within the framework outlined above this may not happen or, if it does, the time at which the law of diminishing returns will operate is postponed into the future. This can be seen by presuming that there is not one type of capital good available, but n varieties. There is, of course, decreasing returns to any specific type of capital. However, the decreasing returns to any one variety of capital can be avoided by switching to a second variety and when diminishing returns set in, switching to a third variety and so on. The availability of these varieties of intermediate or capital goods is dependent upon the degree of specialization occurring in the economy, which is, in turn, dependent upon the existence of a cohesive integrated market system. The logic then is that as coordination leads to the development of an integrated system, the number of varieties of capital goods will rise and the law of diminishing returns can be overcome. Thus the marginal product of capital may actually rise or at least not decline.

This is, of course, what has previously been called Smithian growth. The interesting question concerns whether or not this type of growth can permanently overcome the law of diminishing returns. Theoretically, this is whether the variety of intermediate goods is unlimited or not. If the former, then Smithian growth can occur forever, but if the latter is true, then there are definite limits on Smithian growth. These issues will be discussed further in subsequent chapters.

An Alternative Solution to Market Coordination

The above analysis would seem to imply one pathway through which the coordination problem of market organization can be solved. It is a pathway that emphasizes the agricultural sector and, as a result, it is labeled here as the agrarian path. Its emphasis is on the evolution of the domestic market and argues that agriculture is the birthplace of an integrated national market. Later on in this study it will be shown how such a process can drive an industrial revolution. More simply, the industrial revolution is driven by the domestic market.

There is, however, an alternative industrialization strategy available that seeks to rely on foreign rather than domestic markets to drive the industrialization process. In this case, the creation of an integrated domestic market would not be necessary and an agricultural transformation would not be essential. That is, this approach seeks to get around the coordination problem outlined above by substituting foreign markets, which are already well developed, for domestic markets. This is an outward-oriented approach in which domestic markets play a small role in the development process and emphasizes the early export of manufactured goods. However, while avoiding the coordination problem involved in creating a domestic market, this approach creates a different form of the traders' dilemma. A clue to the problem and its possible resolution is provided by the recent work of Langlois and Robertson (1995), as well as that of Granovetter (1985) and Feld (1981).

Langlois and Robertson view firms and other types of organization as being made up of two components: intrinsic and ancillary capabilities. The intrinsic core 'comprises elements that are idiosyncratically synergistic, inimitable, and noncontestable' (Langlois and Robertson, 1995, p.7). The ancillary capabilities are those which could be purchased from other sources. What is intriguing here is their description of intrinsic core activities. They describe these activities as being part of the organizational culture of the firm. This culture is made up of habits and routines that individuals acquire through procedures that are unique to the firm, and constitute the essence of the firm.

Compare this to Williamson's (1975) discussion of the boundaries of the firm. The boundary of the firm concerns those transactions that take place via the market and thus occur between firms, as opposed to those transactions which are conducted within the hierarchical firm rather than markets. Of course, as to which side particular transactions fall, within the firm or in the market, depends on relative transaction costs. What is important here is the advantage Williamson attributes to organizing transactions within the hierarchical firm. The hierarchical organization of the firm can be used to tame opportunism on the part of individuals. This opportunism involves pursuit of self-interest even if it results in an inferior outcome for the firm (group). This is, in fact, the traders' dilemma discussed earlier, only it occurs within the firm. Transactions involving the significant possibility for such opportunism would, according to Williamson, be better handled within the confines of the firm where the authority of hierarchical relations can be used to limit the pursuit of self-interest.

There is an important difference between the work of Langlois and Robertson and Williamson. The former refers to the core of the firm as a set of habits and expected behaviors involving reciprocal relationships that have come to be viewed as accepted behavior and are unique to that particular firm. Williamson appeals to authority stemming from hierarchical relations of power. The problem with the appeal to authority is that it is itself subject to the corrosive effects of opportunistic behavior. Alternatively, the reciprocal patterns of behavior outlined by Langlois and Robertson rely less on authority and more on interpersonal, reputational mechanisms.

This is related to the work of Feld (1981) who attempts to explain the patterns found in social networks. In particular, he is interested in explaining clusters of social networks and the connections between such clusters. He argues that clusters of social networks tend to evolve around a focus. 'A focus is defined as a social, psychological, legal, or physical entity around which joint activities are organized (e.g., workplace, volunteer organizations, hangouts, families, etc.)' (Feld, 1981. p.1016). It follows then that as a 'consequence of interaction associated with joint activities, individuals whose activities are organized around the same focus will tend to be interpersonally tied and form a cluster' (Feld, 1981, p.1016). The implication then is that firms can serve as the focus around which dense social networks will arise through continuous interaction of the individuals involved. Thus the core of the firm becomes this dense social network tying individuals together. Within this core informal and formal rules for arriving at cooperative solutions to traders' dilemmas are created via continuous interaction over an indefinite time period. The firm provides the mechanism for coordinating this interaction.

The analysis can be briefly summarized by stating that in those environments in which social networks are not well developed, an extensive system of integrated markets will not exist. However, those social networks can be created within firms with coordination achieved through the organization of the firm. Thus the lack of markets due to widespread existence of traders' dilemmas is overcome by substituting the firm for the market. The firm serves as a focus around which or within which social networks can be created.

The role of the state here is quite different from that outlined in the agrarian path. The goal would not be to create a national market system driven by agriculture, but instead the lack of a market is circumvented via the establishment of large business enterprises within which a core set of social networks would evolve. The government's job of coordinating overall expansion is simplified since only the activities of a small number of large firms needs to be coordinated. This solution to the traders' dilemma by forcing repeated plays of the traders' dilemma within the context of the firm results in the reputational mechanism serving to assure cooperation within the firm. The firm and its core of developing social networks substitutes for the market.[3] The government then uses a variety of protectionist and subsidy programs to promote export expansion among these business conglomerates.

One of the main difficulties of the above solution to the traders' dilemma is that a significant degree of responsibility for success rests upon the shoulders of the state. The latter must create business entities, within which the traders' dilemma will be solved, and use various mechanisms to ensure that their firms operate efficiently, efficient enough to be competitive internationally. It is the ability of these firms to gain access to foreign markets that allows them to avoid or skip over the undeveloped domestic market. However, such reliance upon effective state policy making opens up a significant possibility for state failure. Economics has spent a great deal of time outlining the various ways that markets can fail and thus require state intervention to offset the effects of these failures. However, states can fail as well, with the result being significant economic losses, perhaps larger than those stemming from the original market failure. Thus attempts to regulate monopolies often backfire with the boards set up to control monopoly pricing becoming a vehicle for promoting or strengthening monopoly power. That is, the state may set out to create business groups capable of penetrating foreign markets, but in the end being captured by these business enterprises in the sense of having policy eventually being manipulated by those large business enterprises.

There have, however, been some very successful examples of countries who have followed this nonagrarian road to rapid industrialization. In later chapters these examples are discussed in greater detail. However, for the rest of this chapter and the next the discussion is focused on the first solution to the traders' dilemma, the agrarian path. The experiences of both England and Japan are used to illustrate how agriculture served as the birthplace of integrated national markets in both nations.

5. ENGLAND AND JAPAN

It may be surprising to learn that two such different nations are used to illustrate very similar paths to integrated market development. Indeed, it is surprising, but no less true that the period prior to the industrial revolutions in England and Japan were characterized by many similarities. For England the period discussed is the 17th and 18th centuries, while for Japan the period is the 18th and 19th centuries. These are the time periods prior to the development of modern industry in both nations.

Macfarlane describes well the amazement of scholars comparing the experiences of Japan and England. Speaking as an English historian studying Japan, 'It is therefore a source of considerable surprise to find a civilization at the other end of the world which feels rather familiar. It is particularly challenging because there was little direct contact or diffusion before the nineteenth century to account for the apparent similarities' (Macfarlane, 1997, pp.766-767).

It may, of course, be questioned whether Japanese development was truly autonomous. However, for the time period here, 18th and 19th centuries, Japanese growth basically involved expansion of traditional sector economic activities. Macfarlane argues that what seems to have happened represents 'some kind of ignition of pre-existing material' (Macfarlane, 1997, p.768). Thus by 1868, the Meiji restoration, most scholars are convinced that Japan was already quite an unusual place ready for a massive surge in economic activity.

In comparing the pre-industrial revolution experiences of England and Japan one is first struck by the fact that both nations experienced agricultural revolutions. The word revolution used here, however, is quite misleading. Both countries experienced long periods of agricultural growth. This growth exceeded the rate of expansion of the population, thus generating a surplus capable of feeding a sizable nonagricultural population. In many countries increases in output generated by agriculture are quickly siphoned off by the powerful and transferred out of the agricultural sector. However, it seems that in both Japan and England, farmers benefitted from the increased productivity gains.

Also, both Japan and England experienced long periods of time during which traditional manufacturing enterprises and craft production grew rapidly. This has often been labeled as the development of protoindustry in England and a similar phenomenon also seems to have occurred in Japan. Many of these traditional manufacturing activities were located in and prospered in rural or semi-rural areas. Thus 'the base of much of the massive change lay as much in the countryside as in the cities' (Macfarlane, 1997, p.771).

As this phenomenon of traditional sector growth unfolded in both Japan and England it did so in an environment in which significant urbanization occurred. In particular, both countries experienced the creation of major urban areas capable of exerting considerable economic influence throughout the economy. It was the interaction between rural and urban areas that gave rise to extensive in-country trading networks capable of moving goods throughout either nation. Thus merchant groups became important segments of the population playing crucial roles in the establishment of these trading networks.

The next to last characteristic that will be mentioned here concerns both the level of wealth generated in the pre-industrial period and its distribution. 'One characteristic of England since the twelfth century has been its wealth, and the fact that this has been widely distributed. In terms of housing, clothing, diet and general standard of living, it was a very affluent "pre-industrial" society' (Macfarlane, 1997, p.781). The growing wealth from 1550-1750 would seem to be crucial for the industrial revolution. Although Japan was probably not as affluent as England prior to the industrialization period, it would be good to remember that the slow and steady growth in the 150 years prior to the Meiji restoration created a relatively wealthy society in Japan with significant improvement in diet, clothing and housing. It is also true that the relative affluence of this pre-industrial period was crucial in the industrialization process.

Finally, capitalism in both nations grew out of a pre-existing feudal social and political structure. In both regions the farmers served as the main source of surplus food for the warrior group. The warrior group was stratified into various levels of power and authority. The relationship between each of these layers was, however, in the form of a social contract. The lower layers of society swearing loyalty and support to those above them in return for protection and other services. With this social and political structure power and authority were not concentrated in the hands of a few and neither was it so dispersed as to create chaos and anarchy. There seems to have been a delicate balance between centralization and decentralization, between the center and the periphery.

In the following discussion of market development interest will first be focused on England and then Japan. However, it should be borne in mind the similarities in the experiences of both nations.

England

Classical economics, as represented by Smith, Ricardo and Malthus, seems to represent theorizing which was seemingly out of touch with what was going on at the time, the 17th and 18th centuries as well as the beginning of the 19th century. Specifically, there was an undertone of pessimism in the theorizing. The law of diminishing returns seemed to represent the fundamental problem facing all economies with long-run prospects darkened by the likelihood that population growth would overwhelm economic gains. This seems to be in conflict with what seemed to be actually occurring in England at the time. In particular, economic historians of the 1960s presented a picture in which England underwent an agricultural revolution in the 18th century quickly followed by an industrial revolution. Rostow (1960) presents a view in which the English economy experienced a take-off into long-run growth in the late 18th and early 19th centuries making a decisive break with the past. This decisive break was powered by capital accumulation and technical innovation in a few leading industries. This view seems to indicate that the classical economists were quite disconnected with the important events which would have been occurring all around them.

However, in the 1980s a new historical view began to emerge which seemed to indicate that the classical economists' view of their own times was actually quite accurate. Empirical work seems to indicate that British growth in the late 18th century was much slower than originally thought (Crafts, 1985). The new analysis reckons that a large proportion of the population was employed in traditional, rather than modern manufacturing activities. In addition, many modern inventions seemed to have only a very small impact on the economy. The words 'industrial revolution' were looked upon with great skepticism by this historical view. There seemed to be no revolutionary change in the late 18th century.

Thus the classical economists would seem to have had an accurate view of the functioning of an advanced organic economy. In such an economy land was indeed the key to the economy as the major source of food, energy, construction materials and raw materials for industry. The economy was mainly based on the production of textiles produced from animal and vegetable fibers, leather from animal hides and wood for fuel and building. As manufactured production expanded it placed increased demands on the land to provide fodder for horses, food for workers, wood for building and so on. The energy needs of the economy were largely supplied by a flow of resources from agriculture. The limitations imposed by the law of diminishing returns were quite real and thus the fears well founded (Wrigley, 1988).

However, this organic economy seems to have been quite dynamic in its own right. The increased productivity stemming from specialization and the division of labor, which formed the center of Smith's work, seems to have provided a basis for continuous growth during this time period. This growth was, from a historian's point of view, most obvious in the agricultural sector. However, historians who have analyzed the social organization of production in particular localities rather than constructing macroeconomic aggregates have found that the organization of handicraft production was undergoing major changes. By a close analysis of the organization of domestic outwork in textiles or small metal trades, they have charted shifts in the relationship between workers and employers, between merchants and producers, with continuing adjustments in the design of hand tools which permitted gains in productivity (Daunton, 1995, p.13).

Furthermore, objection is made trying to make a sharp distinction between modern and traditional manufacturing.

A clear distinction between two sectors obscures the gradual transformation of the so-called traditional sectors by their own internal dynamics, as they accumulated capital for investment in factories, adopted power machines in order to escape particular bottlenecks, and utilized different production methods to cater for particular markets (Daunton, 1995, p.13).

This analysis has been rejected by some who presume that an integrated national market already existed in England by 1700. However, more recent research would seem to indicate that this was not true. Specifically, from approximately the mid-16th to the mid-17th centuries small, vibrant, localized markets dominated the English countryside. 'The local character of the marketplace ensured recurrent face-to-face interactions, which provided the social foundation for fairness and trust among traders' (Lie, 1993). There were also formal rules and regulations usually enforced by a market court and Justice of the Peace. The most stringent measures concerned attempts to undermine the openness of the marketplace. The great fear was that private trade, which sought to bypass the open market, would imperil the local food supply. Prices were regulated for quite similar reasons.

There were two significant constraints to the expansion of this type of market structure, one technological and the other social. The important technological problems to expansion were difficulties in both transportation and communication which greatly limited the extent to which trading relations could expand. However, perhaps the more binding constraint was social in nature. 'The structure of local trade critically depended on the context of face-to-face interactions to uphold "fair" trade' (Lie, 1993, p.286). The microfoundations of this kind of trade would not suffice to support the development of integrated trade within the context of an integrated market.

In order to generate an integrated market system, a shift from the traditional to the modern technology for information-gathering had to be made. For this to occur, the coordination problem facing buyers, sellers and interregional traders had to be overcome. The Corn Laws provided one such source of coordination. They provided a mechanism for signaling the various players to enter the integrated market game. Bates (1988) represents British policy during the Corn Law period as follows:

$$max \ (P_d, P_w), \tag{2.1}$$

where P_d is the domestic and P_w the world price of grain, thus under the terms of the policy if the world price was below the domestic price, imports were limited. When the world price was above the domestic price, exports were allowed. The goal of the policy was to generate high prices for grain and to try and stabilize these prices over time. In a sense the Corn Laws represented a subsidy to grain production, tilting the balance of resources in agriculture's favor.

The integration of markets in England began around 1700, but was not really finished until the mid-19th century. It was led by the integration of markets for key grains. This would seem to be no accident given the impact of the Corn Laws. They would have signaled to sellers that relative prices would be adjusted so as to assure the successful and profitable sale of grain either to the domestic or to foreign markets. Buyers were assured that grain would be available to them either from domestic or foreign sources and at a relatively stable price. This was combined with the abolishment of controls over internal trade in 1663. Thus the role of the state was to influence the inflow and outflow of grain into the country through import duties and export bounties and to leave the internal market free of regulation.

Bates (1988) emphasizes how exceptional such a policy was in the context of Europe. For example, French policies towards agriculture were much more representative of those prevailing in the rest of Europe.

> French agriculture was peasant based; productivity was relatively low; the government adhered to a low-price policy; and it maintained a bureaucracy to secure cheap grain to feed its civil servants, its armed forces, and its capital city. The French case - not the English, with its large farms, subsidized rural sector, and relatively free internal trade - better approximates the world of contemporary developing nations (Bates, 1988).

Agricultural productivity began to grow during this period, but this was not the result of a technological breakthrough. It was more the result of institutional and social changes in the structure of agriculture which allowed farmers to supply techniques that were available from medieval times, but could not be effectively utilized in an environment in which there was limited market integration.

As agricultural productivity slowly rose a second coordinating mechanism reinforced the movement towards market integration, with resulting productivity growth stemming from specialization. This mechanism was the growth of cities and towns. 'In Europe, urban growth between 1500 and 1750 was concentrated on large cities, and particularly state capitals; cities with a population less than 40,000 only grew in line with the general rise in population, and the number of small towns of 5,000 to 10,000 actually declined between 1600 and 1750' (Daunton, 1995, p.136). The pattern in England was quite different. The number of small towns doubled between 1600 and 1750 and the percentage of populations living in towns with 10000 or more people rose four times between 1600 and 1800. Of course, urban development in all of England was overshadowed by the growth of London as a commercial center.

The coordination process discussed above resulted in the evolution of a new group of traders and markets which knit the markets of England together into an integrated whole. As previously discussed, trade in grains was highly regulated in local or regional markets to try to prevent shortfalls. This was aided by the establishment of chartered markets where all grain transactions were to take place. However, the chartered markets were increasingly circumvented by mills and merchants who bought grain directly from farmers on the basis of a sample inspected by purchasers or purchased the crop while it was still in the ground. London drew its grain for bread, brewing, and distilling from a variety of areas in England, much of it by ship. Thus the grain trade came to rely upon a complex pattern of specialists and middlemen, who linked farmers with final markets (Daunton, 1995).

The retail and wholesale trade of other commodities also sprang to life. During the 17th and 18th centuries a new type of trader merchant began to appear. 'Traveling merchants forged an interregional network of trade across England in tandem with the rising number of provincial shops' (Lie, 1993, p.288). They expanded their activities into manufactured goods and increasingly brought production under their control in the countryside. They supplied raw materials for household manufacturing which in turn produced finished products. Increasingly, much of this merchant activity became centered in London, as did the grain trade, with trade organized into a complex network of merchants and traders.

These processes of market integration were aided by activities aimed at loosening the constraint on trade and exchange imposed by poor communication and transportation systems. 'State intervention was central to this process' (Lie, 1993, p.293). During the years 1660-1689 there were fifteen parliamentary acts to improve transport. This number rose to fifty-nine from 1690-1719 and to one hundred and thirty in the years 1720 to 1749. There was also a rise in navigable river distance from 685 miles in 1660 to 960 miles in 1700 to 1160 miles in 1730. Also by 1750 the system of turnpike roads, which was centered on London, was complete. Finally, national postal services were also begun (Lie, 1993, p.293).

Thus it seems that there were three coordination mechanisms at work in creating an integrated national market. The Corn Laws represented a subsidy to the agricultural sector and spurred the commitment of buyers and sellers and traders to interregional trade via markets. The rise of London as a major urban center also served as a coordination mechanism stimulating the development of a complex web of merchants and intermediaries spanning the island. Finally, improvements in transportation and communication served to further reduce transaction costs thus spurring market integration.

The end result of this was a growth process that was Smithian in nature, that is, growth was stimulated as a result of the regional specialization in agricultural production as well as the structural change which allowed the growth of and specialization in nonagricultural production. This structural change involved an increasing share of the population earning its living in small-scale manufacturing activities. A similar sort of process also seems to have occurred in Japan and it is this example that we now turn to.

Japanese Experience

One can divide early Japanese history into two time periods: Tokugawa (17th, 18th and 19th centuries) and Meiji (late 19th and early 20th centuries). Prior to the Tokugawa period Japan was wracked by warfare between rival feudal lords. However, a particular warlord, Toyotami Hideyoshi, eventually either defeated or forced peace on his rivals. In order to provide a stable political environment he ordered the warriors, samurai and feudal lords to leave the countryside and locate in centralized castle towns. The samurai could no longer support themselves directly by extracting surplus production from the peasants. Instead, they received stipends paid in rice. In an additional move to promote political stability, the shogunate (dominant family) imposed a system of alternative attendance on the warlords. Specifically, all of the warlords were required to maintain permanent residence in the Tokugawa capital of Edo (modern Tokyo), their wives and children had to reside there, and the warlords themselves and their retainers had to, on a regular basis, alternate their residency between Edo and the castle town of their domains. Finally, Japan closed itself off from the outside world by refusing to engage in trade or other types of interaction with other countries.[4] Thus Japan was isolated from external influence until the beginning of the Meiji period (Vlastos, 1986; Smith, 1988).

The policies outlined above, although politically motivated, had a significant economic impact. The payment of stipends to the warrior class meant that an effective system of taxation had to be designed. This first involved an exhaustive survey of the available plots of land and classification of the land based on productivity and whether it was irrigated. The tax rate was then expressed as a percentage of the estimated productivity of each plot (Vlastos, 1986). It must be emphasized that although this tax was levied on individual plots of land and the farmers that cultivated them, it was the village that was responsible for the collection of the tax. The feudal lord presented the tax bill and it was the responsibility of the village as a group to collect the tax (Smith, 1988). This dependence on the village was necessary since the warrior class had been completely removed from the countryside and thus they were no longer involved in managing and governing village affairs.

Initially, the burden of this tax was extremely high. However, over time it appears that the burden of the tax significantly diminished. Feudal lords found it increasingly difficult to reassess farm land and/or raise the tax rate on assessed yield (Smith, 1988). This inability to extract additional rice tax stemmed from the fact that the administrative structure to carry out such changes no longer existed in the countryside. The warlords and samurai were congregated in castle towns and the responsibility for administering the tax fell upon the village as a whole. The leaders of the villages used this advantage to effectively resist tax increases. The implication of this was that any increase in output produced by farmers would remain in their hands rather than in the hands of the feudal lord.

In a dual economy model, such as developed by Lewis (1954) and Ranis and Fei (1961), a great deal of importance is placed on the terms of trade between the two sectors. This same model (with some modification) can be applied to a feudal economy by presuming that the two sectors are peasant farming and an urban sector made up of warriors, a feudal élite and artisans. Rice is extracted from the peasant farmers via a tax in return for which the feudal élite provides protection of life and property. The terms of trade between the two sectors is represented by the proportion of total rice production collected by the feudal elite. A decline in this proportion represents the terms of trade turning in favor of agriculture and this seems to be what happened in the Japanese case.

In addition to the above, the movement of the samurai and feudal élite into castle towns resulted in a significant degree of urbanization at the beginning of the Tokugawa period (approximately 1600). The result was that Japan became one of the most urbanized societies of the world for that time period with an estimated 17 per cent of its population living in towns of 3000 or more (Macfarlane, 1997). In addition, the alternate attendance system increased the demand for roads, food, and services as the warlords and their attendants made their migrations to Edo.

The effect of the above was to resolve the coordination problem that limited the development of an integrated market in rice. The fact that farmers were able to retain increases in output provided an incentive for increased production. This, combined with the growing demand for rice, from castle towns and the feudal élite, stimulated merchants to serve as intermediaries between suppliers in rural areas and buyers in urban areas, resulting in the establishment of buying and selling networks in rural areas. The rice market tended to center on Osaka, given its location and transportation advantages. As the role of Osaka grew, it also developed as a center for trading other commodities and specialization among merchants began to occur. There were individual traders called Tonya merchants, who served as wholesale agents, consignment agents, or receiving agents, while others supervised processing industries (Hauser, 1974). The resulting commercialization allowed further specialization within the countryside to occur.

The specialization discussed above involved not only agricultural, but also nonagricultural products. Thus farmers in rural areas became increasingly involved in family-based manufacturing activities, in addition to agricultural production. This economic growth in the rural areas combined with the relative weakness of the state in terms of regulating rural activities, meant that rural-based merchants also undertook the growing exchanges involved with market integration. Thus the market moved vigorously into the countryside, escaping attempts by urban-based merchants and the state to regulate and monopolize such trade. This is supported by Smith's (1988) observation that during the 18th and early part of the 19th centuries urban areas stagnated or declined as rural-based exchange in agricultural goods and cottage-manufactured goods flourished.

Thus in the Tokugawa period the turning of the terms of trade in agriculture's favor, combined with urbanization, served as coordinating mechanisms for the creation of an integrated market. It was in agriculture that this new market system was created. The process of sheltering the agricultural sector continued into the Meiji era. Within 20 years of the Meiji restoration (1868), Japan was importing significant quantities of rice. The newly modernizing state enacted a tariff on imported Japanese rice during the Russian-Japanese war. After the war ended, the tariff continued with the provision that rice from Taiwan and Korea was allowed duty free into Japan (they were Japanese colonies). The effect of these policies was to raise the domestic price of rice in Japan above the international price, protecting this sector (Anderson, 1983).

Although Japanese agriculture was protected against foreign competition, the government might have pursued domestic policies that effectively discriminated against agriculture. For example, many governments in less-developed countries today have sought to reduce the price of agriculture relative to nonagricultural goods (turn the domestic terms of trade against agriculture). However, available terms of trade data indicate that the terms of trade, in general, were favorable to agriculture in the Meiji period (Mundle, 1985).

Another tool that governments often use to discriminate against the agricultural sector is taxation. If long-run agricultural growth is to occur farmers must be able to reap as much as possible of the benefit of applying new technology and capital to the production process. Information concerning the land tax shows that revenue raised from this tax remained relatively stable until 1915, but then declined rapidly until the period prior to World War II. In terms of the percentage of total government revenue derived from this tax, it declined throughout the period 1885-1935. If the data is examined on all direct taxes on agriculture net of subsidies to agriculture, the figure is positive, but declines almost continuously throughout the period. All of this indicates that in the Meiji as well as the Tokugawa period benefits stemming from increased agricultural productivity were being retained by the farmers, not extracted by the state. In addition to the above, the state reformed the land tax transforming it from a tax in kind to a tax payable in money. This acted to further spur production for the market and thus further stimulated commercialization.

Agricultural productivity did indeed grow during this time period. The government of Japan devoted resources towards agricultural research and extension. Anderson (1983) indicates that such expenditures more than tripled. Similar investments were made in land infrastructure. The growing incomes, the retention of much of this income by farmers, and the conversion of the tax to a monetary basis all served to spur or coordinate further development of rural markets. Much of this growth in market activity was led by a group of individuals labeled as gono. These were 'rural entrepreneurs who had combined agricultural production, with trade and investing activities, making them the most important entrepreneurial group in Japan by the middle of the 18th century' (Tomlinson, 1985, p.673). It is also significant that this group played crucial roles in the development of the cotton spinning and banking industries. Most of these merchants, although originally rural gono, eventually took on wider and wider roles as the economy evolved (Tomlinson, 1985, p.681). Finally, Yamamura's research into the origins of Meiji entrepreneurs indicates that they had strong connections in the rural agrarian and trading economy (Hanley and Yamamura, 1977).

Thus the protection and encouragement of growth in the agricultural sector, combined with tax reforms, all acted as mechanisms of coordination during the Meiji time period. Market integration increased, and merchants continued to tie the nation into a network of trading relationships that became increasingly dense. Traditional manufacturing activities based in rural and commercial areas continued to thrive and grow. Up until the 1900s much of Japanese growth in manufacturing was driven by these traditional, small-scale, labor-intensive manufacturing activities. Even after World War II small-scale industry, increasingly integrated with large-scale production via subcontracting relationships, continued to be an important factor in overall Japanese economic development.

The experiences of England and Japan would thus appear to exhibit some striking similarities. In both countries the development of integrated markets was the key to an economic growth process which was basically Smithian in nature. It was based upon specialization, the division of labor and the increased productivity stemming from these processes. It seems to have been intimately linked in both nations to what was going on in the agricultural sector. For a variety of reasons, both countries provided environments which were generally protective of the agricultural sector and this, combined with the existence in both countries of unusually large urban areas, provided the coordination necessary for market activity to blossom and for merchant groups to arise. These groups in turn connected local and regional markets by constructing new social links and networks. As this integration proceeded in agriculture and incomes rose, markets for nonagricultural goods evolved and also became integrated into national markets. Thus in both nations agriculture and small-scale manufacturing became integrated in an interdependent process of economic development in which the links between the two sectors were created via activities of traders and other merchant intermediaries.

6. SUMMARY

In this chapter the focus of the analysis has been on the traders' dilemma. It was illustrated with some simple concepts drawn from game theory. The main implication drawn was that market exchange is likely to break down as a result of buyers and sellers behaving in an uncooperative manner, trying to cheat each other. Thus the costs of transacting in markets would be extremely high, posing a barrier to exchange and limiting the degree of specialization which producers and consumers could engage in.

One solution to the traders' dilemma emerges when the game is extended to an indefinite play basis among the same players and it is assumed that the discount rate is low enough so that the future is important for both buyers and sellers. In this context the potential for retaliation by buyer and seller results in cooperation (no cheating) by buyer and seller now becoming a potential equilibrium. When reputation effects are allowed for, the indefinite replay of the game also need not involve the same individuals interacting again and again.   This solution to the traders' dilemma resembles the situations found in small-scale societies represented by small villages, kinship groups and so on. In those types of small groups social interaction between buyers and sellers and the reputational mechanism allows for the evolution of formal and informal rules which limit noncooperative cheating and provide cooperation. Merchants within these societies perform the function of linking buyers and sellers, since they are able to lower the cost of transacting for all parties, and they perform this function by utilizing the existing social network. This allows information to be generated concerning the reputations of buyers and sellers with the merchant tying into this existing system of information generation. Market transactions are thus embedded in existing social relationships.

The process of information generation outlined above was called the traditional technology. However, there are significant difficulties in utilizing this traditional technology in large societies.   Larger societies are characterized by a large number of smaller groups where dense social networks exist linking individuals in each small group, but between these groups there are structural holes, a lack of network links generating reliable information on traders (reputation). As a result, trade will be very intense within each small group and it follows that there will be some productivity increase due to specialization and division of labor. However, this will be quite limited due to the small scale of market integration.

The modern technology for generating information on reputations involves merchants acting as entrepreneurs. They are entrepreneurial in the sense that they must seek to establish new social networks to link previously isolated groups. If this new social network can be established, then reputational mechanisms can operate across groups, integrating them into a more extensive market structure. The difficulty here is that the creation of this new social network is subject to significant increasing returns and these increasing returns create a coordination problem. If only a few buyers, sellers and merchant brokers commit to forming the new social network, then the transaction costs involved will be very high. The system will fail. However, if a large number of buyers, sellers and traders commit simultaneously to the establishment of this new technology on a large scale, then transaction costs will be dramatically lowered and integrated market exchange will evolve. Since exchange would now be occurring on a much larger scale, the division of labor and specialization that occurs would lead to significant increases in productivity. The resulting process has been labeled as Smithian growth and it will succeed only if the problem of coordination can be overcome.

There were two ways discussed in the chapter that the coordination problem afflicting exchange on a large scale can be overcome. The agrarian path or solution recognizes that the bulk of the population of most poor countries resides in rural areas and earns its living from agriculture. As a result the potential for integrated market development is greatest here. Coordination might be provided by international trade, since increased exports of an agricultural commodity produced by the bulk of the population would likely provide a strong enough signal to result in the coordinated entry of large numbers of buyers, sellers and merchants into the market resulting in a switch to the modern technology for information-gathering. The key is that the product exported must involve the bulk of the rural population. In situations where a country has a *potential* comparative advantage in agricultural products produced by a large proportion of the population, coordination could be achieved by infrastructure investment, the creation of a research and extension system and tilting the terms of trade in agriculture's favor. All of this coordination involves the sheltering and nurturing of the agricultural sector.

A second path involves bypassing the creation of an integrated domestic market altogether by substituting the already existing international market. That is resources can be devoted to creating firms from which goods, most likely manufactured goods, will be exported. However, this merely shifts the coordination problem from outside of the firm to inside the firm. Dilemmas arise within firms that are similar to those characterized as traders' dilemmas. The idea here is that the firm would serve as the vessel within which interaction among individuals would lead to the evolution of formal and informal rules restraining the pursuit of self-interest and promoting the pursuit of the interests of the firm. This can be conceived as the evolution of a corporate culture or corporate institutional structure. Thus exchange via the market is minimized with most transactions occurring within or between large firms. The main difficulty with this solution to the coordination problem is that it creates a situation in which corporate rent-seeking (of an unproductive nature) may overwhelm the state. However, there is at least one successful real world example of this solution which will be discussed in a subsequent chapter.

Two examples of the agrarian path to the solution of the coordination problem were discussed in detail: 17th-, 18th- and early 19th-century England and 18th- and 19th-century Japan. They both illustrate a process by which protection of agriculture (unintentional perhaps) acted to coordinate the development of integrated national market systems. This in turn unleashed an evolutionary growth process based on specialization and the division of labor. This was called Smithian growth. Although this growth process allowed rates of growth to exceed population growth and living standards to significantly increase in both Japan and England, there are limitations to this growth process. This is short- and medium-term growth, but it seems unlikely that this can account for long-term growth patterns. Smithian growth is not dependent upon technical innovation as its driving force. Instead, it is presumed that societies such as England and Japan were operating inside their production possibilities curves due to the lack of integrated national markets. As such markets evolved out of the rural sectors, both societies were able to move to the production possibilities curve and thus experience a significant improvement in living standards. However, once the production possibilities curve had been reached, the sources of this type of growth would dry up. Growth rates, *ceteris paribus*, would slow down. The Malthusian problem of the race between population and resources might likely reappear.

Additional growth will be dependent upon possibilities curves shifting outward, thus long-term growth involves technical invention and innovation. Accordingly, technical change must be directly addressed for the analysis to proceed. Technical change involves both invention, the creation of new ideas and innovation, making these ideas economically viable. Once this process begins to rapidly occur, the possibility for widespread income divergence appears. This can be visualized as a rapid shifting out of the production possibility curve, with some countries remaining on or close to the curve while others are left inside, further and further behind the expanding frontier.

Since our main concern is with developing nations, those operating far from the frontier (perhaps falling further and further behind) will be a major concern, so the process by which societies learn to use technologies developed elsewhere will be important. The next chapter looks specifically at understanding long-term growth, technical change and learning.

NOTES

1. Actually, there are more than just two equilibrium solutions for this game depending on the particular circumstances under which the game is played.
2. This interpretation of structural holes is slightly different from but strongly related to Burt's (1993) interpretation.
3. A similar idea is proposed by Levy (1990).
4. This isolation was not complete. Some trade and interaction was allowed with the outside world, but it was very limited and highly regulated.

REFERENCES

Amsden, A. (1989), *Asia's Next Giant: South Korea and Late Industrialization* (New York: Oxford University Press).

Anderson, K. (1983), 'Growth of Agricultural Protection in East Asia,' *Food*

Policy 8 (November), 327-336.

Bates, Robert H. (1988), 'Lessons From History on the Perfidy of English Exceptionalism and the Significance of Historical France,' *World Politics* 60 (July), 499-516.

Burt, Ronald (1993), 'The Social Structure of Competition,' in Richard Swedberg (ed.), *Explorations in Economic Sociology* (New York: Russell Sage Foundation), 65-103.

Crafts, N.F.R. (1985), *British Economic Growth During the Industrial Revolution* (Oxford: Oxford University Press).

Daunton, M.J. (1995), *Progress and Poverty: an Economic and Social History of Britain 1700-1850* (Oxford: Oxford University Press).

Davern, Michael (1997), 'Social Networks and Economic Sociology: A Proposed Research Agenda for a More Complete Social Science,' *American Journal of Economics and Sociology* 56 (July), 287-302.

Feld, Scott (1981), 'The Focused Organization of Social Ties,' *American Journal of Sociology* 86 (March), 1015-1035.

Foster, A.D. and M. Rosenzweig (1995), 'Learning by Doing and Learning from Others,' *Journal of Political Economy* 103 (December), 1176-1209.

Frank, Robert H. (1988), *Passions Within Reason: The Strategic Role of Emotions* (New York: W.W. Norton and Company).

Granovetter, Mark (1985), 'Economic Action and Social Structure: The Problem of Embeddedness,' *American Journal of Sociology* 91 (November), 481-510.

Grantham, George (1993), 'Economic Growth Without Causes: a Re-Examination of Medieval Economic Growth and Decay,' paper presented at the Annual Meeting of the Economic History Association, Tucson, Arizona.

Grantham, George (1995), 'Time's Arrow and Time's Cycle in the Medieval Economy: The Significance of Recent Developments in Economic Theory for the History of Medieval Economic Growth,' paper prepared for the Fifth Anglo-American Seminar on Medieval Economics and Society, Cardiff.

Grantham, George (1996), 'Contra Ricardo: The Macroeconomics of Pre-Industrial Agrarian Economies,' paper prepared for the Yale Program in Agrarian Studies.

Hanley, S.B. and K. Yamamura (1977), *Economic and Demographic Change in Preindustrial Japan 1600-1868* (Princeton: Princeton University Press).

Hauser, W. B. (1974), *Economic and Institutional Change in Tokugawa Japan: Osaka and the Kinai Cotton Trade* (Cambridge: Cambridge University Press).

Hayami, Y. and T. Kawagoe (1993), *The Agrarian Origins of Commerce and Industry - A Study of Peasant Marketing in Indonesia* (London:

Macmillan).

Kreps, David (1990), 'Corporate Culture and Economic Activity,' in James E. Alt and Kenneth A. Shepsle (eds.), *Perspectives on Political Economy* (Cambridge: Cambridge University Press), 90-143.

Langlois, R. and P. Robertson (1995), *Firms, Markets, and Economic Change: A Dynamic Theory of Business Institutions* (New York: Routledge).

Levy, Brian (1989), 'Export Traders, Market Development, and Industrial Expansion,' Research Memorandum Series (Williamstown, Massachusetts: Center for Development Economics, Williams College, March).

Levy, Brian (1990), 'Transactions Costs, the Size of Firms, and Industrial Policy,' *Journal of Development Economisc* 34 (November), 151-178.

Lewis, W.A. (1954), 'Economic Development with Unlimited Supplies of Labour,' *The Manchester School* 22 (May), 139-191.

Lie, John (1993), 'Visualizing the Invisible Hand: The Social Origins of ' Market Society' in England, 1550-1750,' *Politics and Society* 3 (September), 275-305.

Locay, L. (1990), 'Economic Development and the Division of Production Between Households and Markets,' *Journal of Political Economy* 98 (October), 965-982.

Macfarlane, Alan (1997), '"Japan" in an English Mirror,' *Modern Asian Studies* 31 (October), 763-806.

Mundle, Sudipto (1985), 'The Agrarian Barrier to Industrial Growth,' *Journal of Development Studies* 22 (October), 49-80.

Murphy, K.W., A. Shleifer, and R.W. Vishny (1989), 'Industrialization and the Big Push,' *Journal of Political Economy* 97 (October), 1003-1025.

Platteau, Jean-Phillipe (1994), 'Behind the Market Stage Where Real Societies Exist - Part I: The Role of Public and Private Order Institutions," *Journal of Development Studies* 30 (April), 533-577.

Polanyi, Karl (1957), *The Great Transformation: The Political and Economic Origins of Our Time* (Boston: Beacon).

Ranis, G. and J. Fei (1961), 'A Theory of Economic Development,' *American Economic Review* 51 (September), 533-565.

Rosenstein-Rodan, Paul N. (1943), 'Problems of Industrialization of Eastern and Southeastern Europe,' *Economic Journal* 53 (June-September), 202-211.

Rostow, W.W. (1960), *The Stages of Economic Growth: A Non-Communist Manifesto* (Cambridge: Cambridge University Press).

Smith, T.C. (1988), *Native Sources of Japanese Industrialization, 1750-1920* (Berkeley: University of California Press).

Tomlinson, B.R. (1985), 'Writing History Sideways: Lessons for Indian Economic Historians from Meiji Japan,' *Modern Asian Studies* 19, 669-

698.

Vlastos, S. (1986), *Peasant Protests and Uprisings in Tokugawa Japan* (Berkeley: University of California Press).

Williamson, Oliver (1975), *Markets and Hierarchies* (New York: Free Press).

Wrigley, E.A. (1988), *Continuity, Chance and Charge: The Character of the Industrial Revolution in England* (Cambridge: Cambridge University Press).

3. Market Integration and Industrial Revolutions

1. INTRODUCTION

The last chapter dealt with a type of short- to medium-term economic growth driven by specialization and the division of labor - Smithian growth. Long-term growth in per capita income is linked to technical change which involves both invention and innovation. Invention is the actual creation of new ideas whereas innovation is making them economically viable. Without these activities the law of diminishing returns will slow down the long-run growth process.

The second section of this chapter seeks to clarify the distinction between short- and medium-term Smithian growth and long-run, technologically driven growth. This comparison will make use of the simple graphical tools of growth theory to compare Smithian growth, neoclassical growth theory and the new growth theory (sometimes called endogenous growth theory). The new growth theory will then be divided into two types, those dealing with technical change (shifting the best practice production possibilities frontier) and those dealing with technological learning or innovation.

Section three examines a different perspective on technical change involving the notions of macroinventions and microinventions. In section four, an alternative model of economic growth developed by Acemoglu and Zilibotti (1997) is explained. This model links capital accumulation and the degree of market integration. Whether investment in various sectors in an economy succeeds or not depends on the extent to which markets in the various sectors are open and operating. Thus development is a risky process in which the degree of market diversification effects both the rate of development and the stability of the development process. This model is adapted to analyze the process of long-run growth - macro and microinventions. Invention (macroinventions) is viewed as random, exogenous shocks to the economic system, while the speed of innovation (microinventions) is dependent on the degree to which market integration has occurred. Thus invention is viewed as being exogenous in nature while innovation is endogenous.

The above analytical perspective is then used to analyze the development process in both small-scale societies, in which traditional technologies for information gathering are utilized, and large-scale societies, where modern technologies are utilized. The experiences of both England and Japan are utilized to illustrate the theoretical ideas developed in the chapter. The English case is, of course, an example of a first occurrence, the birthplace of an industrial revolution. Japan is a hybrid case, exhibiting elements of both indigenous development of industry combined with learning. This leads quite naturally into considering the catch-up process for those countries finding themselves left behind. This is the topic of Chapter 4.

2. SOME THEORIES OF GROWTH

In this section[1] some simple ideas from neoclassical growth theory will be used to illustrate and compare various theories of economic growth. First, the constant returns to scale production function is written as

$$Y = f(K,L) \tag{3.1}$$

or

$$y = f(k),$$

where Y is output, K and L are the stock of capital and labor, y is output per worker, and k is the capital to labor ratio. It is presumed that the production function has all of the standard features in terms of shape and structure, thus one can draw the production function as $f(k)$ in Figure 3.1 with the declining slope representing the law of diminishing returns.

The second relationship displayed in Figure 3.1 is labeled nk, where n is the rate of population growth (the rate of growth of labor) and k is as defined above. It is presumed that n is exogenous and unchanging. The combination nk represents how much new capital will have to be created in order to keep the capital to labor ratio (k) constant. Thus if $n = 0.1$ and $k = 3$, then capital must growth by 30 per cent each time period to keep k unchanged.

The last relationship illustrated in Figure 3.1 is the $sf(k)$ curves. Here s represents the propensity to save (it is presumed that the marginal propensity and average propensities to save are equal). It is assumed to be exogenous. Of course $f(k)$ represents per capita income and thus $sf(k)$ represents capital formation per worker and it is presumed that savings is automatically invested. Therefore $sf(k)$ merely represents a constant fraction of the $f(k)$

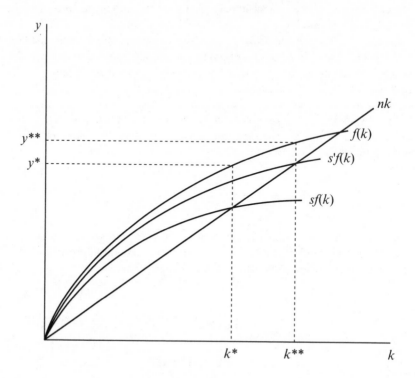

Figure 3.1   Neoclassical Growth Theory

function.

Where $sf(k)$, new capital created per worker, and nk, the capital that must be created per worker to keep the capital to labor ratio constant, intersect represents an equilibrium. At this point, k will remain constant at k^* and, as a result, y (per capita income) will also remain constant at y^*. To verify the stability of the equilibrium pick values for k to either the right or left of k^* and it will be obvious that this economy will return to k^*. Several characteristics of this equilibrium need to be discussed. First, at this equilibrium labor is growing at a rate of n and both K and Y, capital and total output, must be growing at the same rate (since k and y are constant in equilibrium). The second point to note is that changing the marginal propensity to save will alter the equilibrium y and k, but it will not alter the long-run, equilibrium rate of growth of K and Y (which will remain n).

This last conclusion deserves a little more discussion. If the propensity to save should increase from s to s' ($s' > s$), the equilibrium per capita income, y, and capital to labor ratio, k, will rise to y^{**} and k^{**}. However, at the new equilibrium Y and K will be growing at the rate of n since y^{**} and k^{**} are unchanging. If the growth rates of Y, K, and N are all the same in both the old equilibrium (k^*, y^*) and the new equilibrium (k^{**}, y^{**}), how was it the economy could get from the old to the new equilibrium? The answer is, of course, that in the transition from the old equilibrium to the new the growth rates of K and Y rise above n, say to n_t where $n_t > n$. However, as the capital to labor ratio grows, the law of diminishing returns sets in so that by the time the new equilibrium is reached $n_t = n$ once again. Notice the role of the law of diminishing returns here and also note that the model, as of yet, does not include technical change.

The above, of course, is simple neoclassical growth theory without technical change. However, with a slight modification, the same structure can be used to illustrate a variety of growth theories. The typical textbook version of classical growth theory is set out in Figure 3.2. It will be assumed that there are now three factors of production: capital (K), labor (N), and land (L). The initial equilibrium for the classical economy is k_1, with K, L, and Y growing at n. However, with land fixed and the other inputs variable, the law of diminishing returns sets in, rotating $f(k)$ and $sf(k)$ downward. As this occurs, per capita income and the capital to labor ratio will decline continuously.

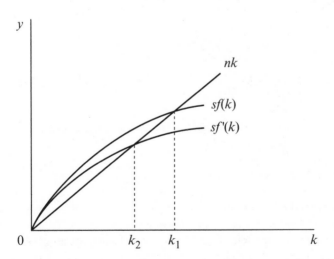

Figure 3.2   Classical Growth Theory

The above version of classical theory does not capture any demographic changes which would accompany this process, but it does illustrate the impact of population growth and the operation of the law of diminishing returns. The above perspective can be compared to the version of Smithian growth outlined in the last chapter. This is presented in Figure 3.3. As can be seen, the production function is presumed to be characterized by three phases. In the initial phase and third phase decreasing returns prevails. Alternatively, in the second phase increasing returns exists. The first phase corresponds to the small society solution to the traders' dilemma problem outlined in Chapter 2. There market exchange does occur with its foundation based upon existing networks and social relationships which are in turn based on kin, extended family and religious links. It works, but attempts to extend transactions beyond this small scale are subject to decreasing returns.

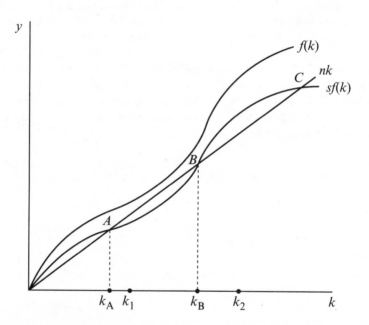

Figure 3.3   Smithian Growth Theory

The second phase represents the large society case discussed in Chapter 2. Presuming that coordination problems are resolved, the modern technology is substituted for the traditional technology of information generation. This involves merchant middlemen behaving in an entrepreneurial fashion establishing new networks of social relationships (not related to kinship, religious affiliation and so on). This process is subject to increasing returns, which is illustrated in Figure 3.3. However, there are limits to this growth and this is represented by the decreasing returns to capital accumulation due to the eventual operation of the law of diminishing returns.

As a result, there are three potential short- to medium-term equilibriums in the Smithian growth model and are represented in Figure 3.3 as *A*, *B*, and *C*. *A* is the low level trap situation in that small increases in the capital to labor ratio, k_A to k_1, will be overwhelmed by population growth and the diminishing returns stemming from the traditional technology for information-gathering. Equilibrium *B* is an unstable equilibrium in that small increases in the capital to labor ratio, k_B to k_2, will set an increasing returns to scale process resulting in economic expansion. This results from the increasing returns from utilization of the modern technology for information-gathering. However, the law of diminishing returns will eventually set in for capital accumulation and equilibrium at *C* will be obtained.

However, equilibrium *C* is not a long-run equilibrium. If a third factor land, which is fixed in supply, is assumed, then long-run diminishing returns will also occur to land since capital and labor will again be growing at rate *n* while land is not growing at all. This will again cause the production function, $f(k)$, to rotate downward. The result will, in the long run, mean a decline in the standard of living. Thus Smithian growth has limitations and this was recognized at the end of the last chapter.

At this point, however, the notion that land is a fixed factor input must be relinquished. In fact, Solow's theory of growth does this by collapsing the three inputs of classical theory into two inputs, labor and capital. This presumes that land is augmentable, just like capital, through savings and investment. In this case diminishing returns to land disappear. This results in the equilibriums for the neoclassical theory in Figure 3.1 and the Smithian theory in Figure 3.3 (equilibrium *C*) becoming permanent, long-run equilibriums. Thus the Malthusian results disappear, but long-term growth in the standard of living is still left as an unsolved mystery in both the neoclassical and Smithian theory. That is, in the long run in both models capital, labor and output all grow at the rate of *n*. Consequently, per capita income will not grow through time. The only possibility to raise per capita income would come from an increase in the propensity to save (*s*). If this should occur, during the transition period, capital and output will grow faster than population, but as the law of diminishing returns again sets in, growth rates will return to *n* as the economy settles into the new equilibrium at a higher level of *k* and *y*.

Long-run growth in the standard of living can be introduced by allowing for technical change. Neoclassical theory did this by assuming that technical change was Harrod-neutral, implying that it augments the productivity of labor so that now one can think in terms of the effective supply of labor. This can be written as

$$N_e(t) = e^{\lambda t}N(t),\tag{3.2}$$

where $N_e(t)$ is the effective supply of labor, $N(t)$ is the number of physical workers, and λ is the constant rate of technical change. Thus the growth rate of the effective supply of labor can be written as

$$\frac{\dot{N}_e}{N_e} - \lambda + n,\tag{3.3}$$

where $\dot{N}_e$ is the derivative of the effective supply of labor with respect to time.

Now since both the neoclassical and Smithian theories of growth will generate equilibriums in which the standard of living will rise through time, y will grow. The figures used to illustrate both types of growth only have to be slightly reinterpreted. In Figures 3.1 and 3.3, the capital to physical labor ratio (k), measured along the horizontal axis, is now reinterpreted to represent the capital to effective labor (N_e) ratio. In the same manner the vertical axis along which output per physical laborer (y) was measured is now output per effective laborer. Now at the equilibriums in both models output and capital will grow at the rate of $(n + \lambda)$ while y and k will grow at the ratio of λ. Thus through time the standard of living will grow.

In the above discussion, the rate of technical innovation is presumed to be fixed and exogenous, thus no explanation of what determines the rate of technical change is given. New growth theory has attempted to fill this void and comes in a great variety of forms. In this chapter simple interpretations of these models developed in the work of Jones (1998) are used to illustrate the operation of these models. The first model will be concerned with technical invention and will presume that once new ideas are created, they can be immediately applied to the production process. Thus it will be presumed that no learning process is required to effectively utilize the technology. The model incorporating these characteristics comes originally from the work of Romer (1990) and is discussed below.

In this model the economy is divided into three sectors: a final goods sector, an intermediate goods sector and a research sector. The production function for the final goods sector can be written as

$$Y - L_Y^{1-\alpha}\int_{j-o}^{A} x_j^{\alpha}dj,\tag{3.4}$$

where Y is final output, L_Y the quantity of labor devoted to final goods production, and x_j represents a number of different capital or intermediate goods. There are A different varieties of these goods and firms in this sector take this number as given. Technical invention, when it occurs, represents the creation of new types of capital (A becomes a larger number). Constant returns to labor and capital (total) are presumed to exist.

In the intermediate goods sector raw capital, generated via savings, is converted into actual capital. This occurs on a one-for-one basis, one unit of raw capital converted into one unit of actual or finished capital of a particular type. In order to do this, however, a new design will have to be purchased from the research sector. It is presumed that the quantity of each type of finished capital will be identical for all types of capital, thus the quantity of each type of capital used can be derived as

$$x - \frac{K}{A}, \tag{3.5}$$

where K is the quantity of raw capital generated by savings. Thus x_j^α in (3.4) is equal to x^α and (3.4) can be written as

$$Y = L_y^{1-\alpha}Ax^\alpha \tag{3.6}$$

or

$$Y = AL_y^{1-\alpha}x^\alpha$$

Substituting (3.5) for x in equation (3.6) gives

$$Y - AL_y^{1-\alpha}\left(\frac{K}{A}\right)^\alpha$$

or

$$Y = AL_y^{1-\alpha}A^{-\alpha}K^\alpha$$

or $$\tag{3.7}$$

$$Y = A^{1-\alpha}L_y^{1-\alpha}K^\alpha$$

or

$$Y = (AL_y)^{1-\alpha}K^\alpha.$$

The reason for pursuing this line of thought in some detail is that it allows us easily to compare this theory of growth with the neoclassical and Smithian theories outlined earlier. In those models technological change (invention) is viewed as augmenting the effectiveness of the supply of labor. In Romer's model technical change (invention), represented by A, is also seen as augmenting the effectiveness of labor. The verbal interpretation is a little more complicated than in the neoclassical or Smithian models. Technology is represented by the number of types of finished capital utilized and as this number rises, output will rise, but in order for this to happen, new designs for the new types of finished capital will have to be created. This leads us to an analysis of the research sector.

In the research sector, new designs for capital are invented. There are many ways to specify this process. Perhaps the simplest way would be to argue that the growth of the new designs depends upon the labor devoted to this work, L_A, and the productivity of this labor in discovering new ideas,

$$\dot{A} - \bar{\sigma} L_A. \tag{3.8}$$

How the determinates of the productivity of labor in creating new designs is explained is critically important. Many theorists have hypothesized that this productivity depends on the stock of designs that have already been created. Thus

$$\bar{\sigma} - \sigma A, \tag{3.9}$$

where σ is a constant with $\sigma > 0$. The rate of change in technology can be derived from substituting (3.9) into (3.8) and dividing by A to get

$$\frac{\dot{A}}{A} - \sigma L_A. \tag{3.10}$$

Thus the rate of expansion in the living standard, which in the neoclassical and Smithian models was unexplained (exogenous), now becomes explainable.

There are a number of reasons for suspecting that equations (3.9) and (3.10) are too simplistic. They imply that as the number of people involved in creating new designs (L_A) rises, the rate of growth of per capita income should rise. There is abundant evidence that this is not true.[2] Thus Jones has hypothesized that the productivity of workers in creating new designs, equation (3.9), can be rewritten as

$$\bar{\sigma} - \sigma A^{\phi}, \tag{3.11}$$

where $0 < \phi < 1$. Thus the body of past knowledge is not completely usable today. Now the rate of creation of new designs is

$$\frac{\dot{A}}{A} - \sigma \frac{L_A A^{\phi}}{A} - \sigma \frac{L_A}{A^{1-\phi}}. \tag{3.12}$$

Along the balanced growth path, $\dfrac{\dot{A}}{A}$ is a constant. Taking logs and derivatives of both sides with respect to time and setting the left hand side equal to zero gives

$$0 - \frac{\dot{L}_A}{L_A} - (1-\phi)\frac{\dot{A}}{A}, \tag{3.13}$$

where $\dot{L}_A$ and $\dot{A}$ represent the changes in these variables with respect to time. Rearranging, one gets

$$\frac{\dot{A}}{A} - \frac{\dot{L}_A/L_A}{1-\phi}. \tag{3.14}$$

If we presume that the rate of growth of workers involved in the creation of new designs is the same as that for population,[3] n, then (3.14) can be written as

$$\frac{\dot{A}}{A} - \frac{n}{1-\phi}. \tag{3.15}$$

Thus new ideas will grow at the same rate as population growth. Those countries generally involved in technical change, the creation of new knowledge, are generally the highly developed countries. The above is a simple model of how the world's production possibility curve evolves through time (the rate at which it shifts out).

The above analysis also has several additional implications. First, new ideas or designs created by the research sector have the characteristics of public goods, they are nonrival and nonexcludable. The latter characteristic implies that unless property rights in ideas can be created (patent system), incentives will not exist for private producers to devote resources to their creation. The second implication is that even if property rights in ideas exist, markets will underallocate labor to the research sector. This is due to the fact that there is an externality in the creation of new designs. In equation (3.11) the productivity of workers in creating new designs is positively influenced by the past accumulation of ideas. In turn, ideas created today will, because they add to the stock of ideas, increase the profitability of tomorrow's designs. Private individuals allocating resources will miss this effect. They will not be rewarded by the market for improving the productivity of future researchers, thus there is an underallocation of resources to research and development.

One final point, a nonrival good is one for which the marginal cost of providing it to an additional individual is zero. From societies' point of view then it should be made available at a price of zero ($P = MC$). However, a positive price must be charged to provide an incentive for production. The charging of a positive price then implies a less than optimal supply of new ideas. Thus there would seem to be an opportunity for the state here to correct this suboptimal allocation of resources to research and development.

The above analysis provides insight as to how technical invention can be brought into the model. However, many nations operate far from the frontier. Their growth will be the result of learning techniques developed elsewhere and catching up. Jones (1998) has constructed a relatively simple endogenous theory of development in which learning plays the driving force in economic growth. In his model the production function is written, in a fashion similar to that of Romer, as

$$Y = L^{1-\alpha} \int_o^h x_j^\alpha dj, \tag{3.16}$$

where h represents the skill level of the population. Thus the range of intermediate goods or the range of designs for such goods that can be utilized depend on the level of human capital. The accumulation of human capital equation is in turn written as

$$\dot{h} = \sigma e^{\psi u} A^\gamma h^{1-\gamma}. \tag{3.17}$$

In this equation $\sigma > 0$ and $0 < \gamma < 1$ and A represents the number of designs that exist (the technological frontier). The key variable in the above equation is u which represents the amount of labor time devoted to accumulating human capital or skills. The above can be written in terms of the rate of growth of human capital by dividing both sides of the equation by h. This will give

$$\frac{\dot{h}}{h} = \sigma e^{\psi u} \left(\frac{A}{h} \right)^\gamma. \tag{3.18}$$

As can be seen, the rate is dependent upon the amount of time workers spend accumulating human capital. However, it also depends upon how close or far away the country is from the frontier, which is represented by the ratio A/h. As the country approaches the frontier this ratio gets smaller, implying a slower rate of skill accumulation.

This section has provided analytical frameworks for looking at a variety of growth theories. The issue now concerns the usefulness of the neoclassical theories of invention and learning. Do they allow for an adequate explanation of the English and Japanese experience? What light do they shed on the process of economic growth in developing nations? It is these issues that we now turn to.

3. AN ALTERNATIVE PERSPECTIVE

It would seem that the neoclassical models of invention and learning discussed above are not very useful in understanding either the experience of Japan or England. Neither, does it seem, do they add much to our understanding of how learning takes place in developing countries. These issues will be explored below and an alternative way of viewing technical change will be presented and analyzed.

Crafts (1996) has strenuously argued that 'growth in terms of both GDP and total factor productivity during the period of the industrial revolution in England (1780-1830) while high by historical standards, were low compared to those in developing countries today - both the successful East Asian economies and some of the frequently criticized Latin American countries' (Crafts, 1996, p.197). On the basis of cross-country regression analysis carried out by Levine and Renalt (1992), the predicted values for growth in England are lower than what was actually achieved. In addition, Britain carried out very little activity that would be considered actual research and development. The legal protection provided by patents in Britain was limited until the 1830s and the cost of taking out a patent remained very high until 1852 (Crafts, 1998). Also if one compares various measures of human capital accumulation in England in 1820 relative to the USA in 1920, it becomes quite apparent that formal training and educational levels in England were very limited (Crafts, 1998). Thus none of the variables emphasized in the endogenous growth theories seem to have been very important in English growth.

The neoclassical endogenous growth theories outlined above do provide some interesting insights. In particular, these theories predict that growth in England would be slow. After all, there was little protection of property rights in ideas and the extent of human capital development was quite limited. However, it leaves a person wondering how England ever became industrialized. Another puzzle concerns one of the key characteristics of English industrialization, the clustering of technical changes during this time period. These theories just do not help much in trying to understand technical change in a society in which a sector for research and development did not exist and formal human capital accumulation was limited.

It must also be remembered that although England certainly was the origin of a number of technical inventions, it was particularly adept at borrowing and adapting ideas developed by others. 'Britain had an unusual proficiency for importing ideas and improving upon them' (Crafts, 1996, p.199). Thus learning as well as invention played an important role in English industrialization. Just as the endogenous growth theories are of little help explaining technical invention, they are also not very useful in explaining

England's learning capabilities. As previously pointed out, formal human capital development in England was quite limited.

With respect to Japan, the emphasis in earlier chapters has been on the great similarities between the early development of Japan and England. They both seemed to have experienced relatively long periods of Smithian type growth. However, while England then experienced a clustering of technical change in the late 18th and early 19th centuries, this failed to occur in Japan (Macfarlane, 1997). In fact, with the Meiji restoration, Japan found itself behind in terms of industrial technology, although not in terms of agricultural technology. Again, the neoclassical theories may be able to explain this lack of invention by the lack of property rights in ideas and the lack of development of human capital. However, it does not explain the technological prowess of Japan in agriculture nor does it explain why the Japanese were so successful at importing and learning technologies developed elsewhere. It is true that the new government placed significant emphasis on education. However, given the nature of the educational process this would have taken a number of decades to have a significant effect. Thus formal schooling does not seem to be a good explanation as to why the Japanese were able to learn so quickly.

Carrying this idea forward these endogenous growth theories do not provide much insight into the growth process in developing nations. They are not on the technological frontier and therefore technical invention is not the driving force behind economic growth. Learning and human capital accumulation is an important factor in this process, but it is clear that there are many ways of generating skills, many of them not strongly linked to the formal educational process.

It would seem that in order to understand 19th-century industrial revolutions and learning in the 20th century an alternative perspective is needed. Mokyr (1990) has pointed out that much of growth theory currently relies upon steady state solutions in which crucial variables grow at steady rates and can be regarded as the dynamic equivalent of equilibrium. Another approach would be to take an evolutionary point of view. He argues that the word evolution encompasses two different meanings, one which emphasizes the gradualist nature of change and the other 'as a specific dynamic model governed by mutation and selection' (Mokyr, 1990, p.273). The latter involves applying a biological analogy to the analysis of technical change. This is not an extremely new notion. Boulding (1981) and Nelson and Winter (1982) have utilized this approach, but they did not apply it to technological change.

Mokyr argues that techniques of production are comparable to the concept of species and thus ideas evolve through time as do species. 'The idea or conceptualization of how to produce a commodity can be thought of as the genotype, whereas the actual technique utilized by the firm in producing the commodity may be thought of as the phenotype of the member of a species. The phenotype of every organism is determined in part by its genotype, but environment plays a role as well' (Mokyr, 1990, p.275). In a similar way, a new idea places constraints on the form that new techniques of production can take, but the circumstances that characterize the environment will help determine the specific form of the new technology.

New ideas represent the equivalent of mutations, but like biological mutations most of them do not survive, that is, given the existing economic environment they do not succeed. Evolution does not ensure survival of the fittest, but survival of the most adaptable. Thus regions that are isolated will create environments in which certain sets of ideas survive for long periods of time with little or no competition from others. However, once the isolation is broken down new ideas will break up this equilibrium with the old rapidly withering away. More important, from the perspective of technological evolution, there may be increasing returns to systems of ideas so that although set A is, in the long run, much more efficient than set B, this does not mean that set A will evolve and B will not. If accidental factors push a society initially towards set B, the increasing returns to this set of ideas may make it impossible to switch to set A at any later time. Thus evolution in the arena of ideas does not assure long-run efficiency. Of course the concept being discussed here is the notion of path-dependent outcomes (Arthur, 1989).

If such a perspective is applied to understanding technological change it would seem then that this model would emphasize the gradualist nature of technical change. However, as Mokyr points out 'biologists have been far from unanimous about the gradual nature of biological evolution itself' (Mokyr, 1990, p.289). The geneticist Goldschmidt (1940) argues that one should make a distinction between macromutations and micromutations. The latter is continuous and cumulative over time and tends to account for change within a species. The former explains great leaps in evolution especially the creation of new species (Mokyr, 1990, pp.289-290). Mokyr applies the same kind of thinking to try to understand the industrial revolution in England. Thus he defines a macroinvention as 'an invention without clearcut parentage, representing a clear break from previous technique' (Mokyr, 1990, p.291). For these inventions to succeed they must be able to successfully compete. This means that the idea must be technically feasible (people must be capable of producing and reproducing it), economically feasible (potential to earn a profit) and socially feasible (a sympathetic social environment).

Once a macroinvention occurs it creates an environment in which it is possible that microinvention will occur rapidly. The problems with the new technology have to be dealt with and it must be adapted to local circumstances. In other words, a learning process will unfold in which new (small) ideas are continuously developed in the application of the macroinvention. However, there is a limit to the learning through microinvention which can occur, that is, a macroinvention opens up significant opportunities for gains from learning by doing. But once the new technology has been completely adapted and learned, the gains will diminish to zero. 'Without microinventions, most macroinventions would not be implemented and their economic rents not realized. But without macroinventions, what would there be to improve?' (Mokyr, 1990, p.292). Mokyr phrases this in a most effective manner. 'Without the macroinventions of the Industrial Revolution, we might have a world of almost perfectly designed stagecoaches and sailing ships' (Mokyr, 1990, p.292).

The distinction between macro- and microinventions is an important one because Mokyr argues that they appear to be subject to different kinds of laws. 'Microinventions generally result from an intentional search for improvements, and are understandable - if not predictable - by economic forces. They are guided, at least to some extent, by the laws of supply and demand and by the intensity of search and resources committed to them, and thus by the signals emitted by the price mechanism' (Mokyr, 1990, p.295). This sounds very much like the explanations of innovation offered by theorists proposing induced innovation models. For example, Hayami and Ruttan (1985) have created a model of technical innovation in agriculture in which relative factor scarcity, reflected in changes in relative factor prices, induce research directed to developing techniques that save on the increasingly scarce factor of production by substituting those factors of production which are becoming increasingly abundant. This process does not, of course, always operate automatically. As discussed in Chapter 1, agricultural technology often has public good characteristics and thus research into these types of technique will often be suboptimal. This is due to the fact that the development of such technology is nonexcludable, it is extremely difficult to establish property rights in some kinds of agricultural technology.

There is a second source of microinvention which stems from the work of Arrow (1962). He hypothesized that the acquisition of knowledge or learning was the product of experience, thus the more experience that one has at producing a commodity, the more learning there will have been. This has been called learning by doing. He used cumulative gross investment as a measure or index of experience. However, as applied today it is often assumed to result from the time devoted to the production of a particular product. As stated earlier, all microinventions have limitations on the extent of learning which can occur, therefore exhaustion of learning possibilities can occur. The other point is that such learning is a by-product or externality connected with the production process. The benefits are generally thought to spill over to other firms producing the same good and also to other similarly produced commodities. Thus this type of knowledge generation will also tend to be suboptimal in a market economy.

Macroinventions are much more difficult to understand and would seem to be governed more by luck than by economic forces. Their occurrence takes on the form of a random event. 'Often they are based on some fortunate event, in which an inventor stumbles on one thing while looking for another, arrives at the right conclusion for the wrong reasons, or brings to bear a seemingly unrelated body of knowledge that just happens to hold the clue to the right solution' (Mokyr, 1990, p.295). Thus the timing and pace of these types of invention seems extremely difficult to explain.

None of the growth theories discussed earlier seem capable of telling a story of macro- and microinventions driving the industrialization process. It must be remembered that they are complementary in nature. Macroinventions in and of themselves cannot have an impact on the economy without the ensuing microinventions and the latter, in turn, run out of steam without the infusion of new macroideas. However, a model recently developed by Acemoglu and Zilibotti provides a structure in which an alternative view of technical change and learning in industrial revolutions can be analyzed. The model is discussed in the next section. Once it has been fully explained, several modifications will be made to the model and then it will be used to analyze the industrialization process.

4. AN ALTERNATIVE MODEL OF DEVELOPMENT

The perspective presented above tended to view macroinventions as positive shocks which bombard an economic system. A model with this sort of characteristic has been developed by Acemoglu and Zilibotti (1997). The model is an overlapping generations model with competitive markets and households that live for two time periods. Production within the economy consists of a single final good sector and a continuum of sectors producing intermediate goods. The final good is produced using labor and capital (the intermediate goods). The intermediate goods sector takes savings by households in time period one and transforms them into varieties of capital for time period two without utilizing any labor. Thus households in time period one (youth) work in the final goods sector and receive a wage. Then they will make a series of decisions with the first being how much of the wage will be consumed and how much saved. The second decision involves how the savings are to be allocated among the various intermediate goods-producing sectors (varieties of capital). Within this sector savings can be allocated to risky intermediate good projects and/or a safe project that pays a guaranteed return of r. That is, the household must decide how much savings to allocate, in a diversified manner, to risky intermediate projects and how much to allocate to a sure thing (safe asset). After this decision is made the uncertainty resolves itself with a certain state of nature occurring and projects in certain intermediate sectors succeeding and paying a large return $R > r$, while the other projects fail (earn $0 < r$). The total value of these investments then becomes the capital stock which the owners (those who allocated some of their savings to these sectors) now sell to the final goods sector. The individuals selling their capital now use these proceeds for consumption in their second period of life while the capital stock is combined with a new group of workers (first period of life for them) to produce final goods for another round of activity and so on.

The key to this model is connected with the risk associated with allocating savings to the intermediate goods sector. It is presumed that households are risk-averse. In addition, it is assumed that there is a continuum of likely states of nature represented by the interval from zero to one. Potential intermediate goods sectors are n in number and are also represented by the interval from zero to one. Intermediate goods sector j pays a positive return (R) only in state j and nothing in any other state of nature. Within this context, households will seek to diversify whatever savings they have allocated to intermediate goods production among risky and safe projects. The extent to which such diversification can occur is, however, limited by the number of intermediate sectors which are actually open and functioning, producing intermediate goods. The greater the number of risky intermediate sectors open, the greater the extent to which risk diversification can occur and thus the higher the expected return from allocating savings to these sectors.

The above analysis can be summarized in Figure 3.4. Along the horizontal axis is measured the proportion of intermediate sectors opened and operating. Along the vertical axis the total savings to be allocated to risky intermediate sector production projects is measured. Curve AB represents that part of total savings allocated to the risky intermediate sector as a function of the proportion of these sectors that are opened and operating. It is upward sloping reflecting the notion that households are willing to allocate more savings to intermediate sector projects as the possibilities for risk diversification increase. It has a positive vertical intercept because it is presumed that if no intermediate sectors were currently open, households would want to devote some savings to open projects in some intermediate sectors if $R > r$. Acemoglu and Zilibotti also assume that at least for some intermediate goods sectors there are minimum size requirements before the sectors can be set up. In Figure 3.4, this is represented by OCD. Those sectors from O to C have no minimum size requirements while C to D minimum size requirements rise in a linear fashion.

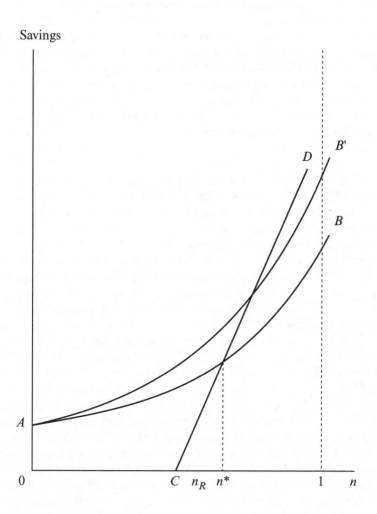

Savings

Figure 3.4 Risk and Growth

The savings curve and minimum size curve intersect at n^*. This represents the equilibrium proportion of all potential risky intermediate sectors that are open at a particular point of time. Sectors beyond n^* cannot be opened because the size requirements are such that there is not enough savings to open them. It is also presumed that those sectors having no size requirement are opened first, followed by those which do, with those sectors having smaller such requirements opening first.

The equilibrium proportion of intermediate sectors open, n^*, is crucial for the long-run development of the capital stock in the model. This is due to the fact that this variable determines how likely it is that an economy will be lucky. An economy is lucky if a state of nature j occurs and intermediate sector j is open. If this occurs, then return R is reaped, income and savings increase, and the capital stock expands (depreciation is ignored in this discussion). Alternatively, an unlucky economy is one in which a state of nature j occurs and sector j is currently not opened. In this situation no return will be reaped on the savings invested in the intermediate sector, income will fall, savings decline and the capital stock bequeathed to the next generation decreases.

The processes discussed above have a certain reinforcing character about them. That is, a lucky economy will find its savings and capital stock growing and this rotates the savings line in Figure 3.4 from AB to AB'. The proportion of intermediate sectors open would thus increase. The latter increases the likelihood that the economy will again be lucky by increasing the probability that success in the risky intermediate sector would occur. Alternatively, if an economy is unlucky, its capital stock and savings would decline and the equilibrium proportion of intermediate sectors open would decline. This in turn increases the likelihood that the economy will be unlucky in the future. There is, however, a downward limit on this latter possibility. It should be remembered that each individual allocates his savings between two broad categories of projects, those that are perfectly safe (yielding r) and those intermediate sectors where the returns are risky (yielding $R > r$). Thus in an economy subject to persistent bad luck, the proportion of savings allocated to the safe project will always yield r and therefore some minimum capital shock can be maintained. More simply, even if the risky investments never pay, at least the sure thing will yield a return which represents a stock of capital which can then be sold to final goods production.

From the above analysis, Zilibotti and Acemoglu show that as this model unfolds and the number of time periods during which the model operates approaches infinity, then the proportion of intermediate goods sector open relative to the total potential number of sectors that could be open approaches 1 or 100 per cent. In this case, all idiosyncratic risk will be removed (since all sectors would be open). The capital stock will then converge to a high-level equilibrium. The intuition to this conclusion is fairly easy to see. If the state of nature which prevails is a random variable, then as the number of time periods grows to infinity, even the unluckiest economies will have some good luck and it should be remembered good luck today tends to promote even better luck in the future. Economies which experience good luck will find that savings will rise, *AB* in Figure 3.4 will rotate upwards, and the equilibrium proportion of intermediate goods sectors open will rise. The larger the proportion of open intermediate good sectors the more likely that when a particular state of nature *j* occurs, that sector *j* will be open. Thus in the long run (time periods approaching infinity), the economy will approach a high-level equilibrium in which all intermediate sectors are open.

There are two important implications that follow from the model. As the number of sectors that are open increases, the economy is luckier. This means that it is likelier that a return of *R* will be reaped in the intermediate sector and then the more likely the capital stock will grow. Second, the variability of growth will also decline as the number of sectors open increases.

The above theoretical analysis can, with some modification, also be useful in our understanding of technical invention or macroinventions. Specifically, it will be assumed that such inventions are truly random and thus not predictable. A state of nature *j* occurring, as discussed previously, is reinterpreted as a particular macroinvention becoming available to sector *j* and only in sector *j*. These technological shocks are assumed to occur at a certain rate per time period and this rate will be called the natural rate of invention. Thus this rate is exogenous just as the rate of technological change was exogenous in the neoclassical model of growth. However, whether these macroinventions become economically viable is dependent upon the proportion of the intermediate sectors that are open.

The proportion of sectors that are opened will be assumed in this model to represent the number of markets that are open and functioning. In terms reminiscent of the last chapter, it will be presumed that the less integrated a national market system is, the fewer markets for intermediate goods that will be open and vice versa. Thus as market integration increases, the number of intermediate goods sectors open and operating rises and the higher the actual rate of technical innovation will be. In the extreme case, where in Figure 3.4 if the equilibrium value of *n* becomes equal to one and complete market integration occurs, the actual rate of technical innovation becomes equal to the natural rate of technical change. Thus in this model it is the actual rate of technical innovation that becomes endogenous, not the potential rate of technical change.

Two implications follow from this reinterpretation of the model. First, as market integration increases the economy as a whole tends to become luckier. However, in the interpretation used here, it would be more appropriate to say that the actual rate of technical innovation approaches the natural rate of invention. Second, the variability of the actual rate of technical innovation would also decrease as market integration occurs.

Another reinterpretation must also be made concerning how sectors or markets are opened up. To recall the earlier discussion of Figure 3.4, individuals in the first stage of their lives earn income by working in the final goods sector. They then decide how much of this income to save and then how to allocate savings among safe and risky sectors. It is presumed that this savings is automatically invested and that this, along with the minimum size requirements per sector, determines the equilibrium proportion of intermediate sectors (n^*) that will be opened up. This is a completely supply-side explanation of when intermediate goods sectors or markets begin operation. It presumes that once the savings become available then they will be immediately invested in as diverse a portfolio of sectors as possible. The only risk that has to be dealt with here is the risk that a technical invention will occur in an unopened sector. However, there is a second kind of risk that cannot be insured against via diversification. This is the risk that producers of intermediate goods, those doing the saving and investing in production projects in the various sectors, may find that there are no buyers for their products. The buyers of intermediate goods are reluctant to commit to the purchase of intermediate goods, unsure that specialized producers would actually arise. As a result, producers will find that they have no buyers for their products. Of course, this was the coordination problem characteristic of the traders' dilemma discussed in the previous chapter.

Thus one must reinterpret Figure 3.4 in the light of the traders' dilemma. Now n^* represents a potential equilibrium. It shows how many sectors may actually be able to open if indeed there was demand for the output produced. Thus it represents only a supply-side potential that remains to be actualized. This modification of the analysis changes one of the conclusions of the model developed by Acemoglu and Zilibotti. In that model as the number of time periods approaches infinity then the proportion of intermediate sectors open approaches 100 per cent. Thus it is inevitable, even for unlucky economies, that full commercialization of the intermediate goods sector will eventually occur. However, this inevitability disappears in the reinterpretation of the model utilized here. Whether the n^* (equilibrium number of sectors open) determined by the supply side in Figure 3.4 becomes an actual real equilibrium depends upon the extent to which the traders' dilemma problem is resolved through coordination. If only a small degree of coordination is achieved, then the actual n achieved or realized (n_R) will be much below the n^* in Figure 3.4. Now it is not inevitable that as time approaches infinity that the proportion of sectors open will become 100 per cent. Instead this proportion will remain low (n_R). The economy will remain caught in a low-level trap situation. If coordination is achieved on a large scale then n_R

would approach 1 or 100 per cent. Now it becomes inevitable that n^*, the level determined by savings, will eventually also approach 1 or 100 per cent through the savings and capital accumulation process.

As previously mentioned, there are two types of general solutions to the problem of the traders' dilemma; small-scale society solutions and large-scale society solutions. Small-scale societies have evolved networks of kinship, village and religious relationships over long periods of time. Merchants link into these networks and use them to generate information about potential buyers and sellers. Thus cooperators will be linked with cooperators and the cooperative solution becomes an equilibrium in the traders' dilemma game. However, this only works on a small-scale basis, implying that the n actually achieved or realized (n_R) in Figure 3.4 will be small. The implication will then be that small-scale societies will tend to be unlucky, that is, the actual rate of technical innovation will tend to be relatively low, much below the natural rate of technical change.

Compare the above situation to that of a large-scale society solution. Remember that in this situation traders and merchants behave as entrepreneurs. Instead of taking the network of social relationships generating information as a given, they seek to construct new networks of relationships that link otherwise disconnected groups. Their behavior bridges the structural gaps or holes in society. Thus information on a much larger population of potential buyers and sellers can be gathered and the potential for market exchange is much enhanced. This new technology is, however, subject to increasing returns. As a result, a coordination problem arises. If only a small number of buyers, sellers and traders commit themselves to market exchange, then the cost per transaction of utilizing the modern technology will be very high, all participants will tend to revert back to the traditional technology, and n actually achieved or realized (n_R) will be small. Alternatively, if a large number of buyers, sellers and merchants connect themselves to the new technology, then cost per transaction will be low and n_R will be high (high degree of market integration) approaching 1 or 100 per cent. In this case the supply-side determination of n^* through savings and capital accumulation will operate as suggested by Acemoglu and Zilibotti. A high n^* (with $n_R = 1$) implies that the economy will over time tend to be lucky with respect to technical change, savings will rise and capital will grow eventually pushing $n^* = n_R = 1$. As this occurs the growth rate will be increasingly less susceptible to variation. Thus the key to development would involve coordinating the activities of buyers, sellers and traders so as to generate a commitment to market exchange on the part of large numbers of those individuals.

The conclusion that follows from this story is that the movement from a small-scale society solution to a large-scale society solution, via some form of coordination, results in the actual rate of technical innovation approaching the potential rate of technical change. However, market integration via coordination has another important influence that has yet to be discussed (see Figure 3.4 for an explanation). In that figure OCD showed the minimum size requirements before sectors can be opened up. For sectors OC there was no minimum size requirement, while from C to D the size requirement is assumed to rise in a linear fashion. Thus minimum size requirements become important at point C.

There has, up to this point, been no discussion as to what determines the position of point C. Specifically, if point C moves to the right then, *ceteris paribus*, minimum size requirements occur for a smaller proportion of the intermediate goods sector and the equilibrium number of sectors that will open (n^*) will increase (the intersection point will move to the right). This is very important since as n^* increases it increases the likelihood of technical change which in turn enhances capital accumulation and rapid growth.

Alternatively, if C moves to the left, then a larger proportion of the intermediate sector is subject to the minimum size requirement. This implies, *ceteris paribus*, that the equilibrium number of sectors that will open (n^*) will decline. Again, this is important since if n^* declines it increases the likelihood that an economy will be unlucky with respect to technical change. Such an economy would then accumulate capital slower and develop slower. Thus the determinants of the location of C would seem to be important for the overall development process.

The question concerning the location of point C would seem to be closely related to the extent to which transactions are internalized within the firm as compared to those transactions that occur outside the firm. This is the issue of what determines the boundaries of the firm. It will be hypothesized here that the more extensively developed a market system is and, therefore, the lower the transaction costs per transaction, the more likely firms will disaggregate their activities, relying more upon the market. Thus the number of sectors subject to minimum size requirements will decline and point C will move to the right. In turn, n^* increases and the economy will be luckier with respect to technical change.

Alternatively, if market development is not extensive then the costs of carrying out transactions in the market will be extremely high. Firms will then move to internalize these transactions within the firm. The proportion of intermediate sectors subject to minimum size requirements would increase and point C would move to the left. It follows then that n^* would decline and the economy would thus become unluckier with respect to technical innovation.

Once again the movement from small-society to large-society solutions via coordination creates an extensive integrated market system. As pointed out above this mechanism operates to lower the cost of transacting leading firms to disaggregate. As this disaggregation occurs, minimum size requirements decline and this, therefore, enhances further market development. Actual technological innovation approaches more closely the potential or natural rate of technical invention.

The model outlined above is consistent with Mokyr's notion that the timing and combination of various macro technical innovations cannot be explained by individuals or firms allocating resources to research in the pursuit of the goal of profit maximization. Instead, these macroinventions are unpredictable and random and what was important in England's industrial revolution was the responsiveness of English society to these inventions. The model implies that this responsiveness was related to the degree to which market integration had occurred. The more integrated the market system, the more likely inventions, when they occurred, would be profitable to pursue through innovation. This coincides with our previous discussion of early English experience prior to the period of rapid technical change. This period was characterized as Smithian growth and its main characteristic was the extensive development of an integrated market system.

Thus it can be envisioned, that the basis for English growth was slowly shifting through time. Initially, rapid market evolution resulting from various coordination mechanisms led to productivity growth and growth in overall output mainly via division of labor and specialization. However, as the proportion of production sectors commercialized rose, England began to experience more rapid technical innovation. Macroinventions, while being random in nature, became more likely as intense commercial activity grew. Consequently, intense market activity increased the economic feasibility of these new innovations and the likelihood that they would prosper increased.

The same model would also seem to shed significant light on the process of early Japanese economic development. As mentioned earlier, Japan, too, underwent a long period of extensive market integration resulting from a series of coordinating factors similar to those in operation in England. This market integration also had a significant positive impact on growth via specialization and the division of labor. Thus income rose in Japan prior to the Meiji restoration (1868) in such a fashion that the standard of living was quite high by historical standards. However, the income level achieved was, most historians believe (Smith, 1986), not as high as that achieved by England prior to its period of industrial (technical) revolution. However, as discussed earlier and as pointed out by Macfarlane (1997), one of the significant differences between Japan and England is that the former did not experience a technical revolution until after the Meiji restoration. He attributes this to the absence in Japan of a tradition of experimental science. This absence he argues was probably due to two forces. 'In England there grew up from the twelfth century a well-endowed and separate set of institutions whose aim was to pursue knowledge as an end in itself' (Macfarlane, 1997, p.804). These were the universities and related educational systems which arose in England. According to Macfarlane, there was no similar institutional development in Japan.

The second important factor referred to concerns of England's location. Both Japan and England were island nations situated close to continental land masses. 'It is obvious that England on its own, without the developments all over the rest of Europe would not have achieved much' (Macfarlane, 1997, p.804). Japan was situated in regions where intellectual ferment and knowledge flows from region to region were limited. 'We have only to undertake the thought experiment of swapping the islands, putting Japan alongside Italy, France, Germany and Holland, and England alongside China, to realize how much the chance of the neighboring continent was responsible for what happened' (Macfarlane, 1997, p.804).

An additional factor is that during the Tokugawa period Japan deliberately closed itself off from the rest of the world. This, in combination with its location, implies that the natural rate of technical invention in Japan was much lower than in England. Specifically, the rate at which randomly occurring macroinventions occurred in Japan was much lower than that of England. Japan's location and the fact that it closed itself to the outside world lowered the rate at which random technical invention impinged upon the Japanese economy. Thus although the development of an extensive integrated market system provided a fertile soil for the seeds of new technology to fall on and sprout, its location and its intentional withdrawal from the world dramatically lowered its natural rate of technical invention.

5.   SOME EXTENSIONS

It must be noted at this point a simplification in the analysis above which as yet has not been explicitly recognized and discussed. It has been argued that integrated market development increased the likelihood that random macroinventions would be successful. Thus if a particular intermediate goods sector experienced such an invention and if that sector was open and operating, then that innovation would succeed. What is really being argued is that if a sector is open and technological invention impacts on that sector, then the individuals making up that sector will immediately know how to successfully use this technology (innovate). If the sector is not open, then no one will know how to use the technology (no innovation). Thus it is the knowing how to use the technology (innovation) that is dependent upon the existence of integrated markets. It is presumed in the above work that the knowing occurs instantly if the sector is open and does not occur if it is closed. This, of course, is highly unrealistic.

How do individuals learn how to use technologies (innovate)? The most common mechanism, discussed earlier, is learning by doing or experience. As experience with a particular new technique of production increases, firms and individuals learn better how to utilize the new technology. So, what is being argued is that market integration creates situations in which rapid learning by doing occurs. Open and operating markets provide opportunities to utilize the new technique in the production process and thus to learn how to use it effectively. Alternatively, if a technical invention occurs in a sector and that sector's market is not operating, then the new technology will not be usable since there is no mechanism that allows individuals and firms to learn how to use the new technology.

This learning by doing for a particular technique of production is, however, generally thought to be bounded. This implies that as experience is accumulated, the reduction in cost of producing a particular product utilizing a new technique will approach zero. However, the productivity benefits gained by such learning are thought by a number of scholars (Young, 1993) to spill over across other intermediate good sectors. In particular, the learning accumulated in the production of less sophisticated products lowers the cost of producing technologically more sophisticated products and vice versa. Thus as technical change occurs in other sectors the learning of the new technology will be promoted both by the experience of producing the good itself and the experience gained in mastering previous new technologies. The ultimate conclusion here is that the expansion of the intermediate goods sector is subject to increasing returns.

The main implication of these ideas is that history will matter very much here. Those countries which initially develop extensive systems of integrated markets will also reap significant productivity gains stemming from learning by doing. An extensive system of sophisticated intermediate goods-producing sectors will likely have arisen. These countries are, therefore, likely to have comparative advantages in those final goods which intensively use such intermediate goods. Thus the actual rate of technical innovation will be driven, through rapid learning by doing, to equality with the natural rate of technical invention.

The natural rate of technical change will also likely undergo a metamorphosis. The development of property rights in ideas combined with the formalization of the research process is likely to lead to a process of invention more directly driven by the pursuit of profit. Thus the neoclassical model, discussed earlier, in which a share of societies resources is devoted to technical research may be a more appropriate way of looking at the process of technical change. As seen in equation 3.4, technical change was represented by an increase in the number of intermediate goods. New intermediate goods sectors would be created via research and development. As these new sectors became integrated into the national market learning by doing would occur, thus allowing the technology to be successfully utilized. Again, this implies that such a country would likely have a comparative advantage in final goods which intensively uses sophisticated intermediate goods.

Contrast this with countries in which extensive development of markets has failed to occur. This implies that the number of intermediate goods sectors that are open (the extent of the integrated market system) is limited. This in turn implies that most of the technical inventions that become available will not be successfully utilized because there is limited learning by doing which can occur. Thus the growth process will be slow and a relatively small intermediate goods sector will evolve. It follows that these countries will tend to develop comparative advantages in final goods which tend to use intermediate goods less intensively. Therefore, they will tend to export less sophisticated final goods.

These nations are likely followers that generally engage in little or no research and development directed at creating new technologies. Instead, the key to their long-run economic development is the ability to borrow technology created elsewhere and learn how to use it in their particular country. However, the limited development of markets for intermediate goods implies that such learning will likely be quite slow.

The implication of the above analysis is that as history unfolds the world will tend to be divided into a rapidly growing center and a slow growing periphery. This conclusion may be objected to by arguing that the countries left behind (developing countries) in the periphery could challenge the center (developed countries) in the production of sophisticated final goods by importing the necessary intermediate goods from the center. Thus the periphery could benefit from technical invention in the center not by borrowing and learning technology, but by merely importing the intermediate goods which have been improved through technical change in the center. However, it is argued here and by others (Rodrik, 1996; Rodríguez-Clare, 1996) as well that such intermediate goods are only imperfectly tradable. For the production of many of these intermediate inputs it is essential that the supplier be near the producers of the final goods. Producer services such as banking, auditing, consulting, wholesale services and transportation are good examples of such inputs. They are also generally thought to be nontradable. In addition, buying physical intermediate goods not produced in the local economy can be quite costly. There is 'a higher risk that they will not arrive at the right time or with the correct specifications, forcing firms to hold high inventories of such inputs' (Rodríguez-Clare, 1996, p.5). Also Pack and

Westphal (1986) have pointed out that new technology embodied in intermediate goods is generally very specific in nature. It was designed to work in particular ways in the production of final goods. As conditions within the periphery are quite different from those in the center, significant adjustments in operating procedure and design are often necessary in order to make the technology work in such different circumstances. 'The consequence is that the downstream producers need to establish geographically close relationships with suppliers' (Rodrik, 1996, p.3). Porter (1990) has also argued that the presence of domestic suppliers of intermediate goods is an important determinant of comparative advantage since it allows quick and efficienct access to cost-effective inputs.

If we accept the arguments made above then after the English technical revolution much of the rest of the world, including Japan, would have been peripheralized. Indeed, with the Meiji restoration and the trade agreements enforced upon Japan by various Western nations, the Japanese mainland was opened up to the process of trade according to the principle of comparative advantage. Therefore, the tendency was for Japan to specialize in relatively technologically simple products which were not intensive in the use of intermediate goods. Thus the borrowing and learning of new technologies would have been slowed. However, this marginalization of Japan was somewhat muted by a number of factors related to both geography and culture.

With respect to geography, Japan was located far from the major groups of industrial nations, Western Europe and the USA, during the period of the Meiji restoration. Thus the high cost of transporting goods to the Japanese market provided the latter's young manufacturing activities with a natural form of protection from external competition.

In addition to geographical protection, there is a cultural factor involved as well. Strong preferences by the Japanese population were exhibited for traditional Japanese goods. The tenacity of traditional consumer preferences reflected the deep cultural cohesiveness of Japanese society, the result of a long experience as an isolated economy before the Meiji restoration (Felix, 1974). This conclusion is borne out of the work of Ohkawa and Rosovsky (1961). They sought to examine the indigenous components of the Japanese economy in the 1950s. By indigenous components they meant the sectors or characteristics of the Japanese economy which were native in origin. The quantitative analysis was divided into two parts. The first related to an examination of the production side of the economy while the other looked at the demand or consumption side. The latter was relatively simple to carry out because types of commodity and service provide an objective mechanism for comparison through time. The supply-side analysis involved a number of different elements. The criteria here involved examining the mechanism of organization (household versus factory), size of establishment (small scale versus large scale), types of job and methods of production.

Indigenous occupations were defined as those normally existing in Tokugawa Japan, before 1868. Thus in 1955 62 per cent of Japanese workers were still engaged in traditional, indigenous occupations. With regard to the use of family workers, in the 1950s one-third of all workers were indeed family workers. In addition, in all industries the proportion of establishments having between 4 and 29 workers was 85.4 per cent in 1955. On the consumption side the results also indicate a strong presence of traditional, indigenous goods. Again, the definition of indigenous goods was one which included goods that had been in general usage in the 1860s. By this definition in 1955 approximately one-half of total consumer expenditures were for indigenous commodities. Thus the evidence of Rosovsky and Ohkawa's work indicated that indigenous, traditional Japanese goods still played an extremely important role in the 1950s. This implies that in the latter part of the 19th century as well as the early part of the 20th century such strong traditional sector preferences by Japanese consumers provided a natural form of protection for the Japanese economy.

The natural levels of protection provided by geographical location and culture were augmented by activities carried out by the government. Sinha gives a broad account of the activities of government in the period following the Meiji restoration. Railway construction was begun by the state and then taken up by private companies. In this latter case the government provided the land and guaranteed payment of interest up to 10-15 years. In 1906 the railway system was nationalized. Japanese merchant shipping owed its origin to government initiative. Financial support was provided in terms of subsidized loans as well as the outright gift of ships. The banking system, with substantial resources placed in special banks, was used by government as a policy tool. Government also purchased a large share of the capital goods, including machinery, produced in the Japanese economy. In the period 1911-1915, the total expenditure by the state on capital goods and construction equaled two-thirds of the total value of capital goods and construction materials produced in Japan. These capital goods were used in the creation of infrastructure and new industries. The state often constructed modern factories in various areas of production only to later turn them over to private owners.

There is hardly any industry which did not owe its origin to government support, financial or technical: the government owned and operated coal and other mines, shipbuilding yards, textile factories (including silk, cotton, wool, spinning and weaving mills) as well as factories for the manufacture of paper, glass, cement, and bricks. Even after some of these were transferred to the private sector, the government saved a number of enterprises i.e., electrical industries, cements, bricks, paper, glass, and leather from bankruptcy in the critical years prior to 1895 by placing large orders with them (Sinha, 1969, p.144).

Thus it would seem that in Japan the learning process was aided by two factors. First, geographical and cultural factors provided a sort of natural protective environment for the development of early Japanese manufacturing. Second, this seems to have been augmented by certain activities of the Meiji government. However, further discussion of these issues will be delayed until the next chapter where the main focus will be on the learning process and the role that the state can play. From this chapter's perspective it is important to see that early Japanese manufacturing activities were built upon the rapid development of an integrated domestic market linked to the development of agriculture. It would seem that this did provide an atmosphere very conducive to the learning of new knowledge and technologies imported from elsewhere.

By the time of World War II, Japanese firms in a number of major industries had clearly made considerable progress in acquiring the capacity to produce products of the standards and qualities required by a modern industrial power, and in developing the necessary scientific and technical infrastructure. The ability to produce quite a wide range of machine-tools had emerged by the late '30s and reliance on imports had substantially declined (Francks, 1992, p.192).

The perspective outlined views Japanese economic development as being basically internally driven, that is, the growth of agricultural production involving the bulk of the population led to the creation of a vast, integrated, national market. This integrated market combined with certain cultural and geographical advantages as well as a state dedicated to the promotion of technological learning, led to rapid overall economic growth. This is a significantly different story relative to the conventional explanations of early Japanese success. This conventional view argues that Japanese economic growth was export-led both in the prewar years and in the 1950s and 1960s (Shinohara, 1962). However, recent empirical work by Boltho (1996) does not support this position. In fact the implication from this work is that growth in Japan was internally driven.

The results from Boltho are based on applying five approaches to Japanese time series data for the time period 1885-1990. The first method uses Granger causality techniques that seek to empirically determine the direction of causality between exports of goods and GDP. The second uses price-quantity data for this time period to determine the extent to which price changes are the result of changes in demand or changes in supply. If demand predominates then domestic prices should rise with quantities. Alternatively, if supply shifts predominate then declining prices should accompany output increases. The third method examines the concentration of exports and seeks to determine whether these goods have faced strong growth in terms of the world market. Fourth, an examination is made of Japanese exchange rates to determine whether a low international rate served as the basis for rapid export growth. Finally, the last method utilized sought to use microeconomic evidence by analyzing the exports of specific sectors. Specifically the idea was to examine the pattern of imports, import substitution and exports. If imports of a particular good are followed by periods of import substitution and then exports, then this is strong evidence that exports depended on domestic growth that is, growth in Japan was internally driven.

Overall the results indicate a fairly clear conclusion. For most of this time period it appears that Japanese economic growth was driven by internal factors and that it is not appropriate to consider Japan as an example of export-driven growth. Specifically, it was Japan's ability to import and quickly learn how to use new technologies that allowed it to grow rapidly. As the production processes for various manufactured goods became increasingly cost-efficient, exports of manufactured goods began to grow rapidly. In this chapter rapid learning was related to the development of integrated market systems. However, it seems that there is a role for the state to play in this learning process and it is to this topic that we turn in the next chapter.

6.   SUMMARY AND CONCLUSIONS

This study began by comparing various theories of economic growth: the textbook classical theory, the Smithian theory, the neoclassical theory and several simplified versions of new growth theory. The latter involved a version of new growth theory in which research created new technology and a version in which technological learning occurs for a country that operates inside the technological frontier. It was argued that the early growth experiences of neither Japan (17th and early 18th centuries) nor England (17th, 18th and 19th centuries) seemed to resemble the stories told by either of the endogenous or new growth theories. Instead, the early experiences of these two countries resembled the discussion of Smithian growth in Chapter 2 and the simple model outlined at the beginning of this chapter.

In addition, none of the models provided a good explanation of the technical innovations that occurred in England in the 18th century and in Japan in the 18th and 19th centuries. Neither country engaged in significant formal research and neither had accumulated significant amounts of human capital. In addition, the systems for protecting property rights were underdeveloped and crude in nature.

The work of Mokyr (1990) provided a useful perspective for analyzing the technical revolutions which occurred in these two countries. Specifically, he divided technical innovation into two types or categories: macroinventions and microinventions. The former represented inventions which were significant breaks with past practice. Most importantly, these could not be explained by the allocation of resources in the pursuit of profits by maximizing firms. They were, to a great extent, random occurrences that were basically unpredictable. Microinventions cluster around macro-inventions and result from attempts to deal with the problems and difficulties involved in making the technology work. In other words, microinventions are the result of a learning process.

An alternative model of economic growth was put forward to better describe this process. It originates as a modification of a model developed by Acemoglu and Zilibotti (1997). This modified model viewed final goods production as utilizing a series of intermediate inputs produced in a variety of separate markets. Technical invention was viewed as random, thus effecting particular intermediate goods sectors in an unpredictable manner. If the market in that particular sector was open and functioning, the new macroinvention would be effectively learnt through a series of microinventions generated by the learning by doing process. If the market in that particular sector was not open, the macroinvention would occur, but there would be no learning by doing to operationalize the new technology and it would fail.

A number of important conclusions were drawn from this model. First, learning by doing is a skill, a kind of human capital. However, it is not accumulated in a formal educational process. Instead, taking part in market activities is presumed to generate a familiarity with products, how they work and how they are sold, that leads to additional small (micro-) inventions. This is what drives the process of technical innovation. Second, the more markets that are open and operating, the greater probability that a random technical invention will occur in a setting in which markets are already active. Thus the greater likelihood that invention will be transformed into innovation and, therefore, spur economic growth (natural rate of technical change and the rate of technical innovation become equal). Third, the opening up of additional markets (creating an integrated market structure) is dependent on solving the sorts of coordination problem outlined in the previous chapter. Thus Smithian growth provides the mechanism for altering the foundation of growth. Smithian growth is based on specialization and the division of labor driven by market integration. However, as markets integrate the actual rate of technical innovation will begin to rise such that growth in per capita income will be primarily determined by innovation.

This theoretical perspective seems to explain England's technical revolution and also why Japan's technical revolution was delayed until after the Meiji restoration. Japan had closed itself to outside contact, thus lowering the rate at which technical change would randomly impinge upon the economy (the natural rate of technical change). The model also highlights the problems of late developing nations, which Japan certainly was. This problem arises by extending the model to incorporate comparative advantage. If the world is divided into two regions, one where an extensive system of integrated markets exist and one in which such a system is limited, then the regions will follow two different growth paths. The highly commercialized region will develop a comparative advantage in those goods which intensively use intermediate goods. Growth there will be driven by the process of macro and microinventions. Alternatively, the region where integrated market development is limited will tend to develop a comparative advantage in those final goods which are not intensive in the use of intermediate goods. Growth via technical change and innovation will tend to be relatively slow. There will be a tendency for a center and periphery to develop.

This is certainly what happened to Japan. However, its place in the periphery at the time of the Meiji restoration was characterized by a number of special circumstances. First, an extensive system of markets had developed in Japan. Its relegation to the periphery resulted from closing itself off from the rest of the world. Thus the structure of the Japanese economy was such that it was a fertile ground for rapid learning by doing to occur once it was opened to the rest of the world. Second, it was protected from external competition during the early Meiji period by certain natural factors. Specifically, its geographical location dramatically raised the costs of transporting goods to the Japanese market and its cultural homogeneity created a strong demand for traditional, Japanese goods. Third, the Japanese government engaged in a number of activities which promoted further market development (agricultural growth) and subsidized and promoted manufacturing. As a result, Japan was able to quickly import and learn technologies developed elsewhere so that by the late 1930s the industrialization process was quite advanced. This view of Japanese development highlights the fact that this process was internally driven and not the result of exports leading growth and development.

The analysis of Japanese development leads us to the topic of the next chapter. Most developing nations in the periphery are likely to have a more difficult time catching up than Japan for the simple reason that they are so much further behind. In addition, systems of integrated national markets have not yet been developed. They also tend to lack the natural sources of protection which sheltered early Japanese industrial development. Finally, the state through its policies seems to have worsened the situation whereas the state seems to have played a positive role in the catch-up process in Japan. It is to the issue of the state and the learning process that we now turn.

NOTES

1. The discussion of the neoclassical growth theory concepts is taken from Jones (1976).
2. See Jones (1998), pp. 94-95.
3. If $L_A/L_A > n$, then the entire population would eventually be creating designs. If $L_A/L_A < n$, people who create designs would disappear from the population.

REFERENCES

Acemoglu, Daron and Fabrizio Zilibotti (1997), 'Was Prometheus Unbound by Chance? Risk, Diversification, and Growth,' *Journal of Political Economy* 105 (August), 709-751.

Arrow, Kenneth (1962), 'The Economic Implications of Learning By Doing,' *Review of Economic Studies* 29 (June), 153-173.

Arthur, Brian (1989), 'Competing Technologies, Increasing Returns, and Lock-in by Historical Events,' *Economic Journal* 99 (March), 116-131.

Boltho, Andrea (1996), 'Was Japanese Growth Export-Led?' *Oxford Economic Papers* 48 (July), pp. 415-432.

Boulding, Kenneth (1981), *Evolutionary Economics* (Beverly Hills, California: Sage Publications).

Crafts, Nicholas (1996), 'The First Industrial Revolution: A Guided Tour for Growth Economists,' *American Economic Review* 86 (May), 197-201.

Crafts, Nicholas (1998), 'Forging Ahead and Falling Behind: The Rise and Relative Decline of the First Industrialized Nation,' *Journal of Economic Perspectives* 12 (Spring), 193-210.

Felix, David (1974), 'Technological Dualism in Late Industrializers: On Theory, History, and Policy,' *Journal of Economic History* 34 (March), 194-238.

Francks, Penelope (1992), *Japanese Economic Development: Theory and Practice* (London: Routledge).

Goldschmidt, Richard (1940), *The Material Basis of Evolution* (New Haven: Yale University Press).

Hayami, Y. and V. Ruttan (1985), *Agricultural Development: An International Perspective* (Baltimore: Johns Hopkins University Press).

Jones, Charles (1998), *Introduction to Economic Growth* (New York: W.W.

Norton and Co., Inc.).

Jones, Hywel (1976), *An Introduction to Modern Theories of Economic Growth* (New York: McGraw-Hill).

Levine, Ross and D. Renalt (1992), 'A Sensitivity Analysis of Cross-Country Growth Regressions,' *American Economic Review* 82 (September), 942-963.

Macfarlane, Alan (1997), '"Japan" in an English Mirror,' *Modern Asian Studies* 31 (October), 763-806.

Mokyr, Joel (1990), *The Lever of Riches: Technological Creativity and Economic Progress* (New York: Oxford University Press).

Nelson, Richard and Sidney Winter (1982), *An Evolutionary Theory of Economic Change* (Cambridge, Massachusetts: Belknap).

Ohkawa, Kazushi and Henry Rosovsky (1961), 'The Indigenous Component in the Modern Japanese Economy,' *Economic Development and Cultural Change* 9 (April), 476-503.

Pack, Howard and L. Westphal (1986), 'Industrial Strategy and Technological Change: Theory versus Reality,' *Journal of Development Economics* 22 (June), 87-128.

Porter, Michael (1990), *The Competitive Advantage of Nations* (New York: Free Press).

Rodríguez-Clare, Andrés (1996), 'The Division of Labor and Economic Development,' *Journal of Development Economics* 49 (April), 3-32.

Rodrik, Dani (1996), 'Coordination Failures and Government Policy: A Model with Applications to East Asia and Eastern Europe,' *Journal of International Economics* 40 (February), 1-22.

Romer, Paul (1990), 'Endogenous Technical Change,' *Journal of Political Economy* 98 (October), S71-S102.

Shinohara, M. (1962), *Growth and Cycles in the Japanese Economy* (Tokyo: Kinokuniyo).

Sinha, R.P. (1969), 'Unsolved Issues in Japan's Early Economic Development,' *Scottish Journal of Political Economy* (June), 109-151.

Smith, T.C. (1986), *Native Sources of Japanese Industrialization, 1750-1920* (Berkeley, California: University of California Press).

Young, Alwyn (1993), 'Invention and Bounded Learning by Doing,' *Journal of Political Economy* 101 (June), 443-472.

4. Market Integration and Catching Up: the State

1. INTRODUCTION

It was pointed out in the previous chapter that, as the process of technical change unfolds, there is a tendency for divergence to occur with some countries marginalized, locked into patterns of production in which there are few increasing returns and little technical change and learning by doing. However, falling behind creates a situation in which it is possible to have growth miracles. In Figure 4.1 society *B* falls behind as the production frontier shifts outward through time. However, there is also the possibility that a country can rapidly propel itself from deep inside the frontier to a point on the frontier through a rapid process of learning by doing. This requires an institutional structure that allows for and encourages such learning.

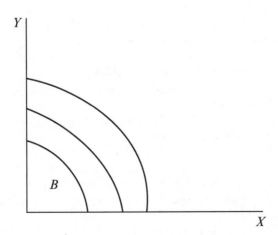

Figure 4.1   Catching Up

Japan is a prime example of a nation that has achieved miraculous rates of growth in such a manner. Its learning process was perhaps easier since the technological frontier at the beginning of the 20th century was not shifting out nearly as rapidly as it seems to be doing recently. However, there are some more recent examples of other nations that have also succeeded in generating miraculous rates of growth via learning - South Korea and Taiwan. Their problems would seem to have been more difficult given how far behind they had fallen, but in a sense the potential for miraculous growth was perhaps even greater than that for Japan. However, in all three of these cases the state seems to have played an important role in creating an environment conducive to learning. Some discussion of these state activities in the Japanese case was presented at the end of the last chapter. In this chapter the state's role in the process is discussed in greater detail.

Section two of the chapter examines a variety of theories concerning the role of the state. This involves looking at the state as being benevolent in terms of its aims and goals, as being driven by special interest groups seeking to control the state for their own benefit, and as being basically predatory in nature with the goal being to enhance the power and wealth of those who hold the reins of power.

Section three puts forward an alternative view known as the developmental state perspective. It argues that states played a crucial role in providing an environment, institutional structures and the leadership necessary for rapid learning to occur. Evidence is presented to support the idea that the states in both Taiwan and South Korea were developmental in nature. Such states were able to independently formulate economic goals (independent of powerful special interests), create organizational structures capable of carrying out plans to achieve these goals, and were flexible enough to alter plans and strategies in the wake of failure. Thus these are pragmatic states. What factors tend to give rise to them? A number of historical circumstances which played a role in the rise of such states in East Asia is discussed. These factors all represent exogenous variables.

Section four attempts to examine some internal factors, endogenous variables which may influence the effectiveness of state policy making. The first factor to be examined is part exogenous, part endogenous. This concerns the technical characteristics of the type of product or products produced with the bulk of a society's resources. This is partly exogenous, since comparative advantage plays a role in the allocation of resources. However, it is also partly endogenous in that state policy can influence this allocation of resources. Certain allocations are likely to result in a state having more independence, in the long run, from powerful interest groups. Other allocations have the reverse effect.

Given that states have some independence in decision making, what then will be its goals? If the typical microeconomic view of individual decision making is accepted and it is applied to members of the state, it would seem that a predatory state is inevitable. However, the traditional model of individual decision making is modified in section five to allow for idealism, concern for societal goals, to figure in the decision-making process. It is argued that the long-run persistence of idealism depends upon the probability of developmental success. The latter is explored within the context of a multiple equilibria model of economic development. The existence of multiple equilibria is related to the variable which underlies much of this study, the degree to which an integrated national market exists. If the latter exists, multiple equilibria are likely and thus the probability of success for state efforts aimed at promoting the development of manufacturing rises dramatically. If such a market system does not exist, state efforts are likely to degenerate into a situation in which policy becomes increasingly predatory rather than productive.

In section six a second set of problems besetting state action related to the timing of benefits and costs is examined. State policy aimed at long-run development generally involves the commitment of resources by the state, but more importantly the commitment of resources by private individuals. The benefits of such activities, if they are successful, are likely to occur in the future. The key to any state policy is often dependent upon how responsive private entrepreneurs are to state policies and incentive arrangements. This responsiveness in turn depends upon whether the state can credibly commit itself to policies which allow private entrepreneurs to retain the benefits of investment. It is argued that a rural-based market integrating environment will create conditions in which such commitment can more easily arise.

In section seven the experience of Taiwan and, to some extent, South Korea is used to illustrate the ideas discussed in previous sections. However, with South Korea, it is argued that it presents, to some extent, a second mechanism or path for solving the coordination problem involved in the traders' dilemma. That is, the problem is solved by promoting a development strategy aimed at exporting manufactured goods to international markets via the vehicle of the large, integrated firm. Thus coordination problems are solved within the borders of the firm. Finally, the dangers of this approach are debated.

Section eight summarizes the chapter and provides some conclusions and speculations. Specifically, the question of the relevance of the East Asian experience for others is addressed. This provides an introduction for Chapter 5 which deals with the development experience of Southeast Asia.

2. SOME THEORIES OF THE STATE

The predominate view of the state that is found in elementary economics textbooks is of an institutional structure run by a bureaucracy whose interests are to promote the welfare of the society as a whole. Within this context the need for state action arises when the market proves inadequate at maximizing society's welfare. These inadequacies have generally been attributed to the existence of public goods, incomplete or missing markets, externalities and imperfectly competitive markets. These inadequacies have been discussed in earlier chapters and in all these activities some sort of government intervention in the marketplace is generally thought to be necessary to achieve optimality.

Some have extended the argument of market inadequacy to even cover difficulties which arise from an extremely unequal distribution of income. Usually when market inadequacies are discussed the term is usually restricted to apply only to deviances from Pareto-efficient outcomes and, therefore, excludes the equity problem. However, Wolf (1982) argues that the concept of a public good can also be applied to considering income distribution. 'An equitable redistribution does not result from freely functioning markets because philanthropy and charity yield benefits not appropriable by donors' (Wolf, 1982, p.111).   Accordingly, if redistribution is left to private individuals the result will be too little redistribution. Thus there would seem to be a role for the state to generate a more equitable distribution.

Much of the literature on market inadequacies has been strongly focused on manufacturing and the urban, industrial sector as being the main location of market inadequacies.   However Myint (1975) has argued that market inadequacies are more characteristic of the traditionally rural sector and, in particular, agriculture than the manufacturing sector. For example, markets are more likely to be missing in the rural traditional sector. The capital market, for example, does not exist in the rural areas of most developing nations. However, it seems to operate quite well in the urban industrial sector, at least for the larger more capital-intensive firms.   The market inadequacies concerning public goods and the existence of externalities also seem to be more likely in the rural areas. This also has been discussed in earlier chapters. Thus the view of the state as being interested in the welfare of society, combined with Myint's notion that agriculture tends to be more afflicted by market inadequacies, would seem to lead to the conclusion that much of state policy would be directed at agricultural development problems.

Earlier discussions have shown that most scholars think that policy in most developing nations is, if anything, biased against the agricultural sector. That is, agriculture and rural sector economic activities actually seem to be discriminated against. Lipton (1977) has labeled this as being urban bias.

How does one explain this result if the state truly seeks to promote the welfare of society? A number of theorists have attempted to explain this by viewing the state and its policies as deriving from the struggle among interest groups for control of the state. From this perspective, the state has no real independence in the decision-making process. It is the interest groups who are successful at gaining control over the policy levers of a society that will make policy.

Perhaps one of the best expositions of this point of view has been put forward by Olson (1971). He argues that the goals of any particular group can best be seen as collective goods. That is, if they are achieved the benefits which follow will be available to all members of the group whether or not they contributed resources to the achievement of the goals. As a result, individuals who will benefit from the provision of the public good and are contemplating contributing resources towards the group, will likely decide not to. These individuals will thus choose to free-ride, benefitting without paying. If the success of the group is dependent upon the extent to which resources are mobilized and if all potential members are governed by the free riding logic, then the group is likely to fail to achieve its objectives.

Olson does, however, make a distinction between large and small groups. Large groups are likely to be most afflicted with the problem of free-riding since in such a large group there is very little interdependence in decision making. Each individual's decision has little or no impact on the decision of others. However, in smaller groups strategic interaction is more likely to occur, that is, if the group is small enough then each individual knows that his or her choices will affect the choice made by others in the group. Thus if an individual chooses to free-ride, others may respond by retaliating in some manner. This possibility increases the likelihood of a cooperative result in which all members contribute to the achievement of the group's goal.

What sort of economic goals will small groups pursue? Olson argues that because of their small size they are highly unlikely to be interested in policies that benefit society in general. Instead they will actually pursue policies detrimental to society if it benefits the members of the small group. The main reason for this is that if a small group pursues a policy that benefits society in general, the group will bear all of the cost with most of the benefits spilling over to nonmembers. It follows then that small groups are likely to be interested in policies that benefit the few at the expense of the many. These would be policies that redistribute wealth or income or the possibilities of earning wealth or income. That these policies harm the rest of society would be of little concern since the cost would be borne by members outside the group.

The likely result of the process outlined above is that as time passes small interest groups will gain control over the policy-making process and it would then follow that the resulting policies would probably be growth-inhibiting in terms of their effects. More specifically, this analysis indicates that policy making in developing countries is likely to be dominated by groups representing urban interests rather than rural interests. The most obvious reason is related to group size. Due to economies of scale and small domestic markets in developing countries it is likely that many industries will be dominated by just a few firms (oligopoly). Alternatively, the agricultural sector is likely to be made up of thousands of farmers. Thus it is possible that industrial groups will organize to defend their interests and highly unlikely that rural groups would be able to do so.

There is a related reason for the relative strength of urban, industrial interests. In most developing countries policy making is not dominated by a single interest group, but by a coalition of such groups. Bates and Rogerson (1980) argue that agrarian interest groups are unlikely to be members of ruling coalitions. This is explained by the proposition that people specialize in production but generalize in consumption. 'That is, they earn their incomes from the production of a particular good and they spend their incomes broadly, allocating only a portion to the consumption of the good which they themselves produce and the remainder to the purchase of a wide variety of other goods' (Bates and Rogerson, 1980, p.215). Thus their real income depends on the price of what they produce relative to the prices of the things which they consume. As a result, the goal of any governing coalition will be to raise the relative price of the products produced by its members.

Now it is possible to see why farming interest groups make unattractive coalition partners. The bulk of the population in most less-developed nations devote a large share of their incomes to the purchase of food. If farming interests became a member of a ruling coalition and the relative price of farm products increased, other members of the coalition would probably suffer greatly. Alternatively, coalitions made up of urban manufacturing interests are less likely to face this problem since no member of such a coalition is likely to spend a large share of its income on a product produced by another coalition member. Thus agrarian groups will be very unattractive partners for ruling coalitions.

Thus the special interest theory of the state implies that policies will generally be aimed at redistribution rather than productivity enhancement and that such policies will favor urban, manufacturing interests rather than rural, agricultural interests. Thus there is likely to be an underallocation of resources to rural economic activities.

The above perspective generally views the state as being identical with the coalition of groups which generates enough influence to dominate decision making. However, the state and the individuals running its agencies and bureaucracies can be viewed as an independent group attempting to pursue its own interests. The interest group view above tends to take a more passive view of the state. Bates (1988) in his analysis of the development process in Africa has the state playing a much more active role. The state seeks to actively engage in policies that are in its own interest, the main one being to remain in power.

If this view is taken then the state's seeming reluctance to utilize markets can now be better explained. Any interference with a market that moves the price away from equilibrium will create either a shortage or a surplus. It prevents the market from serving one of its important functions, to allocate goods and services (and resources) among buyers. By creating a shortage, a new mechanism for allocating the good or service must be developed as a substitute for the market. Now the state can create new institutional mechanisms, under its control, for allocating the scarce product, service or input. The advantage for the state is that it can now utilize this new allocation mechanism to reward its followers and punish its foes. For example, when a country's currency is overvalued the result will be the creation of a shortage of foreign exchange. The state can now use its control over this scarce thing to promote its own power and to undermine the strengths of its opponents. Policies which cripple the operation of the economy often provide the state with the opportunity to gain control over important sources of power and influence, even if they come at the expense of economic growth. Thus the state will behave in a predatory fashion.

The above analysis leads to a rather pessimistic view of the role of the state in the process of economic development. It implies that the influence of the state over the economy should be minimized. However, the miraculous performance of East Asia, Taiwan and South Korea has cast doubt on these pessimistic perspectives. In these countries the state seems to have played a significant and very positive role in the overall process of development. The East Asian experience and the new view of the state that has come out of that experience is examined in the next section.

3. EAST ASIA AND THE DEVELOPMENTAL STATE

By now most social scientists are quite familiar with the economic achievements of East Asia (South Korea and Taiwan). In 1960 South Korea was poorer than many sub-Saharan African nations and Taiwan was not much richer. In South Korea per capita income was $883 and for Taiwan $1359. Since then these two countries have experienced extremely rapid growth with an average annual growth in per capita income of 6.8 per cent in South Korea and 6.24 per cent in Taiwan. As of 1989 real per capita income in

South Korea was $6206 and $8207 in Taiwan (1985 dollars). This growth has been accompanied by a rapid expansion in exports. The export to GDP ratio rose from virtually zero in South Korea in the early 1950s to more than 30 per cent in the early 1980s. For Taiwan, this ratio rose from 10 per cent in the early 1950s to over 40 per cent in the 1980s. In addition, there was a spectacular increase in investment in both nations. Investment in both countries rose from around 10 per cent of GDP in the late 1950s to 30 per cent in the 1980s. This investment effort was roughly matched by an equivalent rise in the rate of savings.[1]

In terms of total factor productivity, from 1966 to 1990 it increased at an annual rate of 1.2 per cent in South Korea and 1.8 per cent in Taiwan. These results are hardly spectacular when compared to countries in other regions of the world (South America). The implications of this, as pointed out by Rodrik (1995, p.60) are that 'once the phenomenal rate of factor accumulation (primarily in capital) is taken into account, there is very little residual left over to explain. The inescapable conclusion is that the proximate determinant of the East Asian miracle is capital accumulation...' This does not mean that there has been no borrowing of technology and that there has been no learning by doing in the development process. Instead, what it means is that most of the increase in output can be attributed to increased physical and human capital. If the imported technology, embodied in equipment, had not been effectively utilized via learning by doing total factor productivity growth would actually have been negative.

There have been a number of theories proposed to try to explain this rapid economic development. Wade (1990) divides these theories into three groups: free market, simulated free market and governed market. The first two views are fundamentally neoclassical in their viewpoint in that they emphasize the importance of relative prices reflecting relative opportunity costs, sometimes referred to as getting prices right. The free market view argues that East Asia succeeded because state interaction in these economies was kept to a minimum. However, for the most part this view has been rejected due to the massive evidence available which illustrates significant government intervention.

An alternative neoclassical view accepts the idea that government intervention has been pervasive, but argues that most of the distortions created were offsetting in nature. Thus the resulting system of relative prices is very similar to what would exist in a free market situation. A related argument is that the common feature in all East Asian policy making is the neutrality of their trade policies, that is, the incentive to export is, on average, equal to the incentive to import. Therefore if there are restrictions on some imports, then the bias against exporters can be reduced by remitting import duties on imports used in export production and the relative prices of traded goods (exports and imports) would not be distorted. However, the relative price of tradable goods would be raised relative to nontradables. The implication is that significant involvement in international trade would occur. As a result, much of this literature tends to view the economic development of East Asia to be trade-driven or, more specifically, export led.

Recently, this view has been somewhat revised by the World Bank (1993). They have indeed recognized the significant presence of the state in these economies and grant that some interventions by the state may have worked to foster rapid growth while maintaining relatively equal distributions of wealth and income. However, they find that the real keys to East Asian success are in terms of its market-friendly approach to policy. Specifically, these countries maintained macroeconomic stability, engaged in significant investment in human capital, and maintained open economies in which production for export could thrive.

However, there are a number of questions that have been raised concerning the above perspective. There is now considerable skepticism concerning the notion that growth in these countries was export-led. As mentioned at the end of Chapter 3 evidence was presented that growth in Japan was internally driven. That is, as capital accumulation and new technologies were incorporated into the production process, the improvements in productivity and efficiency allowed Japanese firms to begin exporting. The same sort of logic is also being applied to the experience of South Korea and Taiwan.

Rodrik (1995) has shown that in both South Korea and Taiwan the export booms began in the mid-1960s. However, most of the incentives provided for export production were already in place in the late 1950s. Thus the spurt in exports does not seem to have been the result of a relative increase in the profitability of export production.

> Of course, export incentives (and in particular a relatively free-trade regime for exports) must have been a necessary condition for exports to take off in Korea and Taiwan; it is hard to imagine the export performance of these countries taking place in the presence of grossly overvalued currencies or high barriers to trade in imported inputs used in exportables. Nonetheless, the delay suggests that the export incentives were not sufficient in themselves (Rodrik, 1995).

Further evidence in support of this contention is provided by the work of de Melo (1985). In a comparative study of South Korea and Taiwan he finds that for manufacturing as a whole and in almost every subsector of manufacturing import substitution preceded export expansion. 'This sequencing lends further support to the theories of the determinants of the pattern of trade which emphasizes the role of demand conditions and internal markets prior to exporting' (de Melo, 1985).

It is also unclear why an export orientation for an economy would have led to an investment boom. Rodrik (1995) provides two important examples which imply that export booms do not lead to increased investment: Turkey and Chile. In Turkey there was a massive increase in the profitability of exports in the early 1980s. These reforms were accompanied by a significant rise in the ratio of exports to GDP, but private investment actually fell. In Chile, export incentives increased significantly after 1982, but private investment did not rise significantly until after 1989. 'In theory, there is no reason to suppose that export orientation should be associated with an increase in investment demand. Export orientation makes some sectors more profitable and others (import-competing activities and non-tradeables) less so. The same is true of import liberalization' (Rodrik, 1995). The net effect on investment would thus be indeterminate.

4. THE DEVELOPMENTAL STATE

This then leads to Wade's third view which attributes the success of East Asia to the state's activities aimed at governing the market allocation of resources. Specifically, the government engages in policies which allocate more resources to a small number of industries than would occur with a free market. As these industries grow and mature, the nation becomes capable of exporting these products to other countries, thus successful industries are not picked, they are made. Comparative advantage does not evolve, instead comparative advantage is created.

The main mechanism for creating comparative advantage involves an import substitution strategy. Certain industries were chosen for development by the governments of East Asia. These industries are protected via the utilization of tariffs, quotas and indirect means of subsidy and support. The latter is likely to include the provision of capital at below market interest rates. In those nations the government either directly controlled the banking system via public ownership or indirectly controlled the system through government influence. As a result, funds could be allocated to favored firms and industries.

The above analysis presumes that the state behaves quite differently from the views of the state presented in the latter part of section two of this chapter. Specifically, the state was either presumed to be under the control of a dominant coalition of special interests or an independent entity acting in a predatory manner with respect to society. That is, the ruling élite try to maximize the benefits that flow to them even if it comes at the expense of the rest of society. Using Myrdal's (1968) terminology a distinction must be made between hard and soft states. Soft states are generally thought to be responsive to a variety of different interest groups, with the latter playing an important role in defining government policy. Hard states are able to resist those influences so as to define autonomous goals and policies and the aim of these goals and policies is to promote rapid economic development.

Rodrik (1992) gives some analytic content to these concepts by likening the interrelationship between the state and the private sector to a game. In this game government and private action are determined in the equilibrium of the game. He argues that the natural way to approach this problem is to consider which group acts as the Stackleberg leader. The latter refers to a game sometimes used to analyze the behavior of duopolists in microeconomic theory. In applying the game to this setting it is assumed that both government and the private sector have control over some particular action. This action influences the utility of each individual player, thus the two players are interdependent. In this context, Rodrik defines an autonomous, developmental state as a Stackleberg leader. By this he means that the state when choosing its policy takes into account the private sector's reaction to this policy. The private sector merely reacts to the policy.

The alternative is, of course, that the state could behave as a follower or behave in a subordinate fashion. In this situation the private sector chooses its policy by taking into account the reactions of the state. The state merely reacts to policies set by the private sector. 'Put differently, the subordinate state lacks a mechanism that would commit it to reward or punish the private sector according to whether the desired behavior is carried out or not' (Rodrik, 1992, p.331). The strong state does, of course, have the ability to commit itself to such rewards and punishments.

This fits in well with Amsden's (1992) explanation as to why East Asian nations have been more successful than the bulk of the rest of the developing world in promoting rapid industrialization. From her perspective, the critical difference between the two sets of nations was not in terms of the types of policy carried out. Both sets of countries (East Asia and the rest of the developing world) have all experienced a significant amount of government involvement in economic activities, usually involving the subsidization of one group of industries at the expense of others. These subsidies reallocated resources from one group of industries to another.

The important difference between the two groups seems more related to the principles used to determine the allocation of subsidies, not in terms of the use of subsidies *per se*. Amsden makes the point that for most developing countries those subsidies are giveaways, that is, they are given to a particular industry or group of industries without the imposition of any performance requirements. 'In the case of financial incentives, for instance, subsidized loans often have not been repaid altogether, or they have been used for purposes for which they were not intended, or they have been bottled up on investments that never approach international standards of productivity or quality' (Amsden, 1992, p.61). In East Asia where successful industrialization has taken place, subsidies were, according to Amsden, allocated on the basis of economic performance. Performance was itself evaluated on the basis of productivity increases, exports, product quality, investment in human capital development and expenditures on research and development.

A number of scholars have attributed the success of East Asia to low wage rates and activities of the state aimed at keeping organized labor weak. However, wage rates are low throughout much of the poorer regions of the world (South America, South Asia, and so on). States in many of these regions have also sought to keep labor divided and weak. 'What accounts for differences in rate of growth of industrial output and productivity among late-industrializing countries is not the degree to which the state has disciplined labor but the degree to which it has been willing and able to discipline capital' (Amsden, 1992, p.331).

The above analysis naturally leads to the following question. How does one explain the rise of hard, developmental states in East Asia while most of the rest of the developing world is cursed with soft states? Factors giving rise to hard states, particularly in East Asia, have been discussed by Migdal (1986). He argues that societies which have undergone significant social upheavals are likely candidates for the development of a strong state. This supposition is further supported by the work of Olson (1971), which was reviewed earlier in this chapter, who argued that the goal pursued by groups can be thought of as a public good for that group. Large groups trying to pursue such collective goods would find it extremely difficult to organize to achieve the goal due to the fact that individual members of such groups are likely to try to free-ride by not contributing to achieving the goal, but enjoying the benefit if the goal is achieved. Alternatively, in small groups strategic interaction occurs among the members. These smaller groups are more likely to organize to achieve their goals than are larger groups and the goals pursued by these small groups are likely to harm society for the benefit of its members. Thus through time, small groups are likely to proliferate within a society leading to policies which are productivity-reducing and aim mainly at redistribution.

The conclusion to be drawn from the above analyses is that for a strong state to evolve that is interested in promoting overall productivity (rather than the interests of small groups), there would have to be a massive social dislocation that sweeps away the small special interest groups. This would allow the state to pursue broad developmental goals. All three nations in East Asia (South Korea, Taiwan and Japan) have gone through such periods of social dislocation. World War II, its aftermath and the Cold War dramatically influenced all three. Japan, of course, lost World War II and was occupied by the US army. Significant changes in social structure were brought about as a result. In Taiwan's case, the retreating Nationalist forces completely transformed traditional Taiwanese social structures after World War II. Finally, the Korean war caused destruction and havoc in South Korea as the superpowers tested each other militarily. It could be argued that such social dislocation swept away the influence of smaller groups, leaving the field open for the development of a strong state.

Related to the above point, in all three nations one of the most powerful groups in any less developed country was eliminated. Specifically, the landlord class in all three nations ceased to exist as the result of land reform (Wade, 1992). One could argue that such reforms swept important and powerful groups from the playing field upon which government policy is created. Thus governments in all three nations felt free to pursue policies which would promote the economic interests of the vast majority of society (through growth) rather than those aimed at the interests of a few.

Once strong, independent national structures existed in these nations, the existence of strong external threats may have served to focus the interests of the state on economic growth as a mechanism to ensure national survival. In particular, both South Korea and Taiwan faced the threat of invasion by truculent neighbors. This threat may have served to make the governments of these nations less lax with respect to promoting overall growth. This same argument has been made with respect to Japan during the Meiji era, when external powers threatened the national survival of Japan.

It may also be maintained that at least part of the success of East Asia is due to the fact that this region received a large share of Western aid, particularly from the USA, during the Cold War years. This aid certainly strengthened the states in these regions. In addition, given the long tradition of education and the evolution of a competent bureaucracy, the effective utilization of such aid was greatly enhanced.

All of these arguments developed by Migdal and others certainly provide some insight as to where strong or autonomous states come from. The evidence from East Asia seems to provide support for the fact that these factors were at least partially to account for the success of government policy in promoting economic development. However, there are several troubling points that need to be addressed. First, most of the influences discussed above find their origins outside the countries examined. Social dislocation, military threats and land reform were all imposed from the outside. Thus little insight is gained concerning those internal factors which might lead to the evolution of economically strong states. More importantly, it seems to imply that weak states can do little to improve their abilities in promoting effective policy. Finally, these explanations do not seem to explain the effectiveness of the Japanese state prior to World War II. Although Japan was threatened by external powers, at no time was colonization imminent. In addition, although the Tokugawa Shogunate was displaced and a new group had come to power, there was no massive social upheaval and there was no land reform, in the sense of a redistribution of ownership rights. How does one explain the effective policy carried out by the state during this period?

5.   SOME ENDOGENOUS VARIABLES

The work of Shafer (1994) sheds some light on at least one factor which is at least partly endogenous (and partly exogenous). He is interested in trying to explain how states restructure their economies. Restructuring refers to efforts by the state to reallocate resources and redirect economic activity by altering the sectoral composition of the economy. Each economic sector has a distinct combination of four variables: capital intensity, economies of scale, production flexibility and asset factor flexibility. Particular combinations of these characteristics produce distinctive state structures.

Of the four characteristics capital intensity and economies of scale need no discussion. However, the terms production flexibility and asset factor flexibility need some explanation. Production flexibility is the ability to meet short-term market shifts by varying output levels or product mix. In microeconomic terms, it is the short run in which the firm adjusts to exogenous shocks by varying output and perhaps by shutting down. Asset factor flexibility refers to the sector specificity of facilities, supporting infrastructure and work force skills. It determines how costly it is to shift resources from one sector to another in the long run.

Using these concepts, Shafer discusses two polar opposite cases: high/high sectors and low/low sectors. The high/high sectors have high capital intensity and large economies of scale which in turn imply production inflexibility and asset factor inflexibility. With regard to the latter two variables some additional discussion is needed. Sectors that are highly inflexible in terms of short-run production decisions are those where fixed costs are very high and where capital facilities are strongly negatively affected by production shutdowns. Sectors which have high asset factor inflexibility are those where production facilities are highly specialized and geographically concentrated, where infrastructure (power grids, railroads, pipelines and so on) is sector-specific and geographically concentrated, where the production technology is useful for the production of a limited variety of goods, and where management is highly specialized in particular services.

Alternatively, low/low sectors have low capital intensity and few economies of scale which implies production flexibility and asset factor flexibility. Production flexibility in the short run results from low fixed costs and production facilities which are not significantly affected by production shutdowns. Asset factor flexibility in the long run results from production processes which have equipment and facilities, infrastructure, technology and management which can easily be reallocated to different types of production.

With these ideas established Shafer argues that the characteristics of the main sectors of an economy influence the extent to which the state has the autonomy to pursue a restructuring of the economy. High/high sector production inflexibility implies that firms in this sector will have a difficult time adjusting to exogenous shocks. Downturns devastate these firms since they find it difficult to dramatically reduce production, via shutting down, in the short run (in light of the high fixed costs). Asset factor inflexibility creates significant barriers to exit this sector in the long run. Most of the facilities, infrastructure and resources have few alternative uses and this affects the state in two ways. First, leading sector firms will, because of the above reasons, have strong incentives to fight restructuring attempts by the state. Second, since states in this type of economy will be dependent upon the firms in the leading sector for the bulk of their tax revenue, their independence is limited and their capacity to promote other sectors is strictly limited.

Perhaps more importantly, in high/high sectors production is usually undertaken by a few firms engaged in a market with oligopolistic characteristics. They use a labor force that has few alternative opportunities and is concentrated geographically. As a result, collective action is relatively easy among both leading sector firms and workers and thus they will be potent political actors. The ultimate objective of such collective action would, of course, be to limit any restructuring activities by the state.

Thus leaders of nations dominated by high/high sectors would seem to have little autonomy. The state is dependent upon a highly specialized sector possessing few alternatives and having significant incentives to penetrate the state. Because of their organizational abilities, groups within this sector also have the political power to successfully penetrate the state. The state's ability to prevent such penetration is extremely limited given their dependence on this sector or sectors for tax revenues.

The situation is exactly the opposite in countries dominated by low/low sectors where economies of scale are minimal and capital intensity is low. This means that exogenous shocks in demand can be easily accommodated by adjusting output or perhaps even shutting some units down, resulting in production flexibility in the short run. In addition, asset factor flexibility implies that resources thrown out of work in those areas experiencing decreasing demand can be easily reallocated to other sectors which are expanding. Thus the incentive by groups to seek to control government policy in order to protect themselves from economic restructuring is much reduced.

In addition to the above, in countries dominated by low/low sectors there is generally a significant degree of competition in production and there are large numbers of firms involved. As a result, labor markets also tend to be less controlled and more competitive. It follows then that collective action by firms and/or labor would be much more difficult and thus neither group is likely to be a potent political actor.

The leaders of nations dominated by low/low sectors would probably have greater autonomy in decision making. The state is *not* dependent on just a few firms for either political support or tax revenue. Groups within the society are also less likely to be harmed by economic restructuring since resources can quickly be moved out of declining sectors and into expanding sectors (at very low cost). Even if such groups would seek to prevent restructuring, the barriers to collective action are likely to be such as to prevent them from successfully organizing.

Shafer argues that the best examples of states characterized by high/high sectors are those dependent upon mining and plantation types of commodities. Whereas those countries dependent upon low/low sectors are those whose dominant sector tends to be peasant agricultural production or simple, labor-intensive manufacturing. Of the first type he discusses the cases of Zambia (copper) and Sri Lanka (tea). Of the latter type he discusses the cases of South Korea (labor intensive manufacturing) and Cost Rica (peasant coffee production.)

This model indicates that the particular product a country happens to have an initial comparative advantage in is crucial in determining the extent to which the state will have autonomy. Those specializing in commodities which are high/high sectors will be states with little autonomy while those specializing in commodities which are low/low sectors will be autonomous in policy making. However, as Shafer recognizes, this is a deterministic logic indicating that states will have a little role in determining their fate. However, the argument that he makes is tempered by reference to the experiences of South Korea and Taiwan. Although both experienced rapid development in the postwar period, as discussed previously, and were characterized by many similarities, there were also some very significant differences.

South Korean economic development has been characterized by significant economic concentration and the development of extremely large firms. In Chapter 2 this represented the second major path to economic development, in contrast to the rural-based growth process. It involved skipping over the coordination problems of creating a national market by targeting the production of these firms for export markets. However, as was pointed out when this path was discussed, this merely moves the coordination problem to within the firm. Thus in this strategy the state promotes interaction and the evolution of a corporate culture within the firm so that the problems of coordination can be overcome. In contrast, firms in Taiwan remained relatively small with little economic concentration. Instead, growth was driven by rural expansion and the creation of an integrated national market. This was the case of a rural-based path of growth which was similar in many aspects to that of Japan.

Shafer accounts for this difference in the following manner. Both countries had comparative advantages initially in labor-intensive agricultural and manufactured goods possessing the characteristics of low/low sectors. Both governments, therefore, possessed significant autonomy in designing and carrying out restructuring programs for their economies. Divergence occurred when Korean policy makers chose to implement policies that 'encouraged economic concentration in order to build national industrial champions' (Shafer, 1994). Taiwan's leaders restructured their economy but minimized increases in firm size and increases in economic concentration. Korea's choices of policies have transformed the economy from one based on low/low sectors to one based upon high/high sectors. This, Shafer would argue, threatens the ability of Korea to restructure its economy as over time it becomes more dependent on interest groups. This is indeed the point that was made in Chapter 2 concerning the second path to economic development and growth.

South Korea's current economic problems, connected with the financial crisis which enveloped Southeast Asia in 1997 and 1998, do seem to stem at least partly from an inability of the state to carry out an economic restructuring of the South Korean economy. Contrast this with Taiwan where the recent financial turmoil in Southeast Asia has, for the most part, had little impact. It seems that the Taiwanese economy is still capable of restructuring itself almost continuously through time. There will be a further discussion on this issue later in the chapter.

Thus it would seem that state policy can influence the extent to which countries allocate resources to low/low versus high/high sectors. Extending this analysis, it can be seen that if this analytical perspective is accepted, then the import substitution policies followed by most less-developed nations after World War II, which were aimed at protecting capital-intensive industries characterized by significant economies of scale, represented a dual disaster. First, such industries were quite inefficient in most of these nations resulting in significant losses. In addition, there was a second significant political cost. These countries basically created a situation which undermined their political autonomy. The industrial sectors created were often not viable without protection and, therefore, there was a great incentive for special interest groups to form around these industries to seek to gain continued protection in the future. This incentive was greatly enhanced by production and asset factor inflexibility. Most of these industries had significant fixed costs implying that shutting down would be extremely painful. Much of the infrastructure, capital stock and labor skills involved could not be easily and quickly transferred to other uses. Also, given the small number of firms involved (oligopolistic structure of industries) and the requirement for concentrations of skilled workers, this created conditions conducive to collective organization.

The above implies that state policy can influence which sectors expand relative to others and, given Shafer's analysis, influence how autonomous the state will be in the future. Pushing beyond these ideas, it should be remembered that prior to World War II, Korea and Taiwan were colonies of Japan. The latter promoted the development of peasant agricultural production so as to serve as a steady source of food for mainland Japan. The strategy followed and techniques of production utilized were those that had been initially developed by Japan during the Meiji period to foster rapid growth in rice productivity within Japan. Thus in all three nations policies were aimed at protecting and promoting productivity growth among large numbers of farmers. This was most effective in the case of Taiwan and less so in Korea. Therefore, prior to the development of labor-intensive manufacturing in all three nations, peasant agriculture achieved development. This sector, peasant agriculture, is one of the low/low sectors discussed by Shafer and this sector involved the bulk of the population and produced a large share of GDP.[2] Thus the basis for autonomous states seems to have been laid by the economic activities and allocation of resources carried out by the Japanese colonial establishment.

As noted above, the development of low/low sectors was more extensive in Taiwan relative to Korea. This was mainly due to the fact that when Japan colonized Korea (1910) its infrastructure, in particular systems of irrigation, was much less developed than that in Japan (Hayami and Ruttan, 1985). As a result, state efforts to raise productivity were much less successful in Korea as compared to Taiwan. Even more importantly, so much rice was extracted from Korea that rice consumption in Korea actually declined. Thus all increases in production as well as additional amounts of rice were directed away from the Korean economy and into Japan (Kuznets, 1977). All of the transactions involving this trade were basically in Japanese hands. Given the sluggish growth of the agricultural sector, combined with the fact that the Koreans were basically excluded from substantial commercial activity (Levy, 1991), implies that at its independence (after World War II) the extensive network of social relationships necessary for the development of an extensive national market had yet to be developed. Therefore, for the most part, the Korean market was fragmented.

It seems that at the beginning of the postwar period Taiwan was perhaps further advanced in the creation of an integrated national market than was Korea. One could speculate that this was perhaps the reason why leaders in South Korea decided to pursue a development strategy based upon the development of large business groups whose focus was the production for sale to foreign markets (Levy, 1991). Biggs and Lavy (1991) label this as a government-directed learning strategy of economic development. Again, this strategy has certainly been successful in terms of growth, but if Shafer's analysis is valid, it undermined the ability of the South Korean economy to restructure the economy in the future.

The above analysis provided some understanding of a factor influencing the autonomy of state decision making which is at least partly endogenous in nature. That is, government choices concerning the allocation of resources today can influence its ability in the future to make independent policy decisions. The key factor involved is the extent to which resources are allocated to economic activities or sectors involving the bulk of the population and characterized by flexibility in production and in asset structure. It was argued that peasant agricultural production is one of these sectors, as well as labor-intensive production of manufactured goods.

However, autonomy does not guarantee a developmental state which means that a state uses its powers to influence resource allocation in order to pursue development for the bulk of the population. An autonomous state could choose predatory policies and thus become a most efficient and vicious predator. In fact, several of the views of the state discussed in section two would indeed argue that this would tend to occur. If it is presumed that individuals seek to maximize their own utility, subject to constraint, then it is likely that if groups of such individuals become members of ruling coalitions they will indeed use the powers of the state for their own benefit, even if it comes at the expense of society. However, in the next section of this chapter this extreme version of the utility-maximizing individual is modified. This modification is based upon the work of North (1990).

6. IDEALISTIC BEHAVIOR AND TRADEOFFS

North sees individual behavior as being constrained by a number of factors other than the individual's budget. There are formal and informal constraints that can be thought of as being part of the institutional and cultural infrastructure of a society. However, there are also self-imposed codes of behavior.

These self-imposed codes of behavior are extremely difficult to explain. North contends that some understanding of this phenomenon can be gained by viewing the problem as one involving marginal tradeoffs. That is, individuals are likely to have a greater willingness to express altruistic motives through their choices if the cost of doing so is relatively low. More simply, he sees a negatively sloped demand curve in which 'the lower the cost of expressing one's convictions the more important will be internal convictions as a determinant of choice' (North, 1990, pp.43-44).

Governments made up of such individuals may indeed be willing to pursue policies aimed at general wealth enhancement, rather than the wealth of a select few and they may, therefore, be willing to replace the individualistic code of behavior with one that sets the good of the group above that of individuals or small groups of individuals. However, the willingness of a governing élite to do this would be a function of its costliness to individuals making up the élite. This costliness in turn would certainly depend, at least partly, upon the probability of success of a productivity enhancement strategy as well as the timing of the benefits stemming from such a policy. Specifically, as the probability of success for a productivity-enhancing policy declines, one would expect governing élites to be reluctant to pursue such policies and vice versa. In addition, most productivity-enhancing strategies require an investment now from which a return is expected at some point in the future. The more delayed this return is, the more costly it will be for a governing élite to follow such a policy. First, attention will be focused on those factors influencing the probability of success.

Amsden (1992) has also argued that the quality of state intervention will depend on the objective conditions surrounding the likelihood that a process of successful growth will occur. 'The higher the probability that investments in industrial development will generate positive returns (in terms of profitability, or at least employment at break-even costs), the greater the likelihood that governments will become developmental' (Amsden, 1992, p.72). The lower the probability of industrial success, the greater the likelihood that governments will remain nondevelopmental. Reinterpreting this in the light of the discussion in this chapter, the less likely that governmental activities aimed at promoting rapid learning will succeed, the more costly the pursuit of such policies becomes for the members of the government. As a result, it becomes much more likely that concerns for personal aggrandizement and power will replace concerns for society's interest.

As discussed above concentration must be focused on the likelihood of success of particular development strategies. Those for which the probability of success is low will likely result in predatory states if they are pursued and vice versa. What can be said concerning the probability of success of broad strategies for economic development? It would seem that for most developing nations strategies aimed at rapid industrialization are likely to have a low probability of success. This becomes most evident by examining the recent theoretical work attempting to explain the success of East Asia in promoting rapid industrial development.

Much of this work currently revolves around the analysis of models characterized by multiple equilibria. Two models of particular interest have been developed by Rodrik and Rodríguez-Clare. These are modern versions of what used to be called theories of the low-level income trap (Nelson, 1956). In these latter models an economy can be caught in a low-income equilibrium in which marginal efforts to move away from it are overwhelmed by forces pushing the economy back to a low-level trap. There is a second, high-income equilibrium that also exists. However, to reach this high-income equilibrium would require some sort of big push effort led by the state.

The models developed by Rodrik (1996) and Rodríguez-Clare (1996) assume that there are two final goods, high-tech and low-tech, and an intermediate good which comes in a continuum of varieties (n) which are all identical. The primary input is labor with the intermediate good representing the capital input to the production process. It is assumed that at all possible relative factor prices the high-tech good uses intermediate goods more intensively than the low-tech sector. Finally, the production functions for these two final goods exhibit a 'love of variety for inputs,' that is, as the number of varieties of intermediate goods increases, total factor productivity in the production of final goods arises. Thus the law of diminishing returns is offset by the utilization of an increased variety of intermediate inputs. This is similar in nature to the discussion in the previous chapter on the process of technical change in which it was argued that the speed of learning was linked to how many intermediate goods sectors are in operation.

These models generally make two additional assumptions that are quite important for the analysis and were also discussed in detail in the previous chapter. First, intermediate goods are assumed to be nontradable because of the tacitness of the technology embodied in intermediate inputs. Thus one cannot master these technologies without using them and users of these inputs must maintain close contact with suppliers. Second, it is presumed that the production of intermediate goods is subject to increasing returns.

The above model structure results in the possible existence of multiple equilibria. In the first equilibrium, the economy has specialized in the low-tech sector. Remember, the intensity of use of intermediate inputs in the production of this good is relatively limited. Thus the variety of intermediate goods produced would be limited and the per unit cost of producing such goods would be quite high. The latter results from the small size of the market for such goods. Any single producer who tries to shift to the production of high-tech goods will thus find his path blocked by the high cost of intermediate goods. Consequently, this country would remain locked into the production of the low-tech good.

There is a second equilibrium that may exist if all of the producers were to shift simultaneously to the production of the high-tech good. If this occurs, then a greater variety of intermediate goods would be produced at a lower per unit cost (increasing returns). This cost advantage may be large enough that it would now be profitable for all the firms producing final goods to produce the high-tech good.

If the above multiple equilibria exist, then a role for the state would emerge. A country stuck in the low-level equilibria (low-tech) will remain stuck there because incentives for individual firms preclude them from making the jump to high-tech production. However, if all producers can be persuaded to make the shift, then the market for intermediate goods would be large enough to make this shift to high-tech production profitable. The state's role would then be to coordinate the expansion of investment spending in the high-tech sector.

However, if multiple equilibria do not exist and the state attempts to coordinate an expansion in investment spending, then a different scenario emerges. Such a transition is impossible due to the nonexistence of the high-tech equilibrium. The strategy of development (coordinated expansion of high-tech production) will fail. In such a situation the government élite are likely to find that predatory policies are more attractive and thus predatory behavior will begin to overwhelm the state. Specifically, it becomes too costly for the leaders to follow a strategy aimed at overall economic development.

Thus the existence or nonexistence of multiple equilibria would seem to be the critical factor. Rodrik has recognized this and has developed a model which sheds light on this issue. He assumes, like Rodríguez-Clare, that the production of intermediate goods is subject to increasing returns. However, he modifies the model such that the per unit cost of producing intermediate goods is negatively related to the skill level of the work force, therefore, the more highly skilled the labor force, the lower the per unit costs of producing all varieties of intermediate goods. Thus a lack of skills on the part of the labor force may offset any cost-reducing impact of an increased market size for intermediate goods. This would effectively eliminate the high-tech production mode as an equilibrium.

This can be made a little clearer. Remember that the second equilibrium will exist if, when all firms shift to high-tech production, the increased market for intermediate goods causes such significant cost reduction (in intermediate goods) that the production of the high-tech good would be profitable. However, the skills of the labor force may be so low as to offset the advantages of market size. In this case then the high-tech equilibrium will not exist. Thus in Rodrik's model multiple equilibria depend on the existence of a skilled labor force. This fits well into an explanation of East Asian economic success since many have noted the relatively high levels of educational attainment achieved in this region.

However, as noted in earlier chapters, human skills incorporate more than just formal learning through schools and other educational institutions. Learning also comes from experience, in and through informal mechanisms. Much of this informal learning involves, as argued in Chapter 2, the creation of networks to gather information and create reputational mechanisms to undergird the creation of integrated national markets. This involves the application of the modern technology as a substitute for the traditional technology for information-gathering. This is critical for both Smithian growth and for making the transition from growth based on the division of labor to growth based on technical innovation, as argued in Chapter 3. In this chapter it is being argued that it is also crucial if state policies aimed at promoting the transition to higher-tech industrial production are to succeed. Thus this kind of informal learning is essential for the evolution of a developmental state.

This analysis can be clarified by referring to Figure 4.2. On the vertical axis the relative price of the low-tech good to the price of the high-tech good (P_L/P_H) is measured. On the horizontal axis the number of varieties of intermediate goods, n, is measured. Curve OA represents the relationship between relative prices and the quantity of intermediate goods utilized when the entire economy is specialized in the production of the low-tech good. Curve OB represents the relationship between relative prices and the number of intermediate goods when the economy is specialized in the production of the high-tech good. Finally, P_L^1/P_H^1 represents the international price ratio for these two goods.

Both OA and OB are drawn to be upward sloping and this can be simply explained. The high-tech good is presumed to be more intensive in the use of intermediate goods than is the low-tech good. Thus as the number of varieties of intermediate goods increases, then the relative price of high-tech goods should fall or the relative price of low-tech goods (P_L/P_H) should rise. This will occur whichever good the country is specialized in.

Note also that the curve OA lies everywhere above OB. This means that for any given level of n, the relative price of the low-tech good is higher when the country is specialized in the low-tech good (OA) than when it is specialized in the high-tech good (OB). This merely reflects the presumed concavity of the production possibilities curve for the low- and high-tech good which is drawn in Figure 4.3. In this figure the vertical axis measures

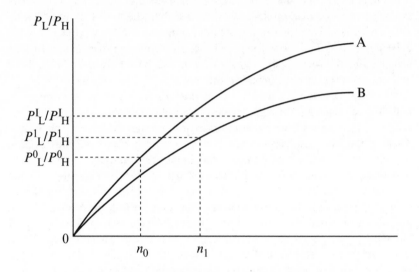

Adapted from Rodríguez-Clare (1996).

Figure 4.2   Low-Tech Equilibrium

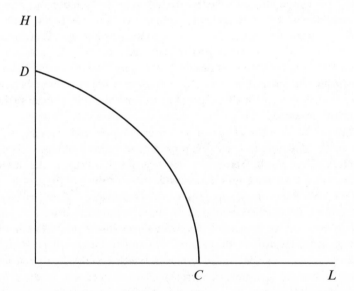

Figure 4.3   Specialization and Relative Prices

the production of the high-tech good and the horizontal axis the production of the low-tech good. When a country completely specializes in the low-tech good (point C), the relative price of the low-tech good is given by the slope of the curve at C. When the country is completely specialized in the production of the high-tech good (D) the relative price of the low-tech good will be given by the slope of the curve at D. Thus the relative price of the low-tech good is always lower if the country is completely specialized in high-tech production, OB is below OA in Figure 4.2.

Given the conditions existing in a particular economy, if it should specialize in low-tech production profits will be maximized with the number of intermediate goods utilized equal to n_0 with relative prices being P_L^0/P_H^0. If a country should specialize in high-tech production profits will be maximized at n_1 with relative prices being P_L^1/P_H^1. Note, it is assumed that $P_L^0/P_H^0 < P_L^1/P_H^1$, that is, as a country switches from specialization in the low-tech good to specialization in the high-tech good, the relative price of the high-tech good will fall (the relative price of the low-tech good will rise). However, as the situation is drawn in Figure 4.2, the only acceptable equilibrium in specialization is the low-tech good. Note that both P_L^0/P_H^0 and P_L^1/P_H^1 are both below the international price ratio, thus it is always cheaper to buy the high-tech good internationally rather than produce it within the country. Consequently, the specialization in low-tech production will be the only equilibrium. This is not a multiple equilibria situation.

Multiple equilibria may come into existence in the following manner. The low-tech sector is assumed to represent traditional sector production activities, while the high-tech sector represents modern manufacturing. If market integration can be achieved in low-tech, as outlined in Chapter 2, it is expected that production in this sector would make greater utilization of intermediate inputs through greater specialization. In Figure 4.2, this would imply that n_0 would move to the right. However, the growth of market integration would also allow high-tech producers (if they were to come into existence) to also make greater use of intermediate inputs. Thus n_1 would also move to the right. As this continues eventually the situation will resemble that outlined in Figure 4.4.

Figure 4.4 represents a situation in which multiple equilibria exist. If the country specializes in the production of the low-tech good, n_0 types of intermediate goods will be used and, as is apparent from the figure, the relative price of the low-tech good will be below the international relative price. However, if producers could be induced to switch to high-tech production, the utilization of intermediate goods would rise to n_1 and the relative price of the high-tech good would now be lower than the international relative price. High-tech production would now be a viable option. Government policies aimed at promoting the expansion of the high-

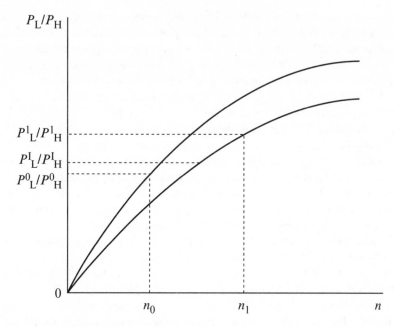

Figure 4.4 Multiple Equilibria

tech sector would have a high probability of success. Given the argument made in this section this increases the likelihood that the state will become developmental rather than predatory.

The previous section made the following simple argument. The autonomy or independence of state decision making is partly dependent upon how governments allocate resources. If they allocate resources to sectors characterized by high capital intensity, significant economies of scale, production inflexibility and asset factor inflexibility, then governments are likely to be dependent rather than autonomous. Alternatively, if resources are allocated to those sectors characterized by a few economies of scale, less capital intensity, production flexibility and asset factor flexibility then government autonomy and independence are likely to increase. Peasant agricultural and manufacturing activities are good examples of the latter. Such an allocation of resources is also likely to provide an environment in which market integration would occur as merchants and middlemen shift from traditional to modern technologies of information-gathering. The number of intermediate goods sectors open and operating would increase. In this section of the chapter it has been argued that this in turn creates an environment in which multiple equilibria between low- and high-tech production are likely to come into existence. In this situation, states are more likely to behave in a developmental rather than a predatory manner.

However, as was pointed out earlier, predatory behavior by the state is influenced not only by the probability of success of general development programs, but also by the timing of the costs and benefits of such programs. This is the issue that is examined in the next section of this chapter.

7.   TIMING AND COMMITMENT

The previous section argued that individuals are willing to sacrifice their self-interest for the good of the group, but this willingness is inversely related to cost.   The cost of pursuing growth and development strategies aimed at general development depends on two factors: the probability of success and the timing of the costs and benefits. The previous discussion concerned the probability of success, this section will be focused on the timing.   The problem of timing is fairly simple.   Government development programs generally require both public and private investment today, while the returns to such investment occur sometime in the future. Farmers and entrepreneurs are reluctant to undertake investment today unless they can be assured that they will be able to keep the bulk of the returns from their risk taking. The state must promise or commit itself to allowing this to occur. However, once the investments are made and the benefits begin to be generated the state has a strong incentive to extract the lion's share of the benefits. Entrepreneurs know this and are thus reluctant to commit resources. This is the commitment problem.

This problem can be illustrated in a simple manner by referring to a form of the prisoners' dilemma game discussed by Kreps (1990). Presume that the state (S) and private entrepreneurs (E) are the two players and the state has promised to provide an environment conducive to investment by entrepreneurs and has promised that the latter will be able to keep their winnings. The private entrepreneurs must now decide whether to believe the state or not. The state in turn must decide whether to honor its promise or not. A simple form of this game is outlined in Figure 4.5.

If the entrepreneurs choose not to believe the state then no investment will occur and nobody gains anything. However, if they choose to trust the state then the state is faced with the choice of honoring its commitment or breaking it. If it honors the commitment, both sides gain and the total benefits from the group are the greatest. However, if it chooses to break its commitment, the state can gain a larger reward (through taxing or confiscating the returns of entrepreneurial activity). Thus the state will, in a single play of this game, always choose to break its commitment. Entrepreneurs realize this and refuse to commit themselves to investment.

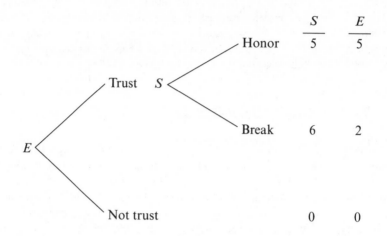

Figure 4.5   State and Entrepreneurs: A Prisoners' Dilemma

As argued previously, in the context of the traders' dilemma, the above result will change if the game is replayed an indefinite number of times and if the discount rate is low enough. Under these conditions, entrepreneurs can exert some influence over the state by retaliating against it whenever the latter chooses not to honor its promises. It is the fear of this retaliation which tempers state behavior and creates the potential for trust and honor to also serve as an equilibrium solution to the game.

However, the problem is much more complex than this. There are multiple groups of entrepreneurs: small farmers, large farmers, merchants, small businesses, large corporations and so on. Within this context a more interesting game presents itself in which the state can play one group against another. Weingast (1995a, b) has analyzed such a situation in which the entrepreneurs are divided into two groups: E_1 and E_2. The state can choose to break or keep its commitment to either group. However, in order to remain in power the state must retain the support of one group. In turn, for either of the groups (E_1, E_2) to try to punish the state will involve a cost for each and will only succeed if they both choose this strategy. Thus if any single group tries to carry out the punishment strategy and the other does not, this strategy fails.

Given the above, an interesting scenario emerges. The state can choose to honor its commitment to one group (E_1) while dishonoring its commitment to the other (E_2). Thus E_1 will support the state and E_2 will not, but the élite making up the state retains their power. It is presumed that the total short-run return to the state of cheating one group and honoring its commitment to another is greater than the return if commitments to both groups are honored. Punishment of the state will fail since the aggrieved party (by itself) cannot possibly succeed in deposing the leaders of the state.

The above bears a resemblance to what political scientists like Kurer (1996) have labeled as political clientelism. This involves the exchange of political support from a client group or groups in return for benefits provided by a patron, in this case the governing élite of the state. The relationship is generally hierarchical in nature with lower levels of patrons being clients of higher level patrons and so on. The ties binding patrons and client are generally informal, of a personal or face-to-face nature, and are entered into on a voluntary basis. Both parties to this relationship are motivated by self-interest and will switch partners if there are gains to be made. Clientelism is compatible with a wide variety of political decision-making systems whether they be of a democratic or authoritarian nature.

Clientelism policies are considered by Kurer and others to have a number of negative economic effects. Patrons have an incentive to try to transform collective goods into private goods. One way of doing this is to try to override bureaucratic rules and structures and allocate collective goods on the basis of political support. Corruption then becomes endemic in such societies with the governing regimes losing credibility or legitimacy. This in turn undermines the stability of the institutional structure. The question then concerns how patron-client political systems can be transformed. In terms of the game outlined above, how can the state credibly commit itself to long-run economic development and keep its promise?

Weingast (1995a, b) has made some progress in analyzing this problem. The difficulty in terms of the game involves the state breaking its commitments (transgressing against) particular groups. Thus the focus has been on which group has been transgressed against and why any attempt by that group to punish the state will fail. If instead of focusing on who is transgressed against one concentrates on what is meant by breaking a commitment, then some progress in the analysis can be made. To actualize this approach it will be assumed that each group and the individuals within each group will challenge the state whenever the state attempts to break a commitment, regardless of the target. The difficulty then in this situation is that there is a high likelihood of a diversity of opinion among groups of individuals as to what is meant by breaking a commitment or engaging in an act of transgression. It is this diversity of opinion which results in a situation in which the Pareto equilibrium solution (best for the whole society) is only one of several possible equilibrium. More simply, it is this diversity of opinion that allows the state to be tempted to play one group against another so as to retain power.

In the situation outlined above the ruling élite learn a very important lesson in governance. The way to maintain power is to construct patron-client links with certain favored groups so as to play one against the other. Learning how to credibly commit to development will become more difficult, rather than less. Is there no way out of this predicament? Specifically, presume that a state is governed by an élite motivated to promote the interests of society, even if it comes at some personal expense. In addition, presume, as argued earlier in this chapter, that this willingness to 'do the right thing' is inversely related to this cost. Then what sorts of policy could such a state follow?

With regard to the costs related with the commitment problem (timing), the key issue revolves around the opinions of groups and individuals making up such groups concerning what constitutes breaking a commitment by the state. If these opinions were similar among the various groups, then the willingness of all groups to oppose what is commonly agreed to be transgressions by the state would eliminate the temptation for the state to try to play one group against another. Thus the incentive to break commitments to long-run development would disappear.

This whole process can be viewed in a more dynamic way. The state and various groups within society are engaged in a dialectical interaction process. It is through this interaction that the state learns what works to maintain its power and what does not. In an environment in which the groups have a great diversity of views as to what constitutes a transgression by the state, the latter learns that it is relatively easy to maintain its power by playing one group against another Alternatively, in an environment where there is a consensus among groups as to what constitutes a breach of promise by the state, the state learns to credibly commit itself to wealth-enhancing policies. How is this consensus to be achieved?

It is here that Timmer's insights (discussed in Chapter 1) concerning the state and learning, in connection with the agriculture sector, seem to be important. He envisioned that the state could learn most how to carry out effective development policy by attempting to carry out a broad-based rural development strategy involving an inflow of resources into the agricultural sector. This inflow of resources must be made available to the bulk of rural producers, meaning small farmers and renters as well as large farmers. The result of this would be to generate broad-based growth throughout the countryside. As a result, all groups would experience similar economic growth stemming from similar sources. It is this similarity of experience that will likely lead to the evolution of a consensus among and within groups in the countryside, as to what is acceptable and not acceptable behavior by the state.

The above ideas can be made clearer by contrasting two different development strategies and what states are likely to learn by following each.

The first strategy is one that is broad-based in nature, involving the bulk of the rural population. The second involves concentrating resources on a small subsector of the economy. If a ruling élite genuinely interested in long-run development chooses the second strategy (resources aimed at a rural élite and so on), extremely divergent views of appropriate government behavior are likely to develop. Those groups that are favored will come to view such discriminatory policies as being perfectly legitimate, as long as they are receiving the bulk of the benefits. Alternatively, groups left out of the development process are likely to view such policies as lacking in legitimacy. Dissimilar experiences create divergent views of appropriate policy. Thus a state which follows this strategy will find itself increasingly tempted to become predatory, to play one group against another.

The first strategy, a broad-based rural process, involves the bulk of the population in similar activities resulting in similar outcomes, rising incomes. These common experiences will result in the evolution of similar views about acceptable and unacceptable government behavior. Thus a state which initially sets out on this path will find the temptation to break commitments much reduced. This is due to the fact that it becomes increasingly difficult for the state to play one group off against another. Thus society's strength serves to counterbalance the strength of the state. Society will then be able to discipline state behavior and the interaction between state and society will teach the state the lesson that credibility pays.

It is often thought that the only mechanism by which groups within a society can resist coercion by the state is via collective action. Such types of action are, however, subject to the free-rider problem. However, buyers and sellers linked in extensive social networks possess an unorganized form of power. For example, state policies which restrain productivity growth can be avoided by moving resources from one line of production to another or from one region to another. In addition, markets and exchange, which are initially overtaxed and regulated by the state, can disappear from the state's view via the establishment of underground economic activities. Thus the cost to the state of engaging in predatory behavior is increased while the gains are reduced as economic participants move resources, hide economic activities and avoid taxation.

The ideas and processes outlined above are similar to the notion of embedded autonomy introduced by Evans (1995). He argues that states indeed need to be autonomous so as to be able to effectively formulate and carry out policy. However, in East Asia the successful development states are 'embedded in a concrete set of social ties that binds the state to society and provides institutionalized channels for the continual negotiation and regeneration of goals and policies' (Evans, 1995, p.12). Evans maintains that either characteristic by itself will not work. A state possessing autonomy, but lacking embeddedness, would not have access to the information embeddedness provides and would lack the ability to rely on decentralized, private implementation of policies. Dense connecting networks of social relationships (embeddeness) without an autonomous state bureaucracy would be incapable of transcending individual and group interests. 'Only when embeddedness and autonomy are joined together can a state be called developmental' (Evans, 1995, p.12).

8.   A LOOK AT TAIWAN AND KOREA

The previous chapter argued that processes connected with technical innovation and learning are likely to lead to divergence in growth experiences between center and peripheral nations.   Center nations are those where integrated national markets have developed resulting in the evolution of a widely diverse set of markets for endogenously produced intermediate goods. It is this that allows for rapid rates of learning.   Alternatively, nations in the periphery are characterized by limited market development, thus learning is a slow process.

Movement out of the periphery is dependent upon the state playing a role in fostering rapid learning.   This, it was argued, was the key to understanding the astonishing East Asian experience.   The states in these countries have been described as developmental.   The conditions giving rise to such developmental states are partly exogenous in nature and partly endogenous.   This chapter focuses its attention mostly upon the endogenous factors.   These include the pattern of allocation of investment resources by the state.   If these resources are allocated to capital-intensive sectors characterized by significant economies of scale, production inflexibility and asset factor inflexibility, then states are likely to become dependent upon interest groups within society and likely to lack the autonomy to design and carry out policies aimed at general development.   Alternatively, if resources are allocated to sectors characterized by low capital intensity, few economies of scale, production flexibility and asset factor flexibility, then states are likely to develop a capability for independent or autonomous decision making.

Investment in peasant agriculture and small-scale manufacturing are likely to provide the most conducive environment for the development of autonomy. Such a broad-based strategy of development is also likely to create conditions, as argued earlier, for the development of integrated national markets.   This in turn creates an environment in which multiple equilibria exist and this dramatically increases the likelihood of success of government programs aimed at promoting the transition from low-tech to high-tech production. This lowers the cost to the governing élite of following a developmental rather than a predatory path and, therefore, increases the likelihood that the state will become developmental.

The final ingredient is the embedding of government decision making within social networks connecting the bulk of economic producers. It is this embeddedness which limits the temptation for the state to break its commitment to long-run development. Once again a rural broad-based strategy of development was seen to provide an environment in which such embeddedness can evolve.

The process underlying the evolution of the developmental state outlined above is perhaps best represented in recent experience by Taiwan. Exogenous factors certainly played a role in creating an environment in which such a state could arise, but there were other factors which are potentially endogenous which were also important. This is to be contrasted with the experience of Korea which represents a developmental state of a different kind. This different kind of developmental state was based on a strategy aimed at using already existing international markets rather than directly creating an integrated national market. This difference reflects the discussion in Chapter 2 concerning two strategies for solving the coordination problem plaguing exchange between buyers and sellers. There the first solution involved a broad-based development of rural production which acts as a coordinating system allowing merchants and intermediaries to commit themselves to market exchange on a large scale. This in turn allows a shift from the traditional to modern technologies for information-gathering and the integration of the national market. This was the basis for widespread Smithian growth. The second solution involved moving many of these transactions inside the firm and using the focal point of production within the confines of the firm to generate a corporate culture within which the coordination problem can be resolved. The state takes a strong role in this process by directing the activities of these large firms to export markets, driving the firms to learn and become internationally competitive.

In this section the foundations for the divergent evolution of different development states in Taiwan and Korea is examined. This involves an examination of the experiences of these two countries during their colonial periods under Japanese rule. This illustrates the contrasting roles played by agriculture in the early process of economic development and sheds light on the directions state development have taken in these two nations. Further discussion of the embeddedness of government decision making in the two countries is also presented, emphasizing the differences. This section closes with an evaluation of these two types of developmental state.

The distinctive experience of Taiwan and Korea during their colonial periods under Japanese rule was briefly discussed earlier. It must be emphasized that Japan in its status as a colonial power was no more enlightened than any other colonial power of the time period. It sought to exploit both Korea and Taiwan for the benefit of the Japanese homeland. This involved using these two colonies as sources of rice for the homeland. As industrialization proceeded rapidly in Japan prior to World War II the demand for rice rose faster than the ability of Japanese agriculture to supply the rice. Consequently, Korea and Taiwan were seen as being the source of rice for the homeland. Thus Japan engaged in a series of institutional reforms aimed at eliminating obstacles to agricultural growth and promoting the commercialization of agricultural production. In addition, resources were allocated to importing and adapting Japanese technology for rice production into these two colonies.

The results of this activity by Japan were, as discussed previously, quite different in the two countries. Agricultural growth and increases in productivity were much more rapid in Taiwan as opposed to Korea. For example, in the period prior to World War II, output in Korea grew at an annual rate of 1.62 per cent, while input usage also grew at about 1.62 per cent annually. The implication is that productivity did not grow at all. Alternatively, in Taiwan during the same period output grew at 3.6 per cent, inputs 2.6 per cent and overall productivity 1.0 per cent per annum (Hayami et al., 1979). Thus the response of Taiwan to Japanese programs aimed at promoting agricultural productivity was much more robust.

The differing responses of the two regions would seem to have been the result of differences in initial conditions, particularly in terms of existing infrastructure. Most importantly, systems of irrigation were much more widely developed in Taiwan compared to Korea. Also Taiwan had been a colony of Japan for a longer period and thus there had been greater opportunity to carry out investment in the Taiwanese rural sector.

Of course this rural investment was not undertaken to improve the welfare of the Taiwanese or the Koreans. The ultimate objective was to provide a greater supply of rice to the Japanese homeland. In this sense, colonial policy was a major success. Imports of rice from Taiwan rose from 636,000 koku[3] in 1915 to 4,962,000 koku in 1938. Imports from Korea rose from 6,870,000 koku in 1915 to 10,127,000 koku in 1938 (Ka, 1995). Thus, as can be seen, Korea served as the major supplier of rice to the Japanese homeland. Given the slow growth of rice production in Korea, relative to Taiwan, this rapid growth in exports posed a significant burden for Koreans. This is reflected in the fact that exports of rice as a share of total product in Korea rose from 9.5 per cent for the time period 1912-1915 to 41.4 per cent for the time period 1931-1935.

The result of the above factors was a decline in the average standard of living for Koreans. Specifically, there was a decline in the average consumption of rice and food grains as a whole in Korea during the colonial period. Before harvests peasants were often forced to eat wild grasses to supplement their food intake. 'The phrase "starvation export" was quite commonly applied... by Japanese food officials' (Kuznets, 1977, p.17). A second result of this process was that much of the rural population left the land and because jobs in manufacturing could not absorb the impoverished tenants, many emigrated to Manchuria and Japan.

The situation in Taiwan was significantly different. The more rapid growth in production and productivity allowed exports to grow without reducing the standard of living. In fact, it seems that the standard of living of the bulk of the rural population improved during the colonial period. This is borne out in the work of Ho (1978). He has examined wage data for this time period and found that real wages in the rural areas grew at between 1.3 per cent and 1.5 per cent per year for the time period. However, this was below the growth of labor productivity for this time period. Although the consumption of rice slightly declined during this period, the increased consumption of other foods was able to make up for the difference. Also the greater diversification of food in the diet (increased consumption of meat and vegetables) indicates the real possibility of nutritional improvement. The per capita consumption of other items such as bicycles, paper and cotton cloth rose steadily. Finally, life expectancy for males rose by 13.4 years and that for females by 16.7 years. Thus the benefits of agricultural growth in Taiwan seemed to have benefitted the Taiwanese, while the reverse seems to be the case for the Koreans. Part of the reason for these divergent experiences was the slower growth of agriculture in Korea relative to Taiwan. However, part of the explanation is also related to how agriculture was organized in the two colonies.

Even before the annexation of Korea in 1910 the Japanese had encouraged their own farmers to emigrate to Korea and this continued during the colonial period. There were two major avenues by which Japanese immigrants obtained arable land in Korea; the arrangements of semi-official institutions and the purchase of land by individuals. Immigrants of the former type were called protected settlers and the latter free settlers. There is still a great deal of disagreement among scholars concerning the extent to which the Japanese were able to gain control over the land. However, it seems likely that a large proportion of the rice land in Korea was owned by large-scale commercial Japanese owners. Rents were generally levied in kind and much of this rice collected via rents to Japanese landlords found its way into exports. In addition, a land tax was also used to direct rice into exports (Suh, 1978). Japanese capitalists also dominated Korean rice milling. They owned large, modern mills that consumed 80 per cent of the horsepower used in rice milling in 1931 (Ka, 1995). Thus the Japanese dominated the commercial rice sector in Korea. However, the situation was much different in Taiwan.

In Taiwan Japanese capital flowed mainly into sugar production and, as a result, rice production and trade remained in the hands of the Taiwanese. This included not only production, but also milling operations as well as domestic trading operations. Thus the 'commercialization of rice production and the separation of industrial activities, such as rice milling, from the farmers household economy thus was affected by Taiwanese miller-merchants. Taiwanese miller-merchants acted as mediators in the rice trade, acquiring unhulled rice from peasants and landlords (who received payment in kind) and selling the processed brown rice' (Ka, 1995, pp.154, 155). They also performed important financial activities. Peasants were generally chronically short of cash and capital and relied on credits from these miller-merchants as a source of funds. It is important to remember that there were few scale economies in the operation of mills and, therefore, there was significant competition among large numbers of these miller-merchants.

The implication of the above is that as the demand for rice in Japan rose and as investments in the agricultural sector in Taiwan increased productivity there, a part of the benefits stemming from this remained in the hands of the Taiwanese. The actual exporting of rice to Japan was handled by Japanese trading companies, but there was enough competition to prevent these trading firms from turning the terms of trade strongly against the rice industry in Taiwan.

The importance of the analysis presented above is the light that it sheds on the development of integrated market systems and the accumulation of human capital related to trading and exchange activities. In Taiwan, merchants and middlemen were actively involved in establishing an integrated system of markets to handle not only the rice trade but also simple consumption goods. The accumulation in skills and experiences benefitted the Taiwanese and provided the foundation for future market development. In the Korean case, the situation was much different. The Japanese displaced Koreans as owners of land and dominated the middleman activities involved in market exchange. Thus the skills and experience of integrating market activities were not accumulated by the Koreans, but by the Japanese. In fact the extraction of large shares of rice production by Japanese landlords via rent and the colonial state via taxes served to suppress indigenous market activities by the Koreans.

The implication of the above is that when both Taiwan and Korea gained independence after World War II the Taiwanese had already moved a long way towards the establishment of integrated market systems. This is further supported in the work of Biggs and Levy (1991). They, too, find that conditions in the two countries were quite different after World War II. Per capita income and levels of education were significantly higher in Taiwan relative to Korea in the early 1950s.

> More fundamental, if less readily measurable, the nineteenth-century population
> of Taiwan - migrants from Fukien located between the major trading ports of
> Hong Kong and Shanghai - appears to have enjoyed more substantial experience
> in business than did Koreans, who at the time were emerging only gradually
> from their status of a "Hermit Kingdom" and, in absence of a fully monetary
> economy, were dependent in part on barter as a vehicle for trade (Biggs and
> Levy, 1991).

The above differences were also important in another way. Government policy making in East Asia was not, in the postwar period, always correct or the result of following a minutely detailed plan of development. Instead, government policy was more pragmatic, following what worked and dropping what did not. Thus there was a dialectical interaction process between policy makers and society, more so in Taiwan than in Korea. This is also reflected in policy making in Taiwan prior to World War II while it was under Japanese control.

In the 1930s the Japanese mainland faced a number of problems in its agricultural sector. Specifically, there were great pressures on the supply-side to drive down the price of rice. In order to ease the political turmoil, the government of Japan spent heavily to sustain the price of rice through government purchase of surplus rice. However, this policy benefitted the producers of rice in the colonies since they could now sell their rice at these prices. This became a significant budget burden on the Japanese government. Thus the central government instructed the colonies to restrict the production and export of rice. This policy had its biggest impact on Korea, but very little impact on Taiwan.

The reason for the differential impact was connected to the organization of rice production in Korea and Taiwan. In the former rice production and trade were firmly in the hands of the Japanese. However, in Taiwan this was not the case, production and trade were in the hands of the Taiwanese. Thus the momentum for growth was maintained by internal accumulation among the indigenous producers. In addition, there were attempts by the colonial state to manipulate the terms of trade for rice. This was partly motivated by the fact that prosperity in rice production threatened the profitability of sugar production in Taiwan and it was in sugar production that Japanese capital was concentrated. Consequently, to protect and promote Japanese capital attempts were made to turn the terms of trade against the rice sector.

> In the face of mounting pressure both from sugar capitalists in Taiwan and rice
> producers in Japan, the Taiwanese landlords and their associates, including

native rice miller-merchants and Japanese export rice traders, formed the major organized power in defending the terms of trade of rice. In the 1930s the possibility of reproducing favorable price conditions for rice development depended primarily on the political power of the Taiwanese landlord class and its associates and on the balance of power with Japanese sugar capitalists (Ka, 1995, p.167).

For much of the 1930s the rice sector was able to effectively resist attempts to turn the terms of trade against rice production. It was only with the onset of World War II that effective regulation was placed on rice production. Thus broad-based development in rice agriculture provided a basis for disciplining state policy even in the prewar period.

Thus at the beginning of the postwar period the newly independent Taiwan and Korea represented two very different economies. In Taiwan significant market integration and human capital accumulation had occurred. The latter was mainly in the form of accumulated experience in market activities. Consequently, the transaction costs involved in engaging in market activity were low and agricultural productivity was quite high. The conditions for multiple equilibria and a coordinated movement from lower-level to higher-level equilibriums (low-tech to higher-tech production) were in place.

The solution to the coordination problem in Taiwan involved rapid agricultural growth combined with a rapid, coordinated expansion of investment spending. The likelihood of the success of such a strategy was quite high given the previous and continued rapid development of the agricultural sector. In the postwar period (1946-1970) output in agriculture grew at an annual rate of 5.6 per cent while input usage grew at 3.9 per cent per annum. The result was that productivity grew at an annual rate of 1.7 per cent. This growth in rural income stimulated domestic demand growth and, as Park and Johnson (1995) have pointed out, growth in domestic demand was the most important source of economic growth and employment in Taiwan up until 1970. Export expansion in this period played only a secondary role in overall growth.

This growth in domestic demand took place within a context in which the net flow of resources was out of the agriculture sector. The resources were transferred via a variety of mechanisms, but the resources themselves were used to carry out investment in the expansion of industry. This in turn served as the basis for a coordinated expansion of investment spending. In Taiwan this investment expansion began in the late 1950s when investment was a little over 10 per cent of GDP, rising to well over 30 per cent of GDP in the late 1970s (Rodrik, 1995). This combination of both increased demand for goods with rising rural incomes and the transfer of resources out of agriculture to stimulate investment was only possible as a result of the prior agricultural growth in the colonial period as well as the continued rapid growth in this sector in the postwar period.

The policies followed by the state in Taiwan resulted not just in the coordinated expansion of investment spending, but in a particular pattern of development in which small- to medium-size firms played a predominant role. Mostly the policies followed aimed at promoting broad categories of industries using mainly fiscal incentives, rather than specific or particular firms (Cheng, 1993). In this process the state often took the lead in establishing capital-intensive upstream industries, while relying upon private entrepreneurs to establish downstream firms. The investment incentives, tax laws, labor laws and a host of other policies presented strong incentives limiting firm size. For example, tax holidays provided investment incentives for new start-up companies rather than expanding already existing firms (Biggs and Levy, 1991). The strategy followed by the Taiwanese state aimed at coordinating an investment pattern based upon or building upon its strength, low transaction costs for market production. Thus firms remained, on average, small as various activities were carried out via market transactions rather than integrated within the hierarchy of the firm. The probability of success of this strategy was enhanced by the broad-based strategy of rural growth in the colonial period as well as in the postwar period.

This rapid rural growth seems to have had a powerful political and social effect as well. Specifically, the structural change connected with Taiwanese agricultural development, the diversification of production and input usage as well as the market integration between various sectors of agriculture and between agriculture and manufacturing, has played a major role in inducing, according to Moore (1988), a shift from statism to pluralism. Statism refers to a high degree of dominance and control by the central government over politics, society and the economy. With pluralism there is a 'degree of symbiosis between individual state agencies and the client populations with which they interact' (Moore, 1988). It also results in a greater capability of the rural population to react through economic or political means. As a result, policy making is more generally the result of a dialectical interaction between various state institutions and groups representing rural interests. The point to note is that the kind of pluralism under discussion has not involved the 'direct incorporation into the policy-making process of representatives drawn from the agricultural population. The increased bargaining power of the agricultural population is mainly of a passive and reactive nature...' (Moore, 1988).

The conditions in Korea were much different. As discussed earlier during the colonial period the rice sector was strictly controlled by the Japanese with the bulk of the Koreans excluded from market activities involving this crop. In addition, agricultural growth was slow and productivity increase nonexistent.   Thus indigenous integrated market development was quite limited and human capital accumulation, in terms of experiences of middlemen-traders, was also quite limited.   The impact of this was that limited market development resulted in significant transaction costs for carrying out market transactions.

The pattern of development in postwar Korea was thus quite different from that of Taiwan. The 1950s and early 1960s were characterized by the state's relative neglect of agriculture. The surplus was, however, transferred out of the agriculture sector via a number of mechanisms including forced delivery of rice by farmers at low prices and exploitative fertilizer-rice barter arrangements. This was a continuation of the prewar experiences in that agricultural growth remained slow, but activity in this sector was burdened by extractive policies. Within this context the resources extracted were used to again coordinate a significant expansion of investment. It rose from about 10 per cent of GDP to 30 per cent in the early 1980s to almost 40 per cent in the late 1980s.

The solution to the coordination problem was not, however, embedding markets in social relationships since integrated market development was limited. Instead, transactions were concentrated within the firm's hierarchy and coordination of decision making was achieved within the firm. Thus the strategy followed by Korea was similar to Taiwan in that select import substituting industries were initially protected with the objective of being eventually able to compete internationally. However, the mechanism utilized was quite different for Korea. Control of the credit system allowed the state to promote certain already existing firms.   In addition, tax breaks were offered on a discretionary basis with export targets often used as a measure of firm performance. This was combined with an extensive use of tariffs and quantitative restrictions to limit imports. Biggs and Levy have labeled this strategy as government-directed learning. This refers to specific efforts on the part of the government to improve the capabilities of individual firms by pushing them to move down their learning curves. 'The Korean strategy of government directed learning appears to have fostered that nations concentrated economic structure by encouraging individual firms to increase their export volumes' (Biggs and Levy, 1991).

Thus East Asia represents two broad strategies of development through learning.   First, a rural path in which coordinated solutions to traders' dilemmas are resolved through government coordination efforts aimed at generating integrated national markets. This extensive market development creates an environment in which governments are both autonomous and yet embedded.   Multiple equilibria exist and it becomes possible and highly likely that government efforts to move the economy from low-tech to high-tech production will succeed.

The second strategy aims at moving transactions within the confines of large firms. It is in this context that coordination efforts, led by the state, can lead to a solution of the traders' dilemma problem within firms. This creates a situation of multiple equilibria within which state policies aimed at a movement from low-tech to high-tech production have a great likelihood of success. However, the difficulties of this approach or path are twofold. First, it seems to be more demanding in terms of its requirements of state capabilities. This is due to the fact that it combines highly selective instruments of intervention and promotion combined with a significant concentration of economic power. Thus there is a significant temptation for members of the state to engage in unproductive rent-seeking. The second danger or difficulty is more long run in nature. It evolves if government-directed learning succeeds. In this situation the growing strength and concentrated power of the economic élite is likely to overwhelm the state. In this case unproductive rent-seeking by the firms is likely to impede effective government policy making.

The rural path is less subject to these criticisms. First, although it still requires significant government efforts aimed at rural sector development, it also depends on inducing private entrepreneurs to carry out tasks. That is, part of the load of entrepreneurial decision making will be borne by private entrepreneurs as they respond to government activities. The impact generated by the state will be felt throughout the economy via the integrated market system resulting in a multitude of entrepreneurial activities by small- and medium-sized firms. In addition, this path fosters both the long-run autonomy of the state as well as embedding that autonomy in a web of social relationship that directs government and private activity into socially productive rent-seeking.

Biggs and Levy (1991) argue that the two distinctive paths followed by Korea and Taiwan were a result of their initial conditions and that each made an efficient policy choice given these initial conditions. That is, an integrated system of markets developed in Taiwan, and thus a strategy relying upon small- and medium-scale firms driven by rapid agricultural growth, was the least cost approach. Alternatively, in Korea the lack of market development indicated that a similar strategy for Korea would be very costly. Instead, government-directed learning allowed the Korean economy to vault over the primitive domestic market and move rapidly into export production, utilizing the international market.

There is certainly some relevance to the idea of initial conditions determining the path of government policy. However, it has been argued in this chapter that an equally important idea is that government choices with regard to development strategies can play a role in determining the structure of the economy and its learning process. Thus choices which emphasize broad-based rural development will lead to an induced process of learning based on small and medium firms. Alternatively, choices which ignore agriculture and emphasize the formation of large firm structures will, if successful, result in government-directed learning within a structure characterized by significant concentrations of economic power.

9. SUMMARY

The previous chapter argued that rapid technical change in England and Japan was not the result of a deliberate process by which resources were allocated to research and development, but more the result of random macroinventions which were translated into economically usable innovations through a process of learning by doing. The latter in turn was spurred by the extensive development of an integrated national market. This sort of process, however, is likely to result in a division of the world into a center and periphery. In the former, well-developed and integrated market systems result in rapid technical change and innovation. In the latter, fragmented and limited natural markets result in a low rate of technical innovation.

For countries to move out of the periphery requires a learning process fostered by the state. This requires a developmental state and much of this chapter has concerned the evolution of such a state. There were a variety of exogenous factors discussed that created conditions likely to give rise to an autonomous developmental state. However, the emphasis in this chapter was on endogenous factors which lead to the development of such a state.

Autonomy by the state allows it to formulate goals and mechanisms independent of attempts by special interest groups to bias policy in favor of their particular interests. If the latter occurs, then the policy-making process will be overwhelmed by unproductive rent-seeking. An endogenous factor influencing the autonomy of state policy making concerns the characteristics of the goods to which the state allocates resources. Goods characterized by significant economies of scale, capital intensity, production inflexibility and asset factor inflexibility result in environments which tend to sap the autonomy of state decision making. Organizations, whether representing firms or labor, have both a greater ability and willingness to oppose policies aimed at altering the structure of the economy. Alternatively, goods characterized by few scale economies, labor intensity, production flexibility and asset factor flexibility create an environment more conducive to autonomy in policy making. Such products reduce the ability and incentives of small groups to organize and engage in unproductive rent-seeking. Thus the strategy followed by the state in allocating resources can influence the degree to which it experiences autonomy in the future.

However, autonomy can be used in a variety of ways. An autonomous state can use its power to promote economic development or to become an efficient predator. It was argued that individuals making up the governing élite are willing to sacrifice their own selfish interests for those of society as long as the cost of doing so is not too great. This cost was related to the probability of success of government strategies aimed at promoting the shift from low- to high-tech production processes. This probability was in turn related to the notion of multiple equilibria. If multiple equilibria (low-level and high-level equilibriums) exist, then government efforts to coordinate a shift will have a high probability of success. The cost of being developmental (instead of predatory) will be low and the state is likely to choose to use its autonomy for development. Alternatively, if multiple equilibria do not exist, then the probability of success in making the shift will be low and the governing élite are likely to choose to use their autonomy for predatory purposes.

The existence of multiple equilibria is the key and it was argued that this was dependent on two factors: the extent to which human capital has been accumulated and the extent to which an integrated national market has developed. The former was emphasized by Rodrik and refers to the formal accumulation of technological skills. The latter can be also thought of as a form of human capital. Market integration, it was argued in a previous chapter, involves the switch from the traditional to the modern technology for information-gathering by intermediaries and traders. This new technology and the skill necessary to use it are learned informally. However, the more well developed these skills and technology the greater the extent of the development of an integrated market system. This dramatically reduces the transaction costs of carrying out market exchange and increases the demand for domestically produced intermediate goods. As the variety of such goods produced increases, it increases the likelihood of multiple equilibria. Thus rural-based development, involving the bulk of the population in an integrated market structure, is a mechanism for creating an environment conducive to multiple equilibria.

An alternative strategy for creating multiple equilibria would involve jumping over the domestic market and aim production mainly at the pre-existing international market. The traders' dilemma problems are internalized by concentrating transactions into large vertically and horizontally integrated production. The interaction within the focus of the firm can, under state guidance, lead to the evolution of a formal and informal institutional and cultural structure within the firm that reins in cheating behavior and promotes cooperation and trust. Now widespread production of intermediate goods occurs within the context of these large firms and thus conditions are established for the existence of multiple equilibria. This second strategy is plagued, however, by several difficulties.

Such a strategy creates significant opportunities for unproductive rent-seeking, especially in the long run. This results from the fact that in the long run this strategy encourages the growth of a few large firms which will eventually dominate the dynamic sectors of the economy. As their economic power grows they are likely to gain the upper hand in dealings with the state. This power erodes the autonomy of state decision making and places significant obstacles to policies aimed at restructuring the economy in the face of exogenous shocks.

Given that the state is autonomous and development-oriented, it must also be embedded in the social structure of the economy. This allows for the possibility of dialectical interaction between the state and society which is necessary to set bounds on state decision making so as to encourage long-run commitment to the development process. In addition, it allows for a process of trial and error learning as information concerning policy performance is fed back to the state via the networks linking the state and society. It was argued that a broad-based rural development strategy creates an environment in which embeddedness can evolve.

Taiwan and Korea were used as examples of the two strategies for state-directed development in which the state coordinates market integration and a shift to high-tech production. Taiwan represents the rural path to market integration and long-run development. Korea in turn represents an example of the second strategy, government-directed learning, based upon the promotion of a small number of large firms. Although successful, the experience of the Korean economy in the late 1990s indicates that a lack of flexibility in policy making has evolved and the sector of large firms has, to some extent, thwarted the restructuring of the South Korean economy. The economic difficulties stemming from this support the conclusion that this strategy is fraught with significant danger.

A variant on the government-directed strategy of development is discussed in the next chapter. This variant is useful in analyzing the economic development of Southeast Asia.

NOTES

1. The above discussion is based on Rodrik (1995).
2. For a detailed discussion of peasant agriculture in East Asia see Hayami and Ruttan (1985).
3. 1 Koku of rice was approximately 140 kg. This varied with the type of rice.

REFERENCES

Amsden, Alice (1992), 'A Theory of Government Intervention in Late Industrialization,' in Louis Putterman and Dietrich Rueschemeyer (eds.), *State and Market in Development: Synergy or Rivalry* (Boulder, Colorado: Lynne Rienner Publishers), 53-84.

Bates, Robert H. (1988), 'Governments and Agricultural Markets in Africa,' in Robert H. Bates (ed.), *Toward a Political Economy of Development* (Berkeley: University of California Press), 331-358.

Bates, Robert H. and William P. Rogerson (1980), 'Agriculture in Development: A Coalitional Analysis,' *Public Choice* 35, 513-527.

Biggs, Tyler and Brian Levy (1991), 'Strategic Interventions and the Political Economy of Industrial Policy in Developing Countries,' in Dwight Perkins and Michael Roemer (eds.), *Reforming Economic Systems in Developing Countries* (Cambridge, Massachusetts: Harvard Institute for International Development), 365-401.

Cheng, Tun-Jen (1993), 'Distinctions Between the Taiwanese and Korean Approaches to Economic Development,' *Journal of East Asian Affairs* 7 (Winter), 116-136.

de Melo, Jaime (1985), 'Sources of Growth and Structural Change in the Republic of Korea and Taiwan: Some Comparisons,' in V. Cerbo, A. Krueger, and F. Ossa (eds.), *Export-Oriented Development Strategies: The Success of Five Newly Industrialized Countries* (Boulder, Colorado: Westview).

Evans, Peter (1995), *Embedded Autonomy: States and Industries in Transition* (Princeton: Princeton University Press).

Hayami, Yujiro and Vernon Ruttan (1985), *Agricultural Development: An International Perspective* (Baltimore: Johns Hopkins University Press).

Hayami, Yujiro, Vernon Ruttan and Herman Southworth (eds.), (1979), *Agricultural Growth in Japan, Taiwan, Korea, and the Philippines* (Honolulu: University of Hawaii Press).

Ho, Samuel P. S. (1978), *Economic Development of Taiwan, 1860-1970* (New Haven, Connecticut: Yale University Press).

Ka, Chih-ming (1995), *Japanese Colonialism in Taiwan: Land Tenure, Development, and Dependency, 1895-1945*, (Boulder, Colorado: Westview Press).

Kreps, David (1990), 'Corporate Culture and Economic Theory,' in James E. Alt and Kenneth A. Shepsle (eds.), *Perspectives on Positive Political Economy* (Cambridge: Cambridge University Press), 90-143.

Kurer, Oskur (1996), 'The Political Foundations of Economic Development Policies,' *Journal of Development Studies* 32 (June), 645-668.

Kuznets, Paul (1977), *Economic Growth and Structure in the Republic of*

Korea (New Haven, Connecticut: Yale University Press).

Levy, Brian (1991), 'Transaction Costs, the Size of Firms, and Industrial Policy: Lessons from a Comparative Case Study of the Footwear Industry in Korea and Taiwan,' *Journal of Development Economics* 34 (1991), 151-178.

Lipton, Michael (1977), *Why Poor People Stay Poor* (Cambridge, Massachusetts: Harvard University Press).

Migdal, Joel (1986), *Strong Societies and Weak States: State-Society Relations and State Capabilities in the Third World* (Princeton, New Jersey: Princeton University Press).

Moore, Mick (1988), 'Economic Growth and the Rise of Civil Society: Agriculture in Taiwan and South Korea,' in Gordon White (ed.), *Developmental States in East Asia* (New York: St. Martins Press).

Myint, Hla (1975), 'Agriculture and Economic Development in the Open Economy,' in Lloyd Reynolds (ed.), *Agriculture in Development Theory* (New Haven, Connecticut: Yale University Press), 327-354.

Myrdal, Gunner (1968), *Asian Drama* (New York: Pantheon Press).

Nelson, Richard (1956), 'A Theory of the Low-Level Equilibrium Trap in Underdeveloped Countries,' *American Economic Review* (December), 894-902.

North, Douglas (1990), *Institutions, Institutional Change and Economic Performance* (Cambridge: Cambridge University Press).

Olson, Mancur (1971), *The Logic of Collective Action: Public Goods and the Theory of Groups* (Cambridge, Massachusetts: Harvard University Press).

Park, Albert and Bruce Johnston (1995), 'Rural Development and Dynamic Externalities in Taiwan's Structural Development,' *Economic Development and Cultural Change* 44 (October), pp. 181-208.

Rodríguez-Clare, Andrés (1996), 'The Division of Labor and Economic Development,' *Journal of Development Economics* 49 (April), 3-32.

Rodrik, Dani (1996), 'Coordination Failures and Government Policy: A Model with Applications to West Asia and Eastern Europe,' *Journal of International Economics* 40 (February), 1-22.

Rodrik, Dani (1995), 'Getting Interventions Right: How South Korea and Taiwan Grew Rich,' *Economic Policy*, (April), 53-108.

Rodrik, Dani (1992), 'Political Economy and Development Policy,' *European Economic Review* 36 (April), 329-336.

Shafer, D. Michael (1994), *Winners and Losers: How Sectors Shape the Development Prospects of States* (Ithaca, New York: Cornell University Press).

Suh, Sang-Chul (1978), *Growth and Structural Changes in the Korean Economy, 1910-1940* (Cambridge, Massachusetts: Harvard University

Press).

Wade, Robert (1990), *Governing the Market: Economic Theory and the Role of the Government in East Asian Industrialization* (Princeton, New Jersey: Princeton University Press).

Wade, Robert (1992), 'East Asia's Economic Success: Conflicting Perspectives Partial Insights, Shaky Evidence,' *World Politics* 44 (January), 270-320.

Weingast, Barry (1995a), 'The Economic Role of Political Institutions: Market Preserving Federalism and Economic Development,' *Journal of Law, Economics, and Organization* 11 (April), 1-31.

Weingast, Barry (1995b), 'A Rational Perspective on the Role of Ideas: Shared Belief Systems and State Sovereignty in International Cooperation,' *Politics and Society* 23 (December), 449-464.

Wolf, Charles (1982), 'A Theory of Non-Market Failure: Framework for Implementation,' *Journal of Law and Economics* 22 (April), 107-139.

World Bank (1993), *The East Asian Miracle: Economic Growth and Public Policy* (Washington, D.C.: Oxford University Press).

5. Developmental Entrepreneurial Groups

1. INTRODUCTION

The last chapter was concerned with the developmental state and what conditions are likely to give rise to such a state. The argument was that an important mechanism by which nations can move out of the periphery is through a process of learning fostered by various investment and protectionist policies carried out by such a developmental state. Taiwan and Korea were presented as two different types of developmental state. In the former the foundations of such a state are rural and agricultural in nature whereas in the latter the foundation is based on the creation of large business groups.

This chapter argues that other kinds of institutional structure, other than states, can also act to promote learning and thus could be characterized as developmental in nature. In particular, large groups of entrepreneurs linked via an extensive social network, based perhaps on ethnic background, can act as an all-encompassing group whose aim will be to promote productive rent-seeking via learning. In this situation states may be soft in that they lack the autonomy and strength to carry out a long-run strategy of development. However, entrepreneurial groups may be extensive enough in their interests, cohesive enough in their organization, and unified enough in terms of their goals so as to at least serve as a partial substitute for a developmental state. It argues that, in fact, just such an analysis provides an explanation for the economic experiences of parts of Southeast Asia, in particular Thailand, Malaysia and Indonesia. In this chapter when reference is made to this region it is always with these three nations in mind.

That Southeast Asia has achieved rapid growth can be easily seen by examining Table 5.1 which includes growth rates for GDP, manufacturing value added, and exports for both Southeast Asia, East Asia (Taiwan and South Korea) and South Asia (India and Pakistan). The growth rates for Southeast Asia in almost all categories are significantly higher than for South Asia, although less impressive than those for East Asia. Thus growth in Southeast Asia is increasingly in terms of manufactured goods and an increasingly large proportion of exports is also made up of manufactured goods. Table 5.2 presents data on investment rates and a very similar pattern

Table 5.1 Average Annual Growth Rates (%)

Country	GDP			Manufacturing (VA)			Exports		
	1961-1970	1971-1980	1981-1990	1961-1970	1971-1980	1981-1990	1961-1970	1971-1980	1981-1990
South Korea	8.7	8.6	9.3	13.5	15.7	11.8	30.1	20.3	11.0
Taiwan	9.6	9.7	8.0	14.6	12.6	8.6	22.0	16.1	11.3
Indonesia	3.9	7.2	5.6	5.0	14.0	11.7	4.7	9.2	1.4
Malaysia	6.0	7.9	6.8	10.8	11.6	8.4	5.3	7.8	9.7
Thailand	8.0	6.7	7.8	9.7	10.1	9.2	8.3	9.6	13.9
India	3.9	3.0	5.6	2.8	4.0	7.3	2.8	7.7	5.7
Pakistan	7.2	4.7	6.4	9.9	5.5	7.2	7.4	1.6	8.1

Source: Adapted from Bradford (1994, p.16).

151

Table 5.2   Gross Domestic Investment (Share in GDP)

Country	1961-1970	1971-1980	1981-1990
South Korea	15.60	25.44	30.14
Taiwan	17.08	23.69	23.20
Indonesia	9.61	16.83	26.22
Malaysia	17.29	23.97	28.25
Thailand	16.49	17.67	18.61
Pakistan	12.37	9.38	9.86
India	12.60	14.38	14.43

Source: Penn World Tables 5.6.

can be observed. Investment rates in Southeast Asia are significantly higher than those found in South Asia, but lower than the rates achieved in East Asia. Thus rapid growth in GDP, manufacturing and exports would seem to be closely linked to high investment in both East and Southeast Asia. The high investment in East Asia was, it was argued in the last chapter, the result of coordination efforts by developmental states. In this chapter it is argued that high investment in Southeast Asia was the result of coordination achieved by developmental entrepreneurial groups.

As discussed in section two, growth in this region prior to World War II, as well as in the 1960s and 1970s, was heavily dependent upon agriculture. As the result of favorable initial conditions (a relative abundance of fertile land) and, in the postwar period, the adaptation of technology to existing conditions, agricultural output grew rapidly and dominated exports. In fact it could be argued that initially international trade served as the coordination mechanism for creating an integrated market system encompassing agricultural trade in much of Southeast Asia. The rapid growth of agriculture created the potential for rapid development of the domestic market as well. However, as is pointed out, much of this potential was unrealized since the rural populations were not allowed to retain the bulk of the surplus in the form of purchasing power.

The rapid development of the trade in agricultural goods in the 1960s and 1970s, as well as labor-intensive manufacturing in the 1980s, was coordinated by ethnic Chinese middlemen, traders. This ethnic group had served this role in the colonial period and thus it was natural that they would play a major role in coordinating trade and carrying out economic activities after independence. It is argued in section three that this represented the evolution of a developmental, entrepreneurial group. In order to explain how this could occur, this section reviews the work of Olson concerning the relationship between group size and the type of rent-seeking being pursued, productive or unproductive. The normal conclusion that it is unlikely that encompassing large groups oriented towards productivity enhancement will arise is reversed. The formation of strong networks of social relationships linking Chinese within Southeast Asia led to the evolution of large, diverse groups who were more likely to be interested in productive rent-seeking rather than redistribution and the unproductive allocations of resources. It was the existence of such networks that allowed the stimulus of international trade opportunities to lead to a successful transition from exporting agricultural goods to exporting labor-intensive goods.

The difficulty with the development process as outlined above was that it led to only limited development of the domestic market, especially the domestic production of intermediate goods, which was due to the slow growth of demand emanating from the domestic economy. Thus the likelihood of the existence of multiple equilibria was reduced and a coordinated shift from low-tech (labor-intensive) to high-tech (intermediate good intensive) production proved to be very difficult.

Foreign investment, which occurred in the agrarian sector initially and subsequently also in manufacturing, did not solve this problem. Instead, given the underdevelopment of the domestic intermediate goods sector, the multinational producers who located in Southeast Asia tended to import the intermediate goods it needed rather than rely on domestic suppliers. Thus foreign investment flows, especially those occurring in the 1980s, had few linkage effects in the domestic economy. Although rapid economic growth was achieved, the foundation for a successful shift to high-tech production was not created. More technically, the conditions for multiple equilibria were not established. These ideas will be developed to a great extent in section four.

The above created a potential problem for the Southeast Asian economies. Deregulation of capital flows allowed for a significant inflow of capital, especially short-term capital, into the region. Firms in the region were thus supplied with large amounts of capital, both from high domestic savings rates and short-run foreign capital inflows. At the same time, in the late 1980s and early 1990s, Southeast Asia was facing increased competition for the production of labor-intensive goods from low-wage regions in China, Vietnam and even India. This competition stemmed from the relative abundance of labor in these regions as well as the fact that successful growth in labor-intensive exports in Southeast Asia had led to rapid growth in real wages there. Thus as firms producing these goods in Southeast Asia found their competitiveness threatened from external sources, they also found it difficult, if not impossible, to move up the technological ladder to technologically more sophisticated products (high-tech goods). Therefore more and more of the funds flowing into this region were being allocated to firms experiencing increasing economic difficulties and a financial collapse became increasingly likely. In addition, the typical high debt to equity ratios prevalent in Southeast Asia, combined with the heavy reliance of this region on bank lending, all provided an environment in which a financial panic, once started, would have strong negative consequences for the region. These issues are discussed in some detail in section five.

Finally, section six summarizes the analysis of the chapter. Some discussion of solutions to the crisis in Southeast Asia are presented. These include a reorientation of investment to production for the domestic market. In particular, it will be argued that a significant flow of resources into the rural sector provides the potential for greater development of the domestic market and, in particular, the development of the domestic intermediate goods sector. This will provide the foundation for multiple equilibria, increasing the probability that the government coordination efforts will succeed in promoting the shift from low- to high-tech production. This will require reflation of the economies in this region and an expansion in domestic demand via rural development.

2. AGRICULTURE AND DOMESTIC MARKETS

By 1870 almost all of Southeast Asia was under the control of European powers. Even independent Thailand had given up a significant amount of its autonomy in economic policy making to Britain under the provisions of the Bowring Treaty. World trade grew rapidly between 1870 and World War I and domestic production for foreign markets expanded rapidly. Most of Southeast Asia followed the typical colonial pattern of exporting a few primary products and importing consumption and capital goods. However, there was also the development of significant interregional trade in rice (Booth, 1991).

In Southeast Asia the indigenous populations tended to respond quite vigorously to the opportunities which international trade presented and rapidly increased their production of export crops. However, living standards prior to World War II increased very little. Several reasons have been attributed to explain this phenomenon. First, most Southeast Asian nations were penalized by deteriorating terms of trade after 1913. In addition, Booth (1991) argues that the large export surplus during this period was balanced by a large capital outflow which effectively limited overall development since this did not allow for investment in the domestic economy. Third, the investment policies of the governments involved were not particularly aimed at overall development. Indeed, most of these activities were aimed at fostering the continued development of crops for export which was in turn reinforced by foreign investment in the primary product sector.

With independence in the postwar period agricultural growth rates attained quite high levels. Table 5.3 indicates that there does, however, appear to be a slowdown in these growth rates in the 1990s. The main reason for the rapid growth in Southeast Asia in the postwar period has been the successful application of the new seed and fertilizer technologies in rice and, to some extent, other cereals such as corn. The success of this program has been attributed to a favorable biophysical environment, a colonial legacy of well-developed irrigation systems, the commitment of governments, in some cases, to incentive pricing policies of both inputs and outputs, and the fact that much farming occurs on small farms, utilizing family labor (Booth, 1991).

Table 5.3   Agricultural Growth Rates

Country	1961-1970	1971-1980	1981-1990	1991-1997
Indonesia	2.68	3.17	4.30	3.21
Malaysia	5.27	4.05	4.40	2.80
Thailand	4.12	4.91	2.00	2.55

In accordance with the arguments made earlier in this study it would have been thought that such rapid agricultural development would have provided the foundation for the development of an integrated system of domestic markets. The vibrant growth of agricultural production would have signaled traders and intermediaries to commit themselves to modern technologies for information-gathering and, as a result of reducing transaction costs, linking local and regional markets into an integrated national market. From this situation it would have been thought that import substitution policies would create opportunities for rapid industrialization followed by a turning outwards with rapid export growth being driven by growth in domestic productivity. In addition, it may have been thought that this situation would give rise to the development of strong states which then could effectively foster import substitution and then export promotion.

However, there were a number of factors which altered the path followed by Southeast Asia in its economic development. First, the process of agricultural development was much less broadly based than in Taiwan or Japan, thus agricultural development was much less even. Second, since there was no land reform, the distribution of the gains from productivity growth were more unequal than in East Asia. Finally, rapid rates of agricultural growth create only a potential for rapid development of the rural-based domestic market. If the rapid growth in income remains in the hands of producers it provides a stimulus for the development of domestically based manufacturing and intermediate goods production. However, this potential will only be realized if the ensuing growth in rural incomes is widely spread among the rural population and only if they are allowed to retain the bulk of the agricultural surplus in the form of purchasing power. However, the evidence presented in Table 5.4 indicates that at least for two of these countries, Thailand and Malaysia, government policy has served to transfer resources and purchasing power out of agriculture via both direct and indirect taxation. Thus much of the impact of agricultural growth on manufacturing oriented to the domestic market would have been muted.

Table 5.4 Taxation on Agriculture (%, annual average)

Country	1960-1972		1976-1984	
	Indirect	Direct	Indirect	Direct
Malaysia	−9.3	−8.1	−6.4	−11.2
Thailand	−13.9	−33.4	−17.7	−17.7

Source: Adapted from Shiff and Valdes (1992).

3.   DEVELOPMENTAL GROUPS

There was a second factor of crucial importance to understanding the economic development of Southeast Asia and this relates to the significant role played in these economies by Chinese immigrants. Their significant presence dates from the 19th century at a time when, under European domination, the region was being incorporated into a rapidly expanding world capitalist system.   Rather than disrupt the production operations and organization of the economies in this region, the colonial powers brought in labor to occupy the lower levels of industry and trade.   The Chinese were easily recruited since for much of this time period their homeland was politically unstable and in turmoil.   Thus in much of Southeast Asia a three-tiered system developed in which the upper levels of business and commerce were dominated by Europeans, the middle by the Chinese, and the bottom by the indigenous population. 'Adapting themselves to their new environment, the Chinese immigrants acculturated to the style of the ruling groups, which in most cases were Western, and this resulted in further estrangement between them and the indigenous elites' (McVey, 1992). As a result, at independence domestic private enterprise and trade was overwhelmingly in the hands of the local Chinese. Since then indigenous participation has increased, but this was largely the result of political pressure and patronage. The bulk of the large firms that are domestically controlled are still in the hands of the Chinese.

Many scholars, according to McVey (1992), find the main reason for Chinese dominance to be a cultural system which places great value on business success and promotes accumulation of capital. This is often then contrasted with the value system of indigenous peoples which is said not to value these characteristics. McVey and others are skeptical of these sorts of argument. They point out that the entrepreneurial success of the Chinese, both outside China and inside China, is a relatively recent phenomenon. 'Any cultural tradition has many strands of meaning, which may be emphasized, forgotten, and reinterpreted over time, providing legitimacy for quite contrary modes of behavior' (McVey, 1992, p.18). Thus it was the social situation that the Chinese immigrants found themselves in during colonial times, which provided the environment for encouraging entrepreneurial behavior such as trading, merchant activity and investing. As noted above, when independence followed, the Chinese prospered even more since most of the recently established regimes were too weak to really effectively interfere and the retreat of the colonial powers generated even greater business and trading opportunities. As McVey states:

> Thus even though Chinese suffered from economic and political measures against them at the outset of Indonesia's Guided Democracy period, their economic role grew, for, either directly or as contractors or agents for state-run enterprises, they moved into the positions formerly dominated by Dutch and British interests, effectively capturing Indonesia's economic heights. In Thailand . . . it was the removal of the Western capitalist presence during World War II which gave Chinese-dominated Thai banking its big chance (McVey, 1992,p 20).

McVey stresses two characteristics resulting from colonial times which strengthened the Chinese position later on. Chinese businessmen were politically dependent since they had no direct access to the levels of political power. Thus the networks and relationships that were formed linking them together into large entrepreneurial business groups did not rely on state enforcement. This, of course, made it difficult for outsiders, indigenous people and Chinese belonging to different speech groups, to penetrate. This difficulty was mainly the result of the fact that the organization depended on enforcement mechanisms based on group identity. The second characteristic was that as a result of their position between Western big business and the local economy, the Chinese business leaders gained the knowledge of trade and manufacturing techniques and the local market. Thus when foreign firms, especially the Japanese, decided to carry out foreign investment it was generally via Chinese business groups. In addition, the overseas links with Chinese business groups throughout Asia and the Pacific rim allowed for increased capital mobilization as well as mobility. This acted as an aid to help protect the Chinese domestic economic position since they could rapidly redeploy capital from one region to another.

The analysis above indicates that large business groups dominated by immigrant Chinese dominate the economies of Southeast Asia. These economies in turn have prospered as these groups have forged the development of international linkages between national markets and have helped to foster significant investment and growth in environments where states have been characterized as being relatively weak (weak in comparison with East Asia). As Doner (1991, p.832) has argued, 'developmentalist organizations need not be confined to public or state sectors.'[1] He argues that most of the crucial difficulties linked to the development process involve collective action problems. 'Even when all parties explicitly recognize the importance of, say, better technical training, actual provision may be blocked by collective action problems - the disincentive individuals have to pay an amount equal to the benefits they acquire' (Doner, 1991, p.821). He argues that collective action problems are generally solved via institutions which are arrangements that go beyond the arm's-length relationships of competitive markets to regularize the processes of cooperation and competition (Doner, 1991, p.821). Thus less developed countries must somehow 'encourage entrepreneurs with often contrasting and entrenched interests to undertake diverse activities for the benefit of the country as a whole; and they must do so where uncertainty is high and information low' (Doner, 1991, p.831).

It is argued that large business groups dominated by Chinese ethnic groups represents just such an institutional structure, serving to solve many of the collective action problems connected with development as discussed above by Doner. In this study these Chinese based institutions are called developmental groups so as to distinguish the term developmental group from that represented by the term developmental states. In this case and in the context of this study these large business groups have internalized many transactions within the group so as to solve the traders' dilemma problem.

In Chapter 2 it was argued that the difficulty involved in the exchange process concerns the possibility of cheating and this can be resolved through a repeated play of the game so that rules, implicit and explicit, arise which restrain opportunistic behavior. The small-society solution involves using existing village, cultural or ethnic ties to embed economic exchange in a network of social relationships. It was argued that generally these solutions will not work on a large scale since village, cultural and/or ethnic ties are not extensive enough to work on a large scale. Two large-society solutions were then discussed. The rural path involved coordinating large numbers of buyers, sellers and traders (the bulk of which are rural and have linkages with urban manufacturing) to enter into market transactions with traders behaving in an entrepreneurial manner establishing new linkages between previously isolated groups. This whole process is characterized by increasing returns. The other large-society solution involves leaping over the domestic market by creating large firms which will then be guided by a developmental state to concentrate on becoming internationally competitive. In this approach the traders' dilemma problem is resolved within large firms through the creation of a corporate culture or ideology.

The Southeast Asian process of development represents a third large-society path to development. It is similar to the second large-society path in that the process of economic growth is driven by and through large firms. However, it is also related to the small-society solution since the large business groups are controlled by a single ethnic group. While it was earlier argued that ethnic groups are generally not extensive enough to resolve the traders' dilemma on a large scale, this argument must now be modified for the case of Southeast Asia. This modification stems from the peculiar colonial experience of the region, that is, the colonial powers created an extensive, business-oriented ethnic group. It created an environment which fostered the development of an extensive network linking ethnic Chinese into a large group. The traders' dilemma is overcome via reputational mechanisms which punish cheaters and reward honesty. Thus trust among members of this group was created in the process.

This analysis can be clarified by reference once again to the work of Olson (1971). In the previous chapter Olson's work was reviewed and he argued that concepts can be used that are drawn from public finance to study how groups form to pursue goals, if one assumes that the goal being pursued is a collective good. If this is accepted, then it follows that all groups are subject to the free-rider problem, the idea being that if the collective goal is achieved then everyone within the group will receive the benefits whether or not they contributed any resources to the achievement of the goal. Thus individuals have an incentive to free-ride, not to contribute resources, but to enjoy the benefits if the goal is achieved. Thus groups will tend not to form.

The above conclusion is modified somewhat when the size of the group is considered. If the group is small, strategic interaction among the individuals becomes likely. In this case each individual realizes that what he does or does not do influences the choices of others (much like an oligopoly or oligopsony) and thus the interaction can result in individuals deciding to contribute resources to the attainment of the public good. With large groups this strategic interaction does not occur, and as a result, Olson argues that small groups will tend to dominate policy making in a country. This is bad news since small groups will tend to pursue goals which harm the bulk of society in order to benefit the small group. This follows from the fact that the negative effects of such a policy fall on outsiders, while the benefits of such predatory policies remain within the group. Alternatively, policy aimed at benefitting society at large will not be pursued by small groups since the benefits fall to individuals outside the group, while the group bears the cost of carrying out the policy. Only large, extensive groups will then have an incentive to promote policies that are socially productive, but they are unlikely to form (free-riding).

The above logic must, however, be modified in the case of Southeast Asia. Large, extensive business groups have formed, based upon ethnic Chinese leadership, that invest in a diverse variety of production activities. Because of this diversity of interests such large business groups are more likely to pursue policies that are socially productive rather than policies which are predatory in nature. In other words, these are large groups in the sense of Olson. What holds such groups together? What prevents free-riding from destroying them or reducing their effectiveness? The cement that holds them together is the extensive network of social relationships based on ethnic identification that were initially forged in the colonial period. These groups of immigrant Chinese can be thought of as being molded into an extensive ethnic group as a result of colonial policy which promoted their function as traders, merchants and organizers of economic activity.

Thus a developmental, entrepreneurial group has led the development process in Southeast Asia. Although effective in organizing economic growth in comparison with South Asia, it was less effective than the developmental states of East Asia as reflected in the growth rates presented in Table 5.1. This is what would be expected since strong developmental states are likely to be more encompassing 'in their interests than developmental, entrepreneurial groups.

So far two aspects of Southeast Asian development have been discussed. The agricultural sector experienced fairly rapid growth, although much of the benefits of this growth were transferred out of the sector, and Chinese-controlled developmental entrepreneurial groups came to dominate trade and manufacturing. These two interacted in a very important way. The rapid growth in agriculture and the transferring of significant benefits from the sector have served to create an environment in which labor was relatively cheap. The explicit and implicit taxes on the agricultural sector kept the earning prospects of rural individuals restrained while the growth in productivity, especially in rice and other crops, has kept the cost of living for workers low.

Neoclassical economists would argue that this would automatically provide Southeast Asia with a comparative advantage in labor-intensive products, in particular labor-intensive manufactured goods. However, Amsden has pointed out that for the East Asian nations the relative cheapness of labor did not automatically provide them with a comparative advantage in labor-intensive manufactured goods in the 1960s and 1970s. This was due to the fact that the argument 'that low wages are a sufficient basis on which to compete in labor-intensive sectors, must rely on the assumption that either exchange rates are flexible, as noted shortly, or that technology (production functions) and productivity are the same in an industry in all countries' (Amsden, 1992). The latter assumption is based on an oversimplified view of technology that implies that it consists solely of capital equipment and product and process designs.

> Nevertheless, technology is multidimensional. It includes not just machinery and designs - call them alpha technology - but also supporting institutions, such as management systems, labor relations, shopfloor practices, subcontractors, and public policies - call them Beta technology. Beta technology is by no means similar in the same industry in all countries and is probably responsible for a large part of the differences in productivity observed around the world (Amsden, 1992, pp.57-58).

Amsden argues that there are always physiological or political limits with regard to devaluation. If wages are close to or at subsistence levels for a large proportion of the population, significant devaluation is not possible without causing tremendous social destruction. There are likely political limits to devaluation as well. Substantial devaluations often trigger wage responses or labor unrest that greatly increases instability and macroeconomic disorder. Such social and political disruption is likely to damage the overall development process. Finally, Myint (1964) has argued that low wages are an obstacle to economic development since they operate to constrain the size of the domestic market and coincide with low productivity.

These concerns are relevant for two reasons. First, for exports based on relatively cheap labor to succeed will require significant learning on the part of the potential producers. Thus, initially, they will have to be protected and resources allocated to the learning process. The coordination of these activities was, in the East Asian process, provided by a strong developmental state. However, in Southeast Asia this coordination has been provided by highly diversified, ethnic-based business groups and large enterprises. These have, in this chapter, been labeled developmental groups. However, the second reason for the importance of the above analysis concerns the financial problems which beset Southeast Asia in 1997 and 1998. Dramatic devaluations of currency have been allowed to occur, especially in the case of Indonesia. As discussed above, and as supported by ensuing events, great political and social unrest has been generated which threatens the social fabric of these societies, based on Chinese entrepreneurial groups, and their future development prospects. This will be further discussed later in this chapter.

The movement by Southeast Asia into the production of labor-intensive exports was indeed quite successful in the 1980s and early 1990s. This has been illustrated in the tremendous change in the composition of exports that have occurred during the time period. Specifically, in the 1970s the bulk of exports were agriculturally based goods. However, by the 1980s and 1990s this had changed dramatically with manufacturing dominating exports in Thailand and Malaysia and growing significantly in Indonesia (Jomo, 1997). This rapid growth in manufactured exports and GDP was given a major push from an additional source in the mid-1980s. Specifically, the rapid appreciation of the yen after 1986 significantly increased the prices of Japanese products in international markets. Faced with declining sales, Japanese firms relocated production into countries with lower manufacturing costs and exchange rates that were unlikely to appreciate against Japan's major trading partners. This resulted in a significant increase in Japanese investment in Southeast Asia. Taiwan's currency also appreciated with respect to the world's major currencies resulting in it emerging as the second most important source of East Asian foreign direct investment in Southeast Asia. A similar story can also be told for South Korea. 'There is indisputable evidence that Japanese and other Northeast Asian investment in Southeast Asia after 1985 gave a tremendous boost to the three second-tier NIC economies in ASEAN - Indonesia, Malaysia, and Thailand' (Jomo, 1997, p.54).

The above analysis can be summarized in the following way. Developmental groups in Southeast Asia played a key role in the rapid development of the region in the 1970s, 1980s and 1990s. This role was significantly augmented by the inflow of foreign investment from Northeast Asia in the mid-1980s. This process of development represented a third path. The first two paths discussed earlier in this study were the rural path (represented by Japan and Taiwan) and the large-firm path (as represented by South Korea). Southeast Asia certainly had the potential to follow the rural path, given the growth in agricultural production. However, the evolution of developmental groups embedded in the social framework of an immigrant ethnic society resulted in a third path. This immigrant developmental group coordinated the expansion of labor-intensive manufactured exports. Thus production and investment were geared to international markets with the development of the domestic market relegated to benign neglect. This third path thus resembles the large-firm path followed by South Korea in that large business groups dominated economic expansion aimed at international markets. The main difference is that the foundation of the large business groups in Southeast Asia was ethnic in nature and these groups operated in environments characterized by relatively weak states. The whole process was significantly strengthened by an inflow of foreign investment form Northeast Asia. This, too, helped to coordinate the transition of the economy into labor-intensive manufactured production aimed at foreign markets.

4.   DIFFICULTIES OF TRANSITION

As outlined above, a number of scholars have argued that there are significant dangers involved with this third path. For example, work by Westphal (1989) on technological capability in Thailand seems to cast doubt on the ability of firms there to make the transition from labor-intensive manufactured goods to more sophisticated goods. Most firms seem to have very weak technological capability because, according to Westphal, they have not developed the necessary capabilities. Thus these exports seem ill-equipped at promoting new opportunities in areas of potential comparative advantage. Despite these problems, the fastest growth in manufactured exports from 1988 onwards has been in medium-term technology products such as computer components, auto parts and electrical goods. However, for most of these products Thailand served only as an assembly base. 'The design, high tech manufacturing process and marketing have generally been done elsewhere' (Jomo, 1997, p.68).

Lall (1995) has suggested a number of worrying features concerning Malaysia's development process. Exports of manufactured goods tend to be concentrated in a few goods. Multinational corporations dominate exports accounting for more than three-quarters of the total value of manufactured exports. Most troublesome is that the local content of most manufactured exports remains low and domestic enterprises perform few technologically demanding tasks. The lack of linkages between the export sector and the domestic economy implies that the Malaysian industrialization process is built on a fragile base.

A similar sort of analysis can be made with regard to Indonesia. In the industries which have become highly export-oriented, large sections of these industries remain traditional in nature. They suffer from a lack of standards and poor quality. Further, design and product development are generally underdeveloped and there is a heavy reliance on imports of complex inputs. In terms of linkages to the domestic economy, Jomo (1997) finds little evidence for their development. In particular, he does not find evidence for the development of industrial clusters which involve interindustry buying and selling.

A good summary statement of this view of Southeast Asian development is provided by Wade (1994). He argues that in all three of these countries most of the investment, both domestic and foreign, was and is oriented to production for export and, therefore, growth is independent of the domestic economy. Foreign subsidiaries account for a very large proportion of manufactured exports and these subsidiaries rely heavily on imported inputs. According to Wade, these subsidiaries constitute foreign enclaves which have little forward or backward linkage with the domestic market.

Rodríguez-Clare (1996) has provided an analysis of the impact of multinational corporations that is useful in the analysis of the process of development in Southeast Asia outlined above. He constructs a multiple equilibria model similar to those discussed earlier in this study, particularly in Chapters 3 and 4. A brief review of the assumptions of this type of model is probably in order. It is assumed that there are two types of good high-tech and low-tech. The production of the two types of good requires labor and intermediate goods. The intermediate goods come in different varieties and are produced under conditions of increasing returns. It is assumed, for reasons discussed in Chapters 3 and 4, that the intermediate goods are nontradable. The high-tech final good uses intermediate goods more intensively than the low-tech good. Both production functions for these goods are assumed to exhibit a 'love of variety' effect, that is, an increase in the varieties of intermediate goods used will increase total factor productivity in the production of both final goods.

In these kinds of model there exists the potential for multiple equilibria. A nation could be caught in an equilibrium in which specialization in low-tech production occurs. In this situation the demand for intermediate goods is limited implying their cost is high. Thus any individual firm contemplating a switch to production of the high-tech goods will find it unprofitable to do so since the cost of intermediate goods is quite high. Alternatively, if all producers decided to simultaneously switch to the production of the high-tech good, this may very well be a profitable equilibrium. This results from the fact that the large demand for a large variety of intermediate goods would so lower the cost of high-tech production that it would be profitable. If this is true, then two equilibriums exist and transition from low- to high-tech requires some form of coordination.

Rodríguez-Clare (1996) extends the analysis to include multinational corporations. In addition to the previously discussed assumptions, it is further presumed that there are two countries, A and B. Country A is already in the high-tech equilibrium, utilizing a large variety of intermediate goods and experiencing a high level of productivity and high wages. Country

B is in a low-tech equilibrium, utilizing a small variety of intermediate inputs, lower productivity and thus low wages. In this case firms could benefit if they could have access to the intermediate inputs in country A and the cheap labor in country B. Domestic firms in country B cannot do this because of the nontradable nature of intermediate goods.

Alternatively, Rodríguez-Clare assumes that firms in A can do this by becoming multinational. They locate their headquarters in country A and a production plant in country B. The headquarters buys specialized inputs produced in country A and utilizes them to construct a composite input, headquarter services, which it then sends to the production plant in country B. The production plant in the latter produces final goods using this composite input, labor and intermediate inputs produced in country B. Thus the multinational in country A is able to take advantage of the availability of a great variety of intermediate goods in their own country and the cheap labor in the poor country.

Within this context, the effect which multinationals will have on the low-tech country (B) will be dependent on the extent of linkages. In this model there are two types of linkage, those generated by domestic firms and those generated by multinational firms. Domestic linkages represent the quantity of each variety of the intermediate good produced in B and purchased by domestic firms per unit of labor hired by domestic firms. Alternatively, multinational linkages represent the quantity of each variety of the intermediate good produced in country B and purchased by the multinational firm per unit of labor hired by that firm in country B.

Assuming for the moment that full employment exists, then the following conclusion emerges. If the linkage effects of a multinational exceed that of the domestic firm or firms which it replaces (by drawing labor away), then investment by multinationals causes the intermediate goods sector to expand and, as a result of the increasing returns in this sector, lowers the per unit cost of intermediate goods. If this impact is great enough, firms in country B will likely find it profitable to shift resources into high-tech production. In this case the economy successfully makes the transition from periphery to center.

Alternatively, if the linkage effects of the multinational firm are less than those of the domestic firm it replaces, then investment by multinationals causes the intermediate goods sector in country B to shrink. As a result, the per unit costs of producing such intermediate goods will rise and domestic firms in country B are less likely to switch to high-tech production. Thus it will become more difficult for a country in the periphery to make the transition to the center.

The discussion above was based on the assumption that full employment exists (no surplus labor). However, if this is not the case then the analysis of the impact of multinational investment becomes more complex. That is, multinational investment would not necessarily displace domestic production, assuming that it utilizes the surplus labor that is available. Thus economic expansion would occur, and the production of intermediate goods would increase, reducing the per unit costs of these goods. If the last effect is substantial enough, domestic firms would then shift to high-tech production. However, one might still argue that a coordinated expansion of production by domestic firms, utilizing surplus labor, would have greater linkage effects (compared to multinationals) and thus have a greater probability of stimulating domestic firms to shift to high-tech production. In this case the coordinator could be the state or perhaps development groups. In any case, the determinants of the linkage effects of multinational relative to domestic firms would still seem to be critically important.

Rodríguez-Clare has suggested several variables which are likely to influence the degree or extent of linkages generated by multinational investment. The multinational firm in A utilizes its relative abundance of intermediate goods to produce a composite good, headquarter services, which is then shipped to B and combined there with labor and intermediate goods to produce a final output. The more of the composite good utilized in this production, the fewer intermediate goods, produced by B, will be used in final production there (the lower the linkage effect). The cost of communicating over great distances as well as difficulties in communication due to cultural differences are likely to reduce the effectiveness of headquarter services. Thus multinational firms are more likely to try to integrate local producers of intermediate goods into the production of the intermediate good. Alternatively, the lower the cost of communication, due to closeness in geography and/or culture, the more likely multinational firms will rely upon headquarter services rather than utilize high-cost domestic intermediate goods suppliers.

There is a second and, for the interests of this study, more important factor influencing linkage strengths. This factor relates to the degree of similarity between the source of multinational firms (A) and the host (B). In this model, similarity has to do with the extent of varieties of intermediate goods that are produced in both nations. The number of varieties of the intermediate good produced in A is greater than that produced in B. This follows by assuming that A specializes in high-tech good production, while B specializes in low-tech production, and there are increasing returns to producing intermediate goods. As the number of varieties produced in A increases, *ceteris paribus*, the decline in cost will induce A to utilize more headquarter services and, therefore, the demand for intermediate goods produced in country B will decline. Alternatively, as country B produces more intermediate goods then, *ceteris paribus*, the decline in cost will induce country A to buy more of its intermediate goods in country B. Thus the more similar A and B, the smaller the difference in the number of intermediate goods produced in A compared to B and this implies that multinational firms from A will have strong linkage effects on host B. Alternatively, the greater the difference between the number of intermediate goods produced in A compared to B, the smaller the linkage effect of multinationals on the host country.

More intuitively, the more well developed the low-tech sector in country B (the greater the variety of intermediate inputs produced and utilized), the more likely multinational corporations will generate very strong linkage effects. The less well developed the low-tech sector in country B (the smaller the variety of intermediate goods utilized), the more likely multinational corporations would have weak linkage effects. If it is assumed that the low-tech sector is domestic agriculture and the domestic, labor-intensive manufacturing linked with agriculture, then the following holds. The transition to high-tech production via multinational investment becomes more likely the more well developed the domestic agro-industrial sector is and is less likely the less developed this sector is.

What has been argued in Chapter 3 is that the number of intermediate goods sectors that are open and operating in an economy is the result of two important sets of factor. The first set includes the amount of savings and the size requirements for each potential intermediate goods sector. This will determine the potential number of sectors which could open. Whether they will actually open will depend on a resolution of the traders' dilemma problem. Producers of intermediate goods will be reluctant to commit resources to such production unless they can be assured that there will be honest buyers and buyers will be reluctant to buy unless they can be assured of finding honest sellers. Middlemen are reluctant to commit resources to developing modern technologies for gathering information so as to identify honest buyers and sellers (identified by reputation) unless they can be assured that enough buyers and sellers will commit to market production.

If this traders' dilemma remains unresolved, then multinational companies entering a less-developed country will have few linkages with the domestic economy. Consequently, it may generate economic growth and employment, but this will be quite fragile in nature, which means that if such multinationals should move their operations to other areas of cheaper labor, growth and development will decline. Thus the domestic foundations for future growth have not been laid.

Alternatively, if the traders' dilemma has been resolved through some sort of coordination process then the number of intermediate sectors open and operating in the domestic economy will be quite large. Domestic production activities will use intermediate goods more intensively. Multinational firms in this kind of situation will have a much stronger linkage effect on the host economy. In this case such foreign investment is much more likely to serve as a coordination mechanism resulting in the transition from low- to high-tech production. Growth is less fragile in nature as the transition to high-tech production becomes more probable.

This section began with a discussion of the views of various scholars who believed that the Southeast Asian growth experience is indeed a fragile thing. They argued that so far this region has developed little capacity for moving up the technological ladder of capability. The previous few paragraphs have argued that this lack of capacity is due to a lack of accumulation of a sort of human capital that can only be accumulated informally. Specifically, the skills connected with producing and modifying intermediate goods have not been readily accumulated. This has been due to a lack of development of the market for domestic production. The potential for development of the domestic market existed, as agricultural production throughout the region has been relatively high. However, much of this potential has instead been utilized by entrepreneurial groups involved in the production of goods aimed at the export market. This surge in export production was significantly enhanced by an inflow of foreign investment in the 1980s. However, given the lack of development of the domestic market, the linkage effects of this investment have been quite limited.

The lack of accumulation of informal human capital was matched by a relative lack of accumulation of more formal sorts of human capital. Nevertheless, this region has certainly done much better than South Asia in terms of equipping its population with knowledge and skills through formal schooling and in providing them with certain social infrastructure: clean water, sanitation and so on. However, its performance only places it within the group of countries classified by the United Nations as medium human development countries. In addition, within this group the countries of Southeast Asia obtain human development levels which are only average at best.

For example, in terms of access to health services, safe water and sanitation (1988-1991), Thailand is below the average for countries obtaining medium levels of human development and Indonesia is well below average. Only Malaysia is above the group average (United Nation's Development Program, 1994, p.132). As far as school enrollments for all levels are concerned, for 1990 Malaysia is above average, while Thailand and Indonesia are below average, for the group of medium human development countries (United Nations Development Program, 1994, p.136). In terms of mean years of schooling Thailand and Indonesia were below average, while Malaysia was above (United Nations Development Program, 1994, p.138). As to tertiary graduates as a percentage of the corresponding age group

(1987-1990), Thailand was above average, while Indonesia and Malaysia were below average. Examining the category of science graduates as a percentage of total graduates (1986-1990) it was found that all three countries are below the average for medium human development countries (United Nations Development Program, 1994, p.138). Thus these three countries, while being classified as a medium human development countries, clearly seem to lag behind in a number of categories crucial for rapid formal human capital accumulation.

This section has argued that the Southeast Asian development process while impressive, is built on a fragile base. This would seem to be borne out by the economic difficulties which seem to have affected this region in 1997 and 1998. The next section briefly discusses the likely reasons for these economic and financial problems.

5.   ECONOMIC COLLAPSE

The economic crisis in Southeast Asia began with the burst of the speculative bubble in assets in Thailand in 1997. This was accompanied by a significant flight of capital from Thailand eventually resulting in a large devaluation of the Thai currency, which was followed by currency crises and financial instability throughout Southeast Asia. This seemed, to many at the time, to be quite surprising since the fundamentals for these economies seemed to be so positive. Savings and investment rates were quite high and these savings funded rates of growth that were also quite high by world standards. In addition, government budgets were generally kept in line with revenues keeping deficits, where they existed, at moderate levels. Inflation rates as well were relatively small.

There were, however, some worrying signs prior to the crisis. For example, since the early 1990s East Asian investors had been shifting their direct investment spending in favor of China and Vietnam and at the expense of Southeast Asia. This was related to the fact that the condition which originally attracted such investment to Southeast Asia, cheap labor, was rapidly changing as the region began to experience growing labor shortages and labor immigration from abroad (Jomo, 1997). In addition to reduced foreign direct investment, these changed conditions also tended to reduce the competitiveness of Southeast Asia's exports, which were generally labor intensive in nature. China's devaluations of 1990 and 1994, together with its lower inflation and faster productivity growth, further worsened this situation. Finally, after 1995 the US dollar appreciated against the yen which further worsened the competitive conditions for Southeast Asia exporters since a number of the currencies in the region were pegged to the dollar

(Wade and Veneroso, 1998).

The decline in competitiveness discussed above resulted in the emergence of very large structural current account imbalances in Thailand, the Philippines, Malaysia, Korea and Indonesia. The financing of much of these deficits took the form of short-term borrowing denominated in foreign currencies, in particular the dollar (Corsetti et al., 1998). This situation was exacerbated by the fact the Asian governments had undertaken a number of significant financial reforms, encouraged by the International Monetary Fund (IMF), the Organization for Economic Co-operation and Development (OECD), and by Western governments, banks and firms. These reforms 'removed or loosened controls on companies' foreign borrowings, abandoned coordination of borrowings and investments, and failed to strengthen bank supervision' (Wade and Veneroso, 1998, p.9).

The financial crisis, which began in 1997 in these circumstances, was heightened in terms of its destructive effects by several characteristics peculiar to the financial structure in Southeast and East Asia. According to Wade and Veneroso (1998) Western financial intermediaries generally carry a debt that is about equivalent to or less than the value of their equity capital. In addition, these companies generally do not lend to companies with high ratios of debt to equity. However, in much of East and Southeast Asia, the debt to equity ratios of firms are multiples of the value of their equity capital. Wade attributes this to several factors. First, savings are much higher in East and Southeast Asia than they are in the West. In addition, these savings are done mainly by households who hold these savings in the form of bank deposits. When neither governments nor households are significant borrowers, the system then becomes dependent on making significant amounts of loans to firms. In addition, 'firms that aim to make an assault on major world industries . . . must get their hands on very large amounts of resources, which they can do only by borrowing' (Wade and Veneroso, 1998, p.7).

The above creates an environment which is highly susceptible to negative, deflationary shocks. Firms that have high debt to equity ratios and banks that are heavily involved in making bank loans to these companies (a high ratio of bank intermediation to GDP) are highly dependent on current cash flows and the supply of bank or portfolio capital. A significant flow of funds out of the system, combined with a rise in interest rates, has the potential to devastate the financial system. Thus, once underway, a financial crisis in this region of the world would have disastrous effects.

Krugman (1998) adds to this the idea that state policies in this region enhanced the danger of this high debt/equity situation through its policies. He uses a highly simplified example to express his ideas. Assume that there are a set of financial intermediaries who are able to borrow money at a low, safe interest rate and invest in risky assets. They are able to do this because it is implicitly assumed by all those involved that the intermediaries are backed by implicit government guarantees. It is further assumed that the intermediaries are not required to put any of their own capital at risk and there are many intermediaries competing to buy risky assets.

Given the implicit government guarantee, the owners of an intermediary will see that investment in any risky asset is profitable if there is any state of nature in which that risky asset yields a return higher than the safe interest rate. After all, even if the investment fails, it is presumed that the government will step in and cover any losses. The competition among the intermediaries is presumed to eliminate any profit. However, because of these implicit guarantees asset values will be driven above expected values. These inflated asset values are then used as the basis for further lending. Within this context, if any doubt should arise as to the government's ability or willingness to guarantee loans made by the intermediaries, then the whole process would run in reverse (the bubble bursts). The value of assets would fall dramatically, the intermediaries would be seen to be insolvent, leading many to cease functioning, resulting in a deflationary spiral. The short-term capital outflow resulting from such a crisis would likely lead to a significant fall in currency values for the country or countries involved.

The discussion above has elements of the notion of crony capitalism, that is, close relationships between political leaders and financial intermediaries led to the evolution of an unsound financial system. Wolf (1998) pushes this idea a little further. He attributes the crisis in Southeast Asia to widespread insulation from market forces. More specifically, governments in these countries have sought to play a significant role in the allocation of resources in order to speed the industrialization process. He believes that such activities have successfully mobilized large quantities of investment and channeled significant amounts of these resources into particular industries and firms. However, these policies have had strong negative efficiency effects resulting in the wasting of substantial quantities of resources.

The negative effects alluded to above include industries which cannot compete (Indonesia's national car and domestic aircraft industry). When faced with the inability to compete, many of these industries and their leaders were bailed out with additional resources provided by public funds or guaranteed by the state. This sort of favoritism and outright corruption has had a corrosive effect on political decision making in the region. In addition, the economies of the region became imbalanced due to overemphasis on export industries and a neglect of the domestic economy.

As discussed above, there are a number of common elements. The financial sector seems to have played an important role in the economic crisis. The underlying problem, at least in Southeast Asia, stemmed from an increasing inability of firms in Southeast Asia to compete in the production of labor-intensive manufactured goods. This was reflected in the current account deficits which plagued Southeast Asian nations. From a simple macroeconomic perspective a current account deficit stems from an excess of investment relative to savings. Normally, current account difficulties generally arise from a fall in savings relative to investment. However, in most of Southeast Asia savings' rates were quite high and there had been no significant decline in these rates. Corsetti et al. argue that these deficits have been the result of increases in investment rates. This generally does not lead to crises, devaluation, and financial instability since such a situation involves creating future production capacity which can be used to service the current account deficit. The problem here, according Corsetti et al. (1998), is that much of this investment in Southeast Asia was wasted via the operation of crony capitalism which pervades the financial system.

The evidence provided to support the above proposition comes in several forms, but it is still quite limited in nature. First, it appears that a significant part of the funds involved in the investment boom went into the nontradable goods sector, in particular, commercial and residential construction, stock investment and so on. Corsetti et al. present evidence implying that throughout the 1990s stock markets in most of the nations were significantly overvalued. In addition, booms in residential and commercial construction led to a glut of vacant buildings (Corsetti et al., 1998). Second, there is also evidence of low rates of profitability for a large variety of investment projects.

A standard measure of investment efficiency at the macro level is the incremental capital to output ratio (ICOR). This is the ratio of investment to GDP divided by the rate of growth of GDP. Thus the lower the ICOR, the more efficient investment is, the more additional output generated for each additional dollar of investment. Table 5.5 presents data on ICOR for two different time periods. As can be seen, with the exception of Indonesia, the ICORs for Southeast Asia seem to have increased sharply. This seems to indicate that the efficiency of investment declined.

There is very little microeconomic evidence concerning profit rates for firms in Southeast Asia prior to the financial and economic collapse. However, there is some evidence from South Korea that the economic crisis was triggered by a series of bankruptcies of large conglomerates who had borrowed heavily to finance their investment projects. Specifically, Corsetti et al. (1998) show that in 1996 20 of the 30 largest firms in South Korea showed rates of return on invested capital below the cost of capital. Similar indicators of low profitability also seem to be provided by the interest coverage rate (ICR) which compares cash flow earned with interest payments due over a specific period of time. Of the top 30 South Korean firms, 11

Table 5.5 Incremental Capital to Output Ratios (ICOR)

Country	1987-1992	1993-1996
Indonesia	4	3.8
Malaysia	3.7	4.8
Thailand	3.4	5.1

Source: Corsetti et al. (1998).

had an ICR below 1 which meant that earnings were below interest payments.

Thus the story that seems to be emerging concerning the Southeast Asian crisis can be summarized in the following way. Investment surged as a result of the operation of crony capitalism. Much of this investment was financed via banks and other financial intermediaries that had close ties with government officials. The intermediaries in turn borrowed heavily from external sources with much of the capital inflow being of a short-term variety. External sources of this short-term credit were assumed to be covered by implicit and explicit guarantees supplied by Southeast Asian governments. Much of this surge in investment was misallocated as the result of corruption and thus investment efficiency significantly declined. The resulting current account deficits, generated by the surge in crony capitalism investment, became increasingly sustainable only through short-term capital inflows. As a result, the entire system became susceptible to financial panic. With the bursting of the asset bubble in Thailand in 1997, the financial panic led to dramatic devaluations in currencies and economic collapse throughout Southeast and parts of East (South Korea) Asia.

Several questions concerning this view immediately present themselves and lead to an alternative explanation of the economic crisis. First, an investment boom, a rise in investment relative to savings, is hypothesized to be the driving factor in the crisis. However, if one examines the data in Table 5.6 concerning investment rates this does not appear to be the case. Investment rates in Southeast Asia were certainly high in the 1990s, but there appears to be an upward trend only in Malaysia, but not Indonesia or Thailand.

Second most of the analyses of this crisis point to crony capitalism as a major cause which of course refers to widespread corruption in the political decision-making process, which significantly alters the allocation of resources. The inefficiency in the allocation of resources, in particular new investment, has an effect on efficiency by lowering productivity. However, most of these concerns are not new. Scholars have for some time now

Table 5.6   Investment Rates (% of GDP)

Country	1990	1991	1992	1993	1994	1995	1996
Indonesia	36.15	35.50	35.87	29.48	31.06	31.93	32.07
Malaysia	31.34	35.79	33.60	37.81	40.37	43.24	43.02
Thailand	41.08	42.21	39.99	41.86	43.36	46.56	42.75

Source: Corsetti et al. (1998).

realized, as discussed earlier in this chapter, that states in Southeast Asia are soft, unlike those found in East Asia.   Thus the development process has always been subject to government activities aimed at directing resources at favored groups with the corruption which often follows.   Financial intermediaries in the region have never operated under rules that would assure adequate capital ratios and eliminate moral hazard. Admittedly, these problems may have become more intense, but again this sort of institutional environment existed during periods of rapid growth in the 1980s as well as during the crisis period of the late 1990s.

An alternative hypothesis is suggested in the previous sections of this chapter, that is, initially Southeast Asia prospered in the 1980s, as a result of the rapid growth of exports of labor-intensive manufactured goods. This process was given added stimulus by foreign direct investment by Japan, South Korea and Taiwan in the mid-1980s.   This inflow of foreign direct investment was stimulated by rising labor costs in East Asia as well as the appreciation of the yen.

However, much of this growth was oriented to external rather than the domestic markets, and as a result development of the domestic market, in particular intermediate goods production, was limited.   Thus there has been little accumulation of the informal type of human capital necessary for the transition from low- to high-tech production.   In addition, there has been little formal accumulation of human capital as well. Given these limitations, Southeast Asia faced a fundamental barrier to growth.

As Southeast Asia succeeded in the production and export of labor-intensive manufactured goods, economic conditions began to change. Labor became increasingly scarce leading to increases in the relative cost of labor. For example, Table 5.7 illustrates how labor costs evolved in Thailand. As can be seen, rapid growth has led to wage growth and rising real wages. In addition, other regions now offered opportunities for foreign investors interested in producing labor-intensive manufactured goods. Thus foreign direct investment in Southeast Asia by East Asia began to decline in favor of countries like China and Vietnam. There was the fundamental dilemma faced by Southeast Asia.   These countries were being squeezed out of the production of labor-intensive manufactured exports since they were increasingly uncompetitive. However, they lacked the human capital, both informally and formally accumulated, to make the transition to the production and export of technologically more complex goods. Consequently, current account imbalances arose and this, combined with significant inflows of short-term capital, created conditions ripe for a financial panic and economic collapse.

Table 5.7   Thailand: Manufacturing, Wage and Productivity Indices

Year	Wage Index	Real Wage Index	Employment Index
1977	68	97	74
1978	70	91	82
1979	80	97	96
1980	100	100	100
1981	109	97	87
1982	117	99	112
1983	131	107	103
1984	144	116	111
1985	144	113	115
1986	153	118	115
1987	148	111	136
1988	171	124	137
1989	167	115	154
1990	180	117	175

Source: Adapted from Jomo (1997).

The IMF has promoted an extensive package of reforms with the goal of resolving the crisis.   This has included the usual program of fiscal and monetary austerity combined with devaluations of the currencies. The actual fall in the values of the involved currencies, however, have been very extreme. Normally, the IMF would then move to promote meetings between the creditor institutions and the countries involved.   This would usually involve debt rescheduling, a resumption of capital inflows and a rolling over of existing debt. However, at least in Indonesia and Thailand, the IMF has taken on a much broader role, similar to the role it has taken in its dealings with Eastern Europe and Russia. It is promoting major structural and institutional reforms. The financial restructuring is aimed at creating financial systems that operate more like their Western counterparts. These include closing down troubled financial institutions, allowing foreign financial institutions to buy domestic ones, and requiring banks to follow Western prudential standards. It seeks to create an institutional environment in which governments are prevented from interfering with the lending decisions of financial institutions. Also restrictions limiting foreign capital inflows are to be further relaxed and restrictions on trade are to be drastically reduced (Wade and Veneroso, 1998).

There are two problems with the IMF approach. First, it represents a broad regime of reform much beyond the scope of IMF activity in the past, with the exception of Eastern Europe and Russia. Feldstein (1998), among others, feels that this is an unwarranted expansion of IMF authority over and interference with the sovereign affairs of independent nations. In particular, Feldstein argues that in deciding to insist on any particular reform, the IMF should ask itself three questions.

> Is this reform really needed to restore the country's access to international capital markets? Is this a technical matter that does not interfere unnecessarily with the proper jurisdiction of a sovereign government? If the policies to be changed are also practiced in the major industrial economies of Europe, would the IMF think it appropriate to force similar changes in those countries if they were subject to a fund program? (Feldstein, 1998).

He argues that unless the answers to these three questions are yes, then the IMF is not justified in requiring changes upon the part of particular client countries.

Beyond the concern that the IMF has overextended its authority, there is a second concern that these reforms will do nothing to solve the underlying fundamental problem. In this chapter it has been hypothesized that this underlying problem is the inability of these countries to make the transition from the production of low- to high-tech goods. This inability stems from a lack of two different types of human capital, that which is formally accumulated via education and that which is informally accumulated via the integration of a national market. The latter results from a learning by doing process related to the production of intermediate goods. The policy reforms proposed by the IMF are unlikely to deal with this underlying fundamental problem. In fact the IMF reforms may likely hinder the solution.

The solution to the problem of transition must, if the hypothesis of this chapter is correct, involve a significant reorientation of economic activity. Resources must be devoted to the development and integration of the national markets in these countries. In all of these countries the lack of adequate infrastructure poses significant bottlenecks in the development process. Such infrastructure investment will provide one mechanism for the coordinated development of the national market. Much of this investment will be rural in nature because the biggest deficiencies in terms of infrastructure are to be found in rural areas. The importance of this is reflected in the fact that although the countries of Southeast Asia have undergone rapid growth in manufacturing, the bulk of the population of each of these countries still resides in rural areas. In Thailand, Malaysia, and Indonesia the rural population as a percentage of the total population is respectively, 77 per cent, 55 per cent, and 70 per cent (United Nations Development Program, 1994). In addition, for at least two of these nations the bulk of the population still earns its living in agriculture. In terms of the percentage of the labor force employed in agriculture, it is 67 per cent and 56 per cent respectively for Thailand and Indonesia, while 26 per cent for Malaysia (United Nations Development Program, 1994). This leads to the second aspect of the solution, investment in broad-based agricultural growth.

The results of such an investment strategy would be a coordinated expansion in national markets resulting in a growth process which at first would be Smithian in nature. However, as the broad-based growth process expands, the state will find its opportunities for a coordinated transition to high-tech production to increase while its ability to carry out such an expansion process will be enhanced as both the autonomy and the embeddedness of the state will be strengthened. This is a process based upon the development of the domestic market, but eventually building the foundation for a process of export-based growth having strong linkages to the domestic economy.

The IMF's policy package poses a basic threat to this process for it seeks to restrain government interference to minimize the state. This, in the long run, will preclude this region from achieving rapid growth. Such long-run economic expansion will require a developmental state linked, in Southeast Asia's case, with developmental entrepreneurial groups. Thus while the current account balances may improve in the short run, as a result of IMF directed reforms, eventually they will return as Southeast Asia persistently runs into problems of transition. Although financial stability may be restored in the short run, the low profitability of investment (due to an inability to make the transition) will again arise. Crony capitalism may be suppressed, again in this short run, but as the probability of successful transition remains low, states will again return to predatory behaviors.

6. SUMMARY

In this chapter it has been argued that Southeast Asia represents a third path of development. It is similar to the second path outlined in the previous chapter, government-directed learning, followed by South Korea. Both involve an emphasis on production for export and the integration of transactions within the confines of large business groups. In the South Korean case, however, it is the state which fosters the development of the large business groups as an attempt to solve the traders' dilemma. The solution is achieved by using these firms as a focal point within which a corporate culture evolves, guided by the state, with the goal being to be able to successfully produce for export markets. This path requires, of course, a strong state capable of driving the process forward. It has two inherent weaknesses. One, in the short run, is that it is subject to great possibilities for unproductive rent-seeking on the part of the state. Alternatively, in the long run, if the firms are indeed successful, then unproductive rent-seeking by these powerful firms may inhibit future growth.

The Southeast Asian development process was not, however, driven by a developmental state. Instead, immigrant groups were utilized by the colonial powers to serve as the middlemen in the colonial economies. Thus an extensive network of social relationships, based on ethnic background, was created in this region and this network served as the basis for overcoming the traders' dilemma in Southeast Asia in the postwar period. Once again, as stated above, large business groups integrated many transactions within the firms, but the firms themselves, rather than the state, served to drive the development process forward. The ethnic links created a strong enough structure to create organizations large enough to be interested in socially productive, rent-seeking, rather than predatory behavior.

The difficulty with this pathway to development is twofold. First, it was built on a network of social relationships based on ethnicity during the colonial period in Southeast Asia. Thus it is historically very peculiar to the particular situation in Southeast Asia prior to World War II, that is, this does not seem a replicable strategy of development that could be followed by other regions.   However, there is one important lesson to take from this experience. Groups other than the state can be developmental in nature, therefore, the potential actors in the drama of economic development are quite varied.

The second difficulty with the Southeast Asian path of economic development concerns it fragility. It is fragile in both an economic and social sense. It is fragile economically because it has bypassed the development of the domestic market, thus the human capital, both formally and informally generated, necessary to provide a basis for rapid learning has not been accumulated. Consequently, the growth that has in the past been driven by the export of labor-intensive manufactured goods has run in to a major obstacle, and by ignoring the domestic market development, has not provided the basis for making the transition from low- to high-tech production. Therefore as labor costs began to rise and regions with relatively cheaper sources of labor began to open to international trade, Southeast Asia has found it increasingly difficult to remain competitive in the production and export of labor-intensive commodities. Current account imbalances arose, the return to investment declined and the banking system became increasingly susceptible to financial panic (an increasing proportion of nonperforming loans).

The IMF has responded to the ensuing crisis with a program of reform which goes well beyond the typical IMF program. Along with fiscal and monetary austerity as well as devaluation, the IMF has sought to persuade, perhaps a euphemism, Southeast Asia to engage in a far-ranging policy of financial and trade reform. The difficulties with this approach are that these far-ranging reforms seem to go well beyond traditional IMF policy and infringe upon the sovereignty of Southeast Asia. More importantly, they are not likely to solve the long-run problem, the inability to make the transition. In order for this problem to be overcome significant investment must be made in the domestic market, in particular in rural infrastructure, agriculture and rural-based manufacturing.

As noted above, the Southeast Asian path would also seem to be fragile in a social sense. The region's economies are dominated by ethnic Chinese and this poses great problems during periods of economic crisis. Such situations place great pressure on a social structure which is at present only weakly tied together. If the current economic crisis cannot be quickly dealt with it threatens to unravel the very structure of these nations.

NOTES

1. This statement which appears in Doner (1991) is actually a quote from Deyo (1987).

REFERENCES

Amsden, Alice (1992), 'A Theory of Government Intervention in Late Industrialization,' in Louis Putterman and Dietrich Rueschemeyer (eds.), *State and Market in Development: Synergy or Rivalry* (Boulder, Colorado: Lynn Rienner Publishers), 53-84.

Booth, Anne (1991), 'The Economic Development of Southeast Asia: 1870-
1985,' *Australian Economic History Review* 31 (March 1991), 20-52.

Bradford, Colin (1994), *From Trade Driven Growth to Growth Driven Trade:
Reappraising the East Asian Development Experience* (Paris:
Organization for Economic Cooperation and Development).

Corsetti, Giancarlo, Paolo Pesenti and Nouriel Roubini (1998), 'What
Caused the Asian Currency Crisis?', manuscript.

Deyo, Frederic (1987), 'Coalitions, Institutions, and Linkage Sequencing -
Toward a Strategic Capacity Model of East Asian Development,' in
Fredric Deyo (ed.), *The Political Economy of the New Asian Industrialism*
(Ithaca, New York: Cornell University Press), 227-247.

Doner, Richard (1991), 'Approaches to the Politics of Economic Growth in
Southeast Asia,' *Journal of Asian Studies* 50 (November 1991), 818-849.

Feldstein, Martin (1998), 'Refocusing the IMF,' *Foreign Affairs*
(March/April).

Jomo, K.S., et al. (1997), *Southeast Asia's Misunderstood Miracle:
Industrial Policy and Economic Development in Thailand, Malaysia and
Indonesia* (Boulder, Colorado: Westview Press).

Krugman, P. (1998), 'Fire Sale FDI,' http://web.mit.edu/Krugman/www/
fireside.htm.

Lall, Sanjaya (1995), 'Malaysia: Industrial Success and the Role of
Government,' *Journal of International Development* 7 (September-
October), 759-773.

McVey, Ruth (1992), 'The Materialization of the Southeast Asian
Entrepreneur,' in Ruth McVey (ed.), *Southeast Asian Capitalists* (Ithaca,
New York: Southeast Asia Program), 7-33.

Myint, H. (1964), *The Economics of Developing Countries* (New York:
Praeger).

Olson, Mancur (1971), *The Logic of Collective Action: Public Goods and
the Theory of Groups* (Cambridge, Massachusetts: Harvard University
Press).

Rodríguez-Clare, Andrés (1996), 'Multinationals, Linkages and Economic
Development,' *American Economic Review* 86 (September), 852-873.

Schiff, M. and A. Valdes (1992), *The Political Economy of Agricultural
Pricing Policy: A Synthesis of the Economies of Developing Countries*
(Baltimore: Johns Hopkins University Press).

United Nations Development Program (1994), *Human Development Report*
(New York: Oxford University Press).

Wade, Robert (1994), 'Selective Industrial Policies in East Asia: Is 'The East
Asian Miracle' Right,' in A. Fishlow, C. Gwin, S. Haggard, D. Rodrik
and R. Wade (eds.), *Miracle or Design? Lessons from the East Asian
Experience* (Washington, D.C.: Overseas Development Council, 1994),

55-79.

Wade, Robert and Frank Veneroso (1998), 'The Asian Crisis: The High Debt Model Versus the Wall Street-Treasury-IMF Complex,' *New Left Review* (March/April), 3-23.

Westphal, Larry B. (1989), *Assessing Thailand's Technological Capabilities in Industry* (Thailand Development Research Institute).

Wolf, Charles (1998), 'Too Much Government Control,' *Wall Street Journal*, February 4.

6. Conclusions

1. SUMMARY OF ARGUMENT

This study set out to examine the role of agriculture in the overall development process. Generally, agriculture is seen as a source of a variety of different things useful for the rapid growth of industry. It can provide labor for the new factories, the food to feed these workers, the means to acquire the capital for the new factories, a market for the output of the new factories and foreign exchange to provide the imported inputs necessary for factory production. However, it was argued that agricultural growth and rural development serve a much more important role in the process of development. In particular, it provides a mechanism whereby the fundamental dilemma facing market exchange can be resolved.

Markets in most less-developed nations are not well developed because the process of market exchange there is afflicted with the traders' dilemma. As previously discussed, this concerns how buyer and seller can learn to commit themselves to cooperative exchange, rather than cheating. This traders' dilemma is overcome on a small scale by embedding this dilemma in an *existing* network of social relationships based upon kinship, village affiliation and ethnicity. This usually works, however, only on a small scale and thus results in fragmented markets, limited specialization and little resulting productivity growth. An alternative solution results from middlemen behaving as entrepreneurs establishing *new* networks of relationships linking isolated groups. This is market integration and is subject, it has been argued, to significant increasing returns.

The above results in a problem of coordination. If large numbers of buyers and sellers commit to market exchange then it will be economically profitable for middlemen to establish new social networks to undergird extended market exchange. This was called the modern technology for information-gathering. Alternatively, if only small numbers of buyers and sellers commit to market exchange, then it is best to rely on already existing social networks, with exchange occurring on a small scale with limited market integration. This is the traditional technology for generating information.

The bulk of the population in most developing nations live in rural areas and earn their living in agricultural production. Initially, most of these countries have comparative advantages or potential comparative advantages in agriculture, thus if market integration is going to occur it will have to involve a coordinated process of agricultural development that involves the bulk of the rural population, not a small élite. As this occurs, middlemen will vigorously respond by linking markets together into integrated networks, specialization will proceed and productivity will rise. This process was labeled as Smithian growth and Japan and England were used as examples of such a process.

Long-run growth must, however, be based on changing technology, invention and innovation. Since most developing countries are not on the technological frontier, it is innovation, the learning of previously developed technologies, that is important. Growth theory, both traditional and new, was found to shed little light on the early development process in either Japan or England. However, a model of development was constructed which assumes that technical inventions (macroinventions) are random in terms of their appearance, but innovation (involving learning by doing) can only occur if the market for that particular product is open and functioning. Intermediate goods are presumed to come in a variety of types and are critical for development. The degree of market integration was related to the number of markets for intermediate goods that are open and operating. The larger the number open and operating, the more integrated the market structure and vice versa.

The story unfolds in the following way. Broad-based rural development results in a coordinated solution to the traders' dilemma. Integrated markets evolve implying that a large number of intermediate goods markets are open. When random macroinventions occur in particular intermediate goods sectors, learning of the technology requires learning by doing and this can only occur if the market for this sector is open and operating. Thus the evolution of an extensively integrated market system creates an environment in which rapid learning is likely to occur, the rate of technical innovation will be high. Alternatively, if broad-based rural development has not occurred, then extensive market integration will have failed to take place. The proportion of intermediate goods markets opened is likely to be quite limited, therefore, when technical invention randomly occurs, it is likely that many of these inventions will occur in sectors that are not in operation. Consequently, little learning by doing can occur and there is little technical innovation.

The process summarized above seems to provide an explanation for much of the development experiences of early England and Japan. Rapid market integration, resulting from rural growth, provided the foundation for Smithian growth which, over time, became dominated by technical innovation (long-term growth) as integrated national markets began to evolve. However, this process also created an environment in which divergence among countries tended to occur, the development of a center and a periphery. A developmental state played an important role as a number of countries sought to make the transition from the latter to the former. Such a state is autonomous in that it can independently pursue goals, but it is also embedded in a network of social relationships. This latter quality allows the state to interact with society so as to assure that the goals are developmental rather than predatory in nature. It was argued that the rural path of development, founded on broad-based agricultural growth, provided an environment in which the state could strengthen its autonomy while at the same time firmly embedding itself in society.

The best current example of the rural-based path of economic development is Taiwan. However, there are other paths of development, as alluded to earlier. States have attempted to sidestep the problem of creating an integrated domestic market by pushing their firms to become competitive in international markets. In this approach, the traders' dilemma is taken out of the marketplace and put within the boundaries of large firms. In this situation, repeated interaction within the confines of the firm is aimed by the state at creating a corporate culture whose goal is export success. The best example of this strategy is provided by the experience of South Korea and was called state-directed learning. This approach is subject to two significant dangers. In the short run, a state powerful enough to carry out this strategy will face great temptations to become predatory. In the long run, this strategy creates economic entities (large business groups) strong enough to resist the economic restructuring that periodically must occur if long-run economic growth is to succeed.

A third path of development, related to the second, is provided by the experience of Southeast Asia. In this region the development of the domestic market has been relatively neglected. Instead, large business groups have formed with many transactions being incorporated within the boundaries of these groups. Again, as mentioned above, within these boundaries the traders' dilemma is resolved through the evolution of formal and informal rules which make up the culture of the firm. However, this process is not driven by a developmental state providing rewards to firms which are using their resources to become internationally competitive and providing punishment to firms who fail to use resources effectively. Instead, this process of economic development is led by developmental groups. These groups, based on ethnicity, were created through the experience of colonization.

The discussion above seems to contradict the idea presented earlier that ethnicity can work to solve the traders' dilemma only in small-scale, but not large-scale societies. However, there is no contradiction here. The colonial experience created a social network tying together diverse members of a particular ethnic group, thus a large, extensive group was constructed for the purposes and aims of the colonial power involved. These large groups were to behave as intermediaries in the colonial economy. When the colonial power departed these pre-existing social networks provided the mechanism for a coordinated movement into international trade.

In the mid-1980s this whole process was given a significant stimulus by the inflow of foreign direct investment from East Asia seeking cheap labor for the production and export of relatively labor-intensive goods. Thus significant growth in manufacturing took place and it appeared that Southeast Asia was following the lead of East Asia. However, this path of development created an economic environment which became increasingly fragile. The relative neglect of the domestic market meant that only limited market integration had occurred. As a result, Smithian growth has been limited and little of the human capital necessary for transition from low- to high-tech production had been accumulated. Then, as the success of export-driven growth led to increased demand for labor and the latter became relatively scarce, the advantage that this region possessed, in the export of labor-intensive goods, began to disappear. This was exacerbated by the opening up of other regions where labor was relatively cheaper, thus Southeast Asia's ability to compete began to decline, but it lacked the ability to make the transition to more complex goods. Current account balances deteriorated, the profitability of investment declined, foreign investment from East Asia shifted to other regions, and short-term capital inflows began to provide the main source for financing the current account. An economic crisis ensued. It was argued that the long-run solution to these problems is likely to lie in the development of the domestic market via broad-based rural growth.

2.   A CRITICAL PERSPECTIVE

The summary presented above ended with an analysis of the fragility of the Southeast Asian path. Thus successful long-run growth will require solving the traders' dilemma on a large scale and this will require a coordinated process of rural development. The coordination necessary for this will require the state to take a significant role. The government-directed path followed by South Korea also has a significant role for the state to play. It fosters the development of large firms and drives them to export success. However, it was argued that such a strategy is extremely demanding on the part of the state in the short run and risks creating predatory firms in the long run. As a result, this path would seem to be beyond the capabilities of most developing countries states.

The rural path would seem to represent a strategy for development which is less demanding on the state in the short run and provides the means to increase state capabilities through time. This is not to imply that this approach can succeed with very limited government activities. This path requires a state capable of carrying out a broad-based strategy of rural investment and growth. However, in some ways it is less demanding than the government-directed path (South Korea). Most governments in developing nations are likely to be more knowledgeable and have greater experience with agricultural activities, relative to manufacturing and industry. In addition, the ingredients of a broad-based rural development strategy are now quite well known. Also, although this path requires significant investment and coordination upon the part of the state, it also relies, to a great extent, on a robust response upon the part of private entrepreneurs. This strategy seeks to create an environment which significantly induces private entrepreneurial response.[1] Finally, this path creates an environment that strengthens state capability through time by augmenting its autonomy and its embeddedness. Thus this book maintains that of these three paths, the rural path has a greater probability of long-run success (unlike the Southeast Asian case) and is less demanding in terms of state capabilities (compared to the government-directed path followed by South Korea).

However, one should not minimize the demands which the rural path places on state capability. The crucial characteristic of this path is that rural development must be broad-based. This runs into a significant problem related to the distribution of land. In those countries where land is extremely unequally distributed, a rural élite may possess a degree of political power which would allow them to effectively oppose any state-led strategy aimed at broad-based rural development. In fact the experience of Taiwan, South Korea and Japan would seem to support this conclusion. In all three cases significant land reform occurred which resulted in the elimination of powerful landlord interests and therefore, they ceased to be an effective political force in government decision making. These reforms were the result, many argue, of external powers, in particular the USA, who used their influence to help bring about these reforms.

The importance of the above argument cannot be denied. The powerful landed élite have sometimes played significant roles in blocking development. However, the prewar experience of Japan provides a very interesting alternative perspective. As previously mentioned, prior to World War II (and its land reform) Japan was able to achieve a very high level of economic development. The broad-based rural growth which occurred in the

Tokugawa and early Meiji period seemed to harmonize the interests of groups within the rural areas. Thus landlords played a significant positive role in the rapid growth of agriculture.

The unintended side effect of this growth was to weaken Japanese landlords. This is reflected in the fact that beginning in 1910 and thereafter 'concerted protest action by organized groups of farmers, usually tenants, had become significantly conspicuous to be regarded as a national issue and to warrant the collection of official statistics and reports' (Francks, 1992). As a result, historians know that such disputes increased from 85 in 1917 to annual totals of over 2000 in the 1920s, peaking at 6800 in 1936 (Waswo, 1977). These disputes ranged from small disputes to outright violent conflicts involving a large number of villages. The traditional explanation provided for these conflicts is the increasing hardship faced by Japanese peasant farmers.

Smethurst (1986) has vigorously argued that this traditional explanation is incorrect. Instead, the rural-based process of economic development in Japan increased the opportunity costs of Japanese farmers. Most simply, the bulk of tenant farmers benefitted not only from the increased agricultural productivity, but also as a result of the increased opportunities for nonagricultural employment in rural areas. These opportunities arose as a result of the growth of rural-based, small-scale manufacturing. Given this greater economic strength Smethurst argues that these protest activities represented attempts by tenants to alter the terms of their contracts by using their collective strength to lower the landlord's share of the crop.

The result was not the elimination of the landlord system. However, most of these disputes ended in compromise which implied a reduction in rents. 'This contributed to the overall tendency for the value of rents to fail to keep pace with rises in yields, let alone farm income from other sources, so that land ownership had become, by the 1930s, a less profitable investment as well as a less gratifying way of life' (Francks, 1992).

The above analysis fits well with the work of Takigawa (1972) on land reform in Japan. He argues that land reform was underway prior to World War II. In particular, peasant unrest had led the government in Japan to establish in 1920 the Research Committee on the Tenancy System within the Ministry of Agriculture to establish measures to deal with the issues giving rise to such disputes. It led to the establishment of the Tenancy Conciliation Law in July 1924. The law's aim was to permit the Tenancy Conciliation Committee and the courts to settle tenancy disputes at the request of any party concerned.

In addition to the above, the government engaged in a number of policies to convert tenant-farmers to owner-farmers and this was the main theme of the agricultural land policy prior to land reform. The achievements of these

programs can be easily summarized. From 1926 to 1945 the Ministry of
Agriculture and Forestry established and maintained 555,000 owner-farmer
households, involving approximately 300,000 hectares of land. The figures
for the number of owner operations established represent 14.5 per cent of the
1926 figure for tenant- and part-owner households. The acreage figures
represent 10.8 per cent of the average available in 1945. Takigawa draws
the following conclusion, 'one can even say that the postwar agricultural land
reform was a successor to the main thrust of the prewar agricultural land
policy' (Takigawa, 1972, p.301). Thus the postwar land reform did not
materialize out of thin air, imposed on a resisting population by a powerful
occupying army. Reform was already occurring in prewar Japan and this
reflected the increased strength of small farmers and tenants relative to
landlords.

Thus it seems possible that a rural-based strategy of development may, in
some instances, undermine the influence of the landed élite. Again,
however, one must not minimize the strength of the landowning élite in a
number of developing countries. In these situations a rural-based strategy of
development involving the bulk of the population may not be viable without
an extensive redistribution of land ownership. Further research into the
process of land reform and those historical circumstances giving rise to it is
needed.

NOTES

1. This notion is, of course, quite similar to Hirschman's (1958) idea of creating
   linkages to stimulate private entrepreneurial activity.

REFERENCES

Francks, Penelope (1992), *Japanese Economic Development: Theory and
    Practice* (New York: Routledge).
Hirschman, A.O. (1958), *The Strategy of Economic Development* (New
    Haven, Connecticut: Yale University Press).
Smethurst, R. (1986), *Agricultural Development and Tenancy Disputes in
    Japan, 1870-1940* (Princeton, New Jersey: Princeton University Press).
Takigawa, Tsutomu (1972), 'Historical Background of Agricultural Land
    Reform in Japan,' *The Developing Economies* 10 (September), 290-310.
Waswo, A. (1977), *Japanese Landlords* (Berkeley, California: University
    of California Press).

Index

Acemoglu, D. 68, 83, 84
Adelman, I. 7
Africa 24
  agricultural growth 6–7
  role of state 109
agrarian interest groups, and coalitions
    108
agrarian path 41–8
  coordination problem 62–3
  see also rural path
agricultural growth 24–5
agricultural production 183
agricultural productivity
  England 55–6
  Japan 60
agricultural-demand-led-industrialization
    programme (ALDI) 8
agriculture
  and economic development, empirical
      evidence 23–5
  and industrial revolution 1
  linkages with manufacturing
      production 8
  linkages with non-agricultural sector
      6–7
  and manufactured goods 7
  and manufacturing industry 8–9
  and markets 16–23
  price stabilization 12
  role in economic development 1
    theoretical perspectives 2–10
  role(s) in development process 5, 7,
      182
  Southeast Asia 155–6
  state discrimination against 44–5, 106
  unimodal strategy 6
alternative technology 37
Amsden, A. 46, 113, 114, 122, 161
Anderson, K. 59, 60
Arrow, K. 82

Arthur, B. 81
ASEAN 162
Asia
  agricultural growth 24–5
  average annual growth rates *151*
  debt equity ratios of firms 170
  financial reforms 170
  gross domestic investment *152*
  investment rates 152
  see also East Asia; Southeast Asia
asset factor flexibility 116–17
autonomy 134, 144, 145
  embedded autonomy 133–5
  of state decision making 121, 128
  uses 145

balanced growth 4–5
Bates, R.H. 55, 108, 109
Bautista, R.M. 24
big push analysis 41–2
Biggs, T. 121, 138, 139, 141, 142, 143
biochemical technology 11
Block 24
Boltho, A. 97
Booth, A. 154, 155
border price paradigm approach 11
border prices 45
Boulding, K. 80
Bowring Treaty, Thailand 154
Bradford, C. *151*
Burt, R. 36, 64

capital accumulation 2
  England 79
capital flows, Southeast Asia 153–4
capital intensity, and state restructuring
    116
capital market 14–15
catching up *103*
center nations 94, 134, 144

Cheng, T-J. 141
Chile, exports 112
China 14
   devaluation 169
   emigration to Southeast Asia 156-9
circular flow *18*
classical growth theory 71-2, *71*
coalitions, and agrarian interest groups
      108
collective goods 107
commitment, state 131-2
comparative advantage 46, 47, 112, 161
cooperation 89
cooperators, and non-cooperators 35
coordination, and the state 45-6
coordination problems 41-50, 182
   agrarian path 62-3
Corn Laws, and British policy 54-5
corruption 131, 171
Corsetti, G. 170, 172, 173, 174
Costa Rica, coffee production 118
Crafts, N.F.R. 53, 101
crony capitalism 171, 172, 177

Daunton, M.J. 54, 56
Davern, M. 36
Dawe 13
de Melo, J. 111
debt equity ratios of firms, Asia 170
decision making process 105, 107
devaluation 161
developing nations, dualism in
      economies 16-17
development strategies 132
developmental groups 158
   Southeast Asia 162, 184
developmental state 112-116, 134-5,
      144, 184
   East Asia 109-12
developmental state perspective 104
Deyo, F. 179
discount rate 32
domestic market 48
Doner, R. 158, 179
dualism
   in developing economies 16-17
   organizational dualism 17-18

East Asia
   and the developmental state 109-12

economic development 110-11
   exports 111
   foreign direct investment 185
   free market 110
   government policy in the post war
         period 139
   import substitution strategy 112
   industrialization and government
         involvement 113-14
   multiple equilibria situation 143
   rice production 136
   rural path 142
   social dislocation 114-15
   state activities 112
   western aid 115
   see also South Korea; Taiwan
economic development, and agriculture,
      empirical evidence 23-5
economic exchange, and social
      relationships 40
economic goals, of interest groups 107
economic growth model 68-9
economies of scale, and state
      restructuring 116
élites 131-2, 133
embedded autonomy 133-5
endogenous growth theory *see* new
      growth theory
England 51-7, 183
   agricultural productivity 55-6
   capital accumulation 79
   compared with Japan 61
   growth 63-4, 91
      during industrial revolution 79
   industrial revolution 91
   integrated national market 54-5
   invention 79
   location 92
   market integration, and state
         integration 56-7
   technical change, during
         industrialization 79
   trader merchants 56
   transport and communication systems
         56-7
   universities 92
entrepreneurial groups 150
entrepreneurs 129, 130, 186
   and state, a prisoners' dilemma *130*
Europe, industrial revolution 43

Evans, P. 133, 134
evolutionary approach, to technological change 80–81
exports, Southeast Asia 164

Fei, J. 4, 17, 58
Feld, S. 48, 49
Feldstein, M. 176
Felix, D. 95
firms
  boundaries 48–9
  instrinsic and ancillary capabilities 48
foreign direct investment, from East Asia 185
foreign investment, Southeast Asia 153, 158, 163
Foster, A.D. 47
Francks, P. 97, 187
Frank, R.H. 35
free market, and East Asia 110
free-riding 107, 133, 159, 160
full employment, in model 165–6

goals, of groups 159–60
Goldschmidt, R. 81
government
  allocation of resources 128
  Southeast Asia 171
  see also state
government decision making, embedding 135
government development programs, investment 129
government directed learning, South Korea 184
government policy 13, 122
  and initial conditions 143–4
  urban bias 1
grain trade, England 56
Granger causality techniques 97
Granovetter, M. 33, 40, 48
Grantham, G. 42–3
groups, goals 159–60
growth
  England 91
  and risk *85*
  Southeast Asia 174
growth rate, and learning 104
growth theory 183

Haggblade, S. 6
Hanley, S.B. 60
hard states 114
Hauser, W.B. 59
Hayami, Y. 11, 33, 82, 136, 146
Hazell, P. 6
high-tech goods 164
high-tech production, in model 124, 125, 127
high/high sectors 116, 117
Hirschman, A.O. 188
Ho, S.P.S. 137
human capital accumulation 168–9
Hwa, E-C. 23

IMF 170
  reforms in Southeast Asia 175–6, 177, 179
import substitution policies 119
import substitution strategy, East Asia 112
income distribution 106
incremental capital to output ratio (ICOR) 172, *173*
India
  agricultural income 6
  average annual growth rates *151*
  economic development 8
  gross domestic investment *152*
individual behaviour 121–2
Indonesia
  agricultural growth rates *155*
  average annual growth rates *151*
  current account imbalance 170, 172
  devaluation of currency 161–2
  development process 163–4
  education 169
  exports 162
  gross domestic investment *152*
  human development level 168
  incremental capital to output ratio (ICOR) *173*
  investment rates *174*
industrial revolution 48
  and agriculture 1
  England 91
  Europe 43
industrialization 9–10, 25
information gathering 45, 125, 182
information generation 36, 37–8, 62, 182

technologies *39*
traditional technology 38
innovation 68-9, 93, 99, 183
innovation models 82
integrated markets 183
    integrated national market, England
        54-5
    Taiwan 138
interest coverage rate (ICR) 172-3
interest groups 107-8, 109, 113, 114
    economic goals 107
    and policy making 108
intermediate goods 93-5, 164, 167
    in model 123-4
international trade 43-4
invention 68, 87, 183
    England 79
investment, in Southeast Asia 162
investment flows 5
investment rates
    Asia 152
    Indonesia *174*
    Malaysia *174*
    Thailand *174*

Japan 51, 57-61, 183
    agricultural productivity 60
    agriculture 120, 139
    economic development 8-9, 100
    economic growth 97-8
    economy in the 1950s 95-6
    emigration to Korea 137
    and England compared 61
    government activities 96-7
    growth 63-4
    integrated market in rice 58-9
    investment in Southeast Asia 162
    and Korea 120
    land reform 115, 186-8
    land tax 60
    learning process 97, 104
    location 92, 95
    marginalization 95
    market integration 91
    rule of Taiwan and Korea 135-6
    social dislocation 114
    state policy 116
    tax under feudal system 57-8
    technical change 80
    Tenancy Conciliation Committee

(1924) 187
time series data (1885-1990) 97-8
urbanization 58
Johnston, B. 140
Johnston, B.F. 5
Jomo, K.S. 162, 163, 169, *175*
Jones, C. 74, 78, 101
Jorgenson, D.W. 5

Ka, C-m. 136, 137, 138, 140, 147
Kawagoe, T. 33
Korea
    current account imbalance 170, 172
    and Japan 120, 137
    see also South Korea
Kreps, D. 32, 129
Krugman, P. 170
Kurer, O. 131
Kuznets, P. 120, 137

labor
    and agriculture 4
    in poorer regions 114
    Southeast Asia 174
labor force, skills 125
labor markets 118
labor-intensive exports, Southeast Asia
    162
Lall, S. 163
Langlois, R. 48
large-scale societies 35-41, 89
learning 80, 82-3, 93, 125, 145
    and entrepreneurial groups 150
    and growth rate 104
    and state 104, 132
learning by doing 93, 99, 103, 183
learning process, Japan 97
Levine, R. 79
Levy, B. 37, 64, 120, 121, 138, 139, 141,
    142, 143
Lewis model 2-4, *3*
Lewis, W.A. 2, 17, 58
Lie, J. 54, 56
linkage effects 165, 166
linkages 25
    between agriculture and
        manufacturing production 8
    between agriculture and non-
        agricultural sector 6-7
Lipton, M. 1, 106

Locay, L. 47
long-run growth 21, 68, 183, 185
low-level income trap, models 123
low-tech equilibrium *126*
low-tech goods 164
low-tech production, in model 127
low/low sectors 116, 117

Macfarlane, A. 51, 52, 58, 91, 92
macroinventions 81, 83, 87, 91, 92, 99
  see also inventions
McVey, R. 157
Malaysia
  agricultural growth rates *155*
  average annual growth rates *151*
  current account imbalance 170, 172
  development process 163
  education 168, 169
  exports 162, 163
  gross domestic investment *152*
  human development level 168
  incremental capital to output ratio
    (ICOR) *173*
  investment rates *174*
  taxation on agriculture *156*
manufacturing industry, and agriculture
  7, 8–9
marginal tradeoffs 122
market coordination, alternative solution
  48
market failure 11, 12, 16
market inadequacy 106
market integration 87–8, 183
  England 56
  Japan 91
markets 26, 33–4, 182
  and agriculture 16–23
  opening up 88
  and state 109
  undervaluation of agriculture 14–15
Mellor, J.W. 5
microinventions 81, 82, 99
  see also innovations
Migdal, J. 114
modern sector, in a developing nation
  2–5, 18–20
modern technology, for information
  generation 38–40, 62
Mokyr, J. 80, 81, 82, 99
Moore, M. 141

moral hazard problems 13
multilateral reputation mechanism 32–3
multinational corporations, impact in
  Southeast Asia 164–7
multiple equilibria *128*, 145–6
multiple equilibria model(s) 123–7, 164
multiple equilibria situation, East Asia
  143
Mundle, S. 8, 9, 60
Murphy, K. 10
Murphy, K.W. 41
Myint, H. 7, 16, 17, 18, 106, 161
Myrdal, G. 112

Nelson, R. 80, 123
neoclassical growth theory 21, 69–71, *70*
new growth theory 47, 68, 74–8, 98
new technology 46–7, 89, 93, 95
Newbery, D. 12
non-cooperators, and cooperators 35
North, D. 27, 121, 122

OECD 170
Ohkawa, K. 95
oligopoly 108, 120, 159
Olson, M. 107, 114, 159
organizational dualism 17–18
overlapping generations model 83

Pack, H. 95
Pakistan
  average annual growth rates *151*
  gross domestic investment *152*
Park, A. 140
Penn World Tables 152
peripheral nations 94, 134, 144
Philippines, current account imbalance
  170, 172
Platteau, J-P. 32, 40
pluralism, in Taiwan 141
Polanyi, K. 40
policy making, and interest groups 108
political clientelism 131
population growth 34, 77
Porter, M. 95
poverty, reduction 15–16
predatory behaviour, by state 129
price stabilzation, in agriculture 12–13
prisoners' dilemma game 129, *130*
private sector, and state 113

producer services 94
production
    flexibility 116–17
    transition from low to high tech 163–8
productivity 14, 15

Ranis, G. 4, 17, 58
Ray, D. 15
relative prices, and specialization *126*
Renalt, D. 79
research sector 77
resources, government allocation 128,
    144
restructuring 116–21
returns, increasing 37–8
rice production
    East Asia 136
    Southeast Asia 139–40
risk 84–5
    and growth *85*
Robertson, P. 48
Rodríguez-Clare, A. 94, 123, *126*, 164
Rodrik, D. 94, 95, 110, 111, 112, 113,
    123, 140, 146
Rogerson, W.P. 108
Romer, P. 74
Rosenstein-Rodan, P.N. 41
Rosenzweig, M. 47
Rosovsky, R. 95
Rostow, W.W. 53
rural households 13, 14–15, 44
rural path 159, 162, 186
    East Asia 142
    Taiwan 184
Ruttan, V. 11, 82, 120, 146

savings rate 2
Schiff, M. *156*
Shafer, D.M. 116, 119
Shinohara, M. 97
shocks, negative and positive 43
Sinha, R.P. 96, 97
small-scale societies 30–35, 89
Smethurst, R. 187
Smith, T.C. 57, 58, 91
Smithian growth 21, 26, 30, 43, 44,
    47–8, 62, 63–4, 99, 183
Smithian growth theory 72–3, *72*
social networks 36–7, 49–50, 89, 150,
    158–9, 178

Southeast Asia 153
social relationships, and economic
    exchange 40
soft states 114, 150
Solow, R. 12
Solow's theory of growth 73
South Korea 105, 109–12
    agriculture 1, 142
    average annual growth rates *151*
    bankruptcies of conglomerates 172
    decline in living standard 136–7
    development 178
    development of large firms 185–6
    developmental state 135
    developmental strategy 121
    economic development 118–19
    economic policies 119
    exports 111
        and investment 112
    government directed learning 142, 184
    gross domestic investment *152*
    growth rate 104
    irrigation systems 136
    Japanese immigrants 137
    labor intensive manufacturing 118
    land reform 115, 186
    per capita income 109
    postwar period
        conditions 138–9
        development 141–2
    rice production 136, 139
    social dislocation 115
    total factor productivity 110
    under Japanese rule 135
Southeast Asia
    agricultural growth rates *155*
    agriculture 152, 155–6
    Chinese immigrants 156–9
    developmental groups 162, 184
    domestic market 168
    East Asian investment 169
    economic crisis 169
        summarized 173
    economic development, fragility
        178–9
    European control 154
    exports 164
    financial problems 161–2
    financial restructuring 175–6
    foreign investment 158, 163

from East Asia 185
government allocation of resources 171
growth 150, 152, 174
IMF reforms 175-6, 177
immigrant groups 178
impact of multinational corporations 164-7
investment 172
    in agricultural growth 177
labor 169, 174
labor-intensive exports 162
living standards 154-5
national markets 176-7
profit rates 172
rice production 139-40
social networks 153
wages 161
specialization 44, 56, 59
and relative prices *126*
Sri Lanka, tea 118
state
    action 106
    bias against agriculture 45, 106
    commitments 131-2
    and coordination 45-6, 50
    decision making, autonomy 121, 128
    and entrepreneurs, a prisoners' dilemma *130*
    intervention 122
        and market integration, England 56-7
    and learning 104, 132
    and markets 109
    policy 105
    predatory behaviour 129
    and private sector 113
    resource allocation 144
    restructuring
        and capital intensity 116
        and economies of scale 116
    restructuring of economies 116-21
    theories concerning role 104
    theories of 106-9
    see also developmental state; government
Stiglitz, J. 12
structural holes 89
    in social networks 37
subsidies, allocation in developing

countries 113-14
Suh, S-C. 137

Taiwan 105, 109-12
    agriculture 1
    average annual growth rates *151*
    economic growth 119
    evolution of developmental state 135
    exports 111
        and investment 112
    gross domestic investment *152*
    growth rate 104
    integrated market system 138, 143
    irrigation systems 136
    land reform 115, 186
    per capita income 109-10
    pluralism 141
    postwar period
        conditions 138-9
        economy 140
        rural growth 141
        state policies 141
    productivity 136
    restructuring of economy 119
    rice production 136, 138, 139
    rise in living standard 137
    rural path of economic development 184
    social dislocation 115
    sugar production 138, 139
    total factor productivity 110
    under Japanese rule 135
Takigawa, T. 187, 188
technical change
    England, during industrialization 79
    Japan 80
    rate 93-4
technical invention, in model 74-7
technology 161
    use of 92
Tenancy Conciliation Committee (1924), Japan 187
Thailand
    agricultural growth rates *155*
    average annual growth rates *151*
    Bowring Treaty 154
    current account imbalance 170, 172
    economic crisis 169, 173
    education 169
    exports 162

gross domestic investment *152*
human development level 168
incremental capital to output ratio
    (ICOR) *173*
investment rates *174*
manufacturing, wage and productivity
    indices *175*
taxation on agriculture *156*
technological capability 163
theories of state 106-9
Timmer, C.P. 11, 12, 13, 14, 16, 24, 26
Tomlinson, B.R. 60
trader merchants, England 56
traders' dilemma 21-3, *21*, 26, 30-32,
    31, 36, 39, 49-50, 61-2, 88-9, 145,
    159, 167, 182
traditional sector 18-20, 33-4, 36
    decision making 5
    in a developing nation 2-5
traditional technology 36
    for information generation 38, 62
transaction costs 19-20, *20*, 90
trust 33
Turkey, exports 112

unimodal strategy, in agriculture 6, 13
United Nations Development Program

168, 169, 177
universities, England 92
urban bias 1, 11, 106

Valdes, A. *156*
Veneroso, F. 176, 169-70
Vlastos, S. 57, 58
Vogel, S.J. 25

Wade, R. 110, 114, 164, 169-70, 176
wage rates, in poorer regions 114
Waswo, A. 187
Weingast, B. 130, 131
western aid, East Asia 115
Westphal, L. 95
Westphal, L.B. 163
Williamson, O. 48
Winter, S. 80
Wolf, C. 106, 171
World Bank 111
Wrigley, E.A. 53

Yamamura, K. 60
Young, A. 93

Zambia, copper 118
Zilibotti, F. 68, 83, 84